Instructor's Resource Manual

for

Press, Siever, Grotzinger, and Jordan's
UNDERSTANDING EARTH
Fourth Edition

Peter L. Kresan

University of Arizona, Tucson

Reed Mencke, Ph.D.

University of Arizona, Tucson (retired)

W. H. Freeman and Company
New York

ISBN: 0-7167-5781-8

Printed in the United States of America

First printing 2003

W. H. Freeman and Company
41 Madison Avenue
New York, NY 10010
Houndmills, Basingstoke RG21 6XS, England

www.whfreeman.com

Contents

Part I: Instructional Design

Part II: Chapter-by-Chapter Teaching Tips

CHAPTER 1

Learning Objectives: How to Define Your Goals for Your Course

If you don't know where you're going, you're liable to wind up somewhere else.

—DAVID CAMPBELL

What is the essential content of your course? This is a deceptively simple question. There may have been a time long ago when geology instructors were free to decide course content from the perspective of the discipline: "What topics, facts, and theories are key to understanding geology?" That time, if indeed it ever existed, is long past. Nationwide, general education reform as well as concerns about student retention at the freshman level have led many universities and colleges to curriculum reform directed toward non-majors and first-year students (new freshmen and transfer students) in introductory courses. As higher education becomes ever more competitive, instructional objectives are likely to be increasingly tuned to the needs of each market segment of students who may decide to take your class. For a typical introductory geology course, these segments will include (1) non-majors, (2) first-year students (new freshmen or transfers), (3) potential majors, and (4) related majors.

Needs of Geology Learners

Ideally, the process of instructional design should begin with a careful review of the students who take the course and a determination of what they need to learn. Such a review might focus on questions such as the following.

Non-majors.   If the course is used to satisfy a general education requirement, then you have a population of non-geologists. What does an "informed citizen" need to know about geology? What kinds of problems confront an ordinary citizen that hinge on an understanding of geology? What do you want those informed citizens to know? How do you hope they would approach those problems as a result of taking your course? Perhaps most important for non-majors: what *attitudes* do you want these "informed citizens" and "future legislators" to develop?

How? Politically speaking, non-majors, who might be better thought of as future informed citizens, are a very important group for the future of the discipline.

What attitudes towards science do you want to foster among non-majors?

At our institution general education reform has focused on functional skills. Assignments in our new curriculum focus on developing students' skills in writing, critical thinking, team work, even public speaking, using technology such as the Internet to find and report information. In every chapter of the resource manual, you will find material and actual assignments that address these issues.

First-Year Students (freshmen or transfer students).   What percentage of the students who take your class do so in their first year at your university or college? What percentage of these students survive their first year of college? At many institutions the freshman survival rate is low enough that legislators and college officials have decided to focus on freshman survival. What policies and programs at your institution bear on first-year survival? How can your course support these efforts?

Freshmen often come to college unprepared for the challenge of intensive academic effort. Many have studied less than six hours per week, few have learned how to learn science on their own, few know how to preview their text in preparation for lecture, almost none have experience taking notes in a large lecture hall. Instructors control the incentives here. Do your assignments and policies encourage desired performance? What have you built into your course to assist freshmen who are trying to bridge the (often very wide) gap between expectations at the high school level and what is expected of them in college? See Part I, Instructional Design, Chapters 5 and 6 in this manual for ideas about how you can do this. Then in Part II, Chapter Resources, we provide materials and assignments for each chapter in *Understanding Earth,* Fourth Edition, that you can build into your class to foster efficient preparation. Finally, look over the Study Guide. Consider urging your students to use it. Better yet, make assignments for credit using the Study Guide.

Potential Majors.   Note the word "potential." What is the role of your course in recruiting new majors? What should it be? What concepts do potential majors taking your class have to know (really have to know) to succeed in the geology classes that will follow? It may be useful to talk about this question with instructors who teach key upper-division courses. Surveys or focus groups with students in upper-division classes can also be helpful. Ask about what they learned well in the intro course and what they wish they had learned better. Finally, a post-enrollment survey of majors employed in geology professions may provide additional perspective about what majors need to learn in their very first course.

Related Majors.   Which other departments require your course? What do students value and take back to their discipline? What content in your course is considered important by the faculty teaching related courses?

Ultimately, the information you get by considering market segments (majors, related majors, non-majors) must be transformed into a list of learning objectives, i.e., what you hope to teach your students. What do the particular kinds of students who take your course need to learn? You need to break learning into components: What *facts* do they need to know? What *skills* do they need to master? How will they/should they *apply* their knowledge of geology (what specific geological phenomena do you expect them to *interpret*?)? What kinds of problem solving should they master? What attitudes toward geology do you hope to impart?

Learning Objectives

Learning objectives for a typical geology course fall into the following categories:[*]

- **Knowledge:** What do you want your students to know and understand?

  Examples:

  ✓ Understand chemical weathering processes.
  ✓ Understand the scientific method.

- **Applications:** What kinds of geological scenarios should students be able to interpret? What kind of problems should students be able to be able to solve?

  Examples:

  ✓ Determine the relative age of strata using the principle of superposition.
  ✓ Determine wind direction in a desert from the orientation of a barchan sand dune.
  ✓ Interpret geologic structures for the type and orientation of stress.

- **Geology Skills:** What should students be able to do by the end of the course?

  Examples:

  ✓ Identify the basic rock forming minerals.
  ✓ Recognize specified landforms in the field.
  ✓ Geology math.

- **General Education Skills**

  Examples:

  ✓ Critical thinking (see the Annotated Bibliography at the end of this manual for helpful sources that deal with critical thinking)
  ✓ Effective writing
  ✓ Teamwork and leadership skills
  ✓ Math reasoning and analysis
  ✓ Public speaking

- **Freshman Survival Skills**

  Examples:

  ✓ Text preview
  ✓ Note taking
  ✓ Exam preparation

- **Attitudes:** What attitudes do you want foster?

  Examples:

  ✓ Develop a lifelong interest in science.
  ✓ Value the scientific method.
  ✓ Value the contribution of scientific information to society.

To educate a man in mind and not in morals is to educate a menace to society.

—THEODORE ROOSEVELT

Thinking about what you want students to learn in each category for each lecture can be a heuristic. It will suggest points you need to make and activities you need to include to ensure

---

[*] Schema adapted for geology from the *Bloom Taxonomy of Educational Objectives* (Bloom, 1956; Crooks, 1988). Note that we have added several categories that reflect nationwide concern with freshman retention and general education.

that students master the skills, applications, and test items that tap higher-order thinking. The acronym "KASA" will help you remember the categories.

It is up to you to decide which level of thinking is appropriate for your objectives and students. But in general, it makes sense to reserve critical thinking and writing assignments for really important concepts.

In Part II of this manual we suggest a set of learning objectives for each chapter of the text. You will find learning objectives representing the entire spectrum (knowledge, skills [geology, general education, freshman survival], applications, and attitudes). Use them to target your lectures and other classroom activities on student performance. More important, formulate your own learning objectives. The idea is to build a course that effectively meets the learning needs of your particular student population and is in tune with the strategic plan of your university or college.

References

Bloom, B. S., ed. 1956. *Taxonomy of educational objectives*. Vol. I: *Cognitive domain*. New York: McKay.

Crooks, T. J. 1988. The impact of classroom evaluation practices on students. *Review of Educational* Research, *58*(4):438–481.

CHAPTER 2

The Importance of Active Learning

Learning without thought is labor lost.
What I hear, I forget.
What I see, I remember.
What I do, I understand.

—CONFUCIUS

Several thousand years ago Confucius stated a proposition about learning that has recently been confirmed in laboratory studies of learning. This principle says that we learn by constructing knowledge. Our brain does not passively receive information; it processes it. Confronted with new material, we subconsciously ask ourselves three questions:

- Have I heard this before?
- Where does this information fit?
- What can I do with it?

It is only when we reach the point of "doing something" with new information that we truly learn. This is one reason why straight lecture is a fairly inefficient vehicle for delivering learning. Studies of attention during lecture paint a discouraging view.

- Lecturers speak at between 100 and 200 words per minute. Students think at the rate of 400 to 500 words per minute. That leaves lots of time for students to wander off into inattentiveness. And most do just that (Silberman, 1996).
- Students are not attentive 40 percent of the time during lecture (Pollio, 1984).
- Student attention decreases with each passing minute. While students retain 70 percent of what is covered in the first 10 minutes of lecture, they retain only 20 percent or less of points covered in the last 10 minutes (McKeachie, 1986).
- Lecture fits only the auditory learning style.[*]
- Lecture encourages memory of facts rather than thought.

---

[*] Lecture here assumes the old style where the instructor just talks. These days, most of us incorporate slides into our lectures, thereby addressing the visual learner. But that still leaves one group of learners underserved. Kinesthetic learners are students who learn by "doing something." Meeting the needs of the kinesthetic learner requires classroom activity (cooperative learning). (See Part I, Chapter 7, How to Teach to Student Learning Styles in this manual.)

Seven Principles for Good Practice in Undergraduate Education

1. Encourage student-faculty contact.
2. Encourage cooperation among students.
3. **Encourage active learning.**
4. Give prompt feedback.
5. **Emphasize active learning.**
6. Communicate high expectations.
7. Respect diverse talents and ways of learning.

Chickering & Gamson (1987)

Active Learning Activities   Should we abandon lecture as a method of instruction? Certainly not! But we do need to vary the pace. Try breaking your lecture into chunks or segments. Stop every 10 to 20 minutes and interject an active learning experience—something other than listening, for example:

- Thinking and writing
- Asking a question
- Solving a problem
- Filling in holes in their notes with the aid of a partner
- Generating a list of questions about the lecture
- Discussing what was just covered

Chapters 3 and 4 provide some specific activities that promote active learning. Chapter 3 suggests some tested ideas about how to encourage a productive classroom discussion. Chapter 4 describes collaborative learning exercises. This manual provides specific active learning activities for every chapter of *Understanding Earth*. You will find these exercises in **Part II, Chapter Resources,** in this manual. Look under **Teaching Tips** for the chapter you are preparing to teach to find the following:

- **Collaborative Learning Exercises** you can use during lecture to vary the pace and ensure active learning on the part of students.
- **Sample Exercises** to stimulate thinking
- **Topics for Class Discussion**
- **Additional Tips and Information**

Finally, we recommend a helpful monograph titled *Active Learning* by C. C. Bonwell and James Eison (1991). Bonwell and Eison first develop a solid case for active learning activities and then provide wonderfully helpful material on how to do it. The monograph is a must read for instructors who desire to improve the quality of learning in their classroom. The former chair of our molecular and cellular biology department liked this book so much that he purchased a stack of copies and handed them out to faculty to encourage instructors to incorporate active learning into their classes.

References

Note: *References marked with a star are references that we think you will find most useful. They are also discussed in the annotated bibliography at the end of the manual.*

★ Bonwell, C. C., & Eison, J. 1991. Active learning: Creating excitement in the classroom. ASHE-ERIC *Higher Education Report No. 1*. Washington DC: George Washington University, School of Education and Human Development.

Chickering, A., & Gamson, Z. 1987. Seven principles for good practice in undergraduate education. *Wingspread, 9*: 1–8.

Crooks, T. J. 1988. The impact of classroom evaluation practices on students. *Review of Educational Research, 58*(4): 438–481.

McKeachie, W. 1986. *Teaching tips: A guidebook for the beginning college teacher.* Boston: D. C. Heath.

Pollio, H. R. 1984. What students think about and do in college lecture classes. *Teaching Learning Issues, No. 53*. Knoxville: Learning Research Center, University of Tennessee.

Silberman, M. 1996. *Active learning: 101 strategies to teach any subject.* Boston: Allyn and Bacon.

CHAPTER 3

Six Things You Can Do to Encourage Classroom Discussion

What we want to see is the child in pursuit of knowledge and not the knowledge in pursuit of the child.

—GEORGE BERNARD SHAW

In his whole life man achieves nothing so great and so wonderful as what he achieved when he learned to talk.

—OTTO JESPERSEN

I have come to a frightening conclusion. I am the decisive element in the classroom. It is my personal approach that determines the climate. It is my daily mood that makes the weather. As a teacher, I possess tremendous power to make a student's life miserable or joyous. I can be a tool of humor, hurt, or healing. My response decides whether a crisis will be escalated or de-escalated, and a [student] humanized or dehumanized. No machine, sophisticated as it may be, can do this job.

–HAIM GINOT, TEACHER, 1972

As Haim Ginot notes in the quote above, the instructor has everything to do with the kind of environment that prevails in the classroom. Most professors I know welcome student questions and interaction in their classes. They understand that students often miss important points, misinterpret information due to misconceptions, or even stop listening altogether during lecture. To counteract these problems, the prevailing solution is to ask, "Does anyone have any questions?" For reasons we get into later, this device by itself is worthless and is best discarded. What does work? Following are six proven strategies. There are, of course, a few caveats. First, no one strategy by itself will guarantee productive discussions. Each depends on one or more of the others. But the impact can be powerful once the whole package is mastered.

The second caveat is that nobody masters the whole package all at once. Be gentle with yourself. Becoming a skillful facilitator of classroom discussion is a long-term project, as is becoming a competent scientist. Most of us have quite a few bad days along the way. Plan to work at your skills in this area over a period of years. Seek mentoring or, even better, team teach with somebody you consider a successful discussion leader. Cooperation is just as key to faculty learning as it is to student learning!

1. **Learn your students' names and always call on them by name.** Doing so sends a strong message that you value and welcome interaction. It is quite wondrous how some students respond to this message.

    How do you learn the names when you have a hundred or more students in your class? Some faculty keep their class roster handy and frequently call on different students (kinesthetic approach). Others use their digital camera, taking time the first day of class to photograph each and every student. Then they keep the pictures in a portfolio sheet to refer to during lecture. The mere fact that you take time for such activities will change the tone of your classroom. It says to the students that you consider interaction a vital part of the learning process and you expect interaction to occur. **Hint:** If you are team teaching, your co-instructor can help you take pictures. If you have undergraduate preceptors (see Chapter 4), consider turning the class over to them for ten minutes while *you take the pictures.*

2. **Use two-minute think/pair/share active learning exercises in every class.** Break up your lecture by stopping to ask students to do something with the information you have given them. These exercises should be designed to help students see what you expect them to be able to know and do with the material. We provide some ideas in **Part II, Chapter Resources,** in this manual.

    Example: Present a lecture about volcanoes. Then ask students to pair up for two minutes. Instruct them to develop a simple chart comparing shape and magma composition of shield volcanoes and stratovolcanoes. Then select one team at random and call on them (by name, of course) to report on their chart. Let students know that it is considered just as valuable to come up with a good question as it is to "get the right answer." See Part I, Chapter 4 in this manual for more about how to build such activities into your class.

3. **Paraphrase student questions.** When you do get a question, be sure to paraphrase it. It is not uncommon to hear professors provide a lengthy, eloquent answer to a question that was not what the student was asking about. This is understandable. Student questions are not always articulate or clear. The antidote is simple: just take a moment to restate the question.

    Example: "I think you are asking me why a stratovolcano is so explosive, is that it?" Paraphrasing helps to ensure that you are on the right plane before you leave the airport! This is obviously fundamental to success in facilitating discussions. But there are other advantages. A good paraphrase *signals empathy* with the questioner. It says that you understand the question and consider it important. Paraphrasing also helps to ensure that all participants hear the entire exchange between you and your questioner (vital, if you expect them to stay involved) and signals to the rest of the class that you expect all to participate. (Why else would you be repeating it?) Finally, paraphrasing buys time for you to formulate a clear response.

4. **Ask open-ended questions.** Open-ended questions cannot be answered with a simple "Yes" or "No." The standard catch-all question "Are there any questions?" is a poor question in part because it is a closed question. Students typically say, "No" or "I'm not sure" in their mind, and the class remains silent.

    Example: Try instead "*What* questions do you have about the different characteristics of stratovolcanoes and shield volcanoes?" You will be more likely to get a response.

    Example: *How* is another good open-ended question word for geology instructors. Use *How* to get students thinking about a process. "*How* does physical weathering (or substitute any other geological process) work?" Compare that with "Do you understand physical weathering?" Which question forces the student to provide some real information? Any question that begins with *What*, *How*, or *Why* is likely to be an open-ended question. The chance that a student will answer with a non-informative "Yes" or "No" is remote.

5. **Probe student responses.** To stimulate thinking and help students flush out their answers, use probing questions.

   Example: To a student answering the question "How does physical weathering work?" ask "Can you give me a specific example of a physical weathering process?" or "Tell me more about how the stream gradient makes a difference."

6. **Allow sufficient wait time.** Instructors often ask questions, then rush on before students have time to formulate an answer. As a general rule of thumb, wait time should be geared to the learners and the complexity of the question you ask. "What's your name?" requires zero wait time. "How does physical weathering work?" when students have just read about weathering for the first time might require a 20-second *or even longer* wait time for formulating a response. Try increasing your wait time to 15 seconds.

   Example: "Which volcano type has viscous lava?" Probably 5 to 10 seconds.

   Example: "What is the major difference between stratovolcanoes and shield volcanoes?" It might take 20 seconds for an average student to answer.

Build interaction into each class. It won't happen automatically. Prime the pump by including a brief 2-minute pair-and-share exercise that requires students to think, check their notes, and answer a question. Follow up with specific open-ended questions that you write out ahead of time in your lecture notes. Use a stopwatch to allow sufficient wait time. Guess how much time it will take students to answer the question, then add 15 seconds to your estimate. Better yet, try out the exercise ahead of time on one of your students and time the response. If you have undergraduate preceptors (see Chapter 4) they can be invaluable for such experiments. Preceptors can also tell you why some of your questions get no response.

Becoming a skillful discussion leader is a lifelong project. Be patient with yourself.

Be patient with your students, too. Be aware that most freshmen are just beginning to learn how to think like scientists, just beginning to learn critical thinking skills, just beginning to learn how to work effectively in a team. Challenge them. But respect them as well. Many will evolve significantly by the time they are graduating seniors. Your course can be a powerful force in their development as human beings.

All the affectionate feelings of a man for others are an extension of his feelings for himself.

—ARISTOTLE

To love one's self in the right way and to love one's neighbor are absolutely analogous concepts, are at bottom one and the same.

—KIERKEGAARD

References

Wilen, W. and Clegg, A. 1986. Effective questions and questioning: A research review. *Theory and Research in Social Education.*

Wilkes, G., ed. February, 1998. Maximizing participation in class discussion. *University of Arizona Teaching Center, Thinking About College Teaching, 1*(1). Tucson: University of Arizona.

CHAPTER 4

Cooperative Learning Teaching Strategies

The best answer to the question "What is the most effective method of teaching?" is that it depends on the goal, the students, the content, and the teacher. But the next best answer is "Students teaching other students." There is a wealth of evidence that peer teaching is extremely effective for a wide range of goals, content, and students of different levels and personalities.

—WILLIAM McKEACHIE IN HIS CLASSIC REVIEW OF LEARNING IN THE COLLEGE CLASSROOM

Many educators who believe that they are using cooperative learning are, in fact, missing its essence. A crucial difference exists between simply putting students in groups to learn and in structuring cooperation among students. Cooperation is not having students sit side by side at the same table to talk with each other as they do their individual assignments. It is not assigning a report to a group of students where one student does all the work and the others put their names on the product as well. It is not having students do a task individually with instructions that the ones who finish first are to help the slower students. Cooperation is much more than being physically near other students, discussing material with them, helping them, or sharing material among students, although each is important in cooperative learning.

—DAVID JOHNSON

Cooperative learning is the use of small classroom groups in ways that encourage students to work together to maximize their learning. Many kinds of learning groups are possible. Two-person learning groups are great for quick (two-minute) classroom exercises. At the other end of the continuum are workshop teams that meet regularly throughout the semester. Students learn and take delight in learning in proportion to the amount of effort they put into application and mastery. Mastery is best achieved by answering questions. Teaching others is the best way to learn material. All these elements are built into cooperative learning teaching strategies. The basic formula for a cooperative learning exercise is to take a problem, one that requires higher-order thinking, and ask students to work on it in collaboration with another student or team of students. Working cooperative exercises into your lecture format is perhaps the best strategy available to increase the amount of active learning that goes on in your class (Bonwell & Eison, 1991). It does this in part by changing the pace of your lecture. Changing the pace helps keep your students' attention.

Ample evidence (well over 600 studies) demonstrates that cooperative learning works. Indeed, one reviewer (Johnson, 1992) notes that we know far more about the effectiveness of cooperative learning than we do about the effectiveness of lecture! Johnson found that cooperative learning

> | **Seven Principles for Good Practice in Undergraduate Education** |
> | --- |
> | 1. Encourage student-faculty contact. |
> | 2. Encourage cooperation among students. |
> | 3. Encourage active learning. |
> | 4. Give prompt feedback. |
> | 5. Emphasize active learning. |
> | 6. Communicate high expectations. |
> | 7. Respect diverse talents and ways of learning. |
> | *Chickering & Gamson (1987)* |

- increases learning and measured student achievement.
- provides an opportunity to teach students teamwork skills.
- creates possible relationships among students.
- promotes students positive adjustment to college.

Revitalize students and faculty by providing a structured environment for sharing some of the responsibility for learning. But one does not achieve these fine results easily. Many instructors have set up what might be described as "loosely structured group work" in their classes with disappointing results. Success depends on "smart structuring." Here we outline some structuring ideas that have worked for us and others. Also see the **Online References** section Web links to key resources that will help you learn how to design and run cooperative exercises.

Cooperative Learning Methods for Geology Classes

Following are three cooperative learning formats we have found particularly useful for constructing geology exercises. There are many others. Check out the online references for additional ideas.

Think/Pair/Share

What is think/pair/share? Group members work on a question individually (think), then pair with a partner (pair), then discuss the question further to reach consensus on the answer (share).

When to use think/pair/share: Perhaps the most useful cooperative exercise for those who teach in large lecture halls with bolted-down seats. Most Cooperative Learning Exercises in the **Part II, Chapter Resources,** in this manual utilize the think/pair/share format.

Tip: Don't rush or omit the "think" part of this exercise. Introverts need to think and organize their thoughts before working with others. Introverts make up one-fourth of a typical college class.

Jigsaw

What is jigsaw? For a jigsaw the class is divided into small groups. Each small group works on some piece of a larger problem, question, or issue. Groups report their part of the solution to the entire class either in a short verbal presentation or in newsprint.

When to use jigsaw: When there is a complicated problem and limited time, the jigsaw method allows all participants to think through at least one aspect in depth and then learn the remainder from other groups. To use the jigsaw successfully you should have *at least one* of the following:

- A small class
- Lots of help, for example undergraduate preceptors
- Exceptionally mature and motivated students

Workshop Teams (sometimes called formal learning groups in the literature)

What do we mean by teams? At the University of Arizona, Peter Kresan and others have set up their geology classes so that students attend lecture two hours each week and spend the third hour in workshops. For the workshop sessions the class is divided into teams of three students and they work cooperatively on projects that culminate in oral presentations.

When to use teams: Use teams when you want students to apply their growing knowledge of geology to problems of appropriate scope.

Frequently Asked Questions about Cooperative Learning

Question: Where do I find exercises?

Answer: Cooperative Learning Exercises are provided in **Part II, Chapter Resources,** in this manual for each chapter of *Understanding Earth.* Look under **Teaching Tips.** Also see the **Online References** at the end of this chapter.

Question: Do I need a special seating arrangement to use cooperative learning exercises.

Answer: Not for the kinds of informal group exercises (e.g., think/pair/share) provided in this manual. Students can sit where they please as long as they have access to a partner. You will need special seating arrangements if you want to form teams. Students must sit together. Some instructors make one team member responsible for physically grouping the team. A classroom with moveable chairs, so that teams can sit in a circle, is helpful but not essential.

Question: How do I set up groups?

For **think/pair/share,** the easiest way is to have students turn to the person next to them. To avoid confusion and shuffling about, direct the students as follows: "Partner with the person sitting next to you for this exercise." Wait a few seconds and then say, "Those without a partner raise your hand." You may need to press the point that everyone *must* find a partner. It may take a reminder or two for those without partners to raise their hands. Then direct those without partners to sit with others with their hands in the air. If movement is not prompt, become more directive: "Jill, move to the back row and sit beside Sam." Often, students are hesitant to move the first time. But they quickly learn that they are going to be moved if they don't move themselves, and they move more rapidly from then on.

For a **jigsaw,** the ideal number of groups should equal the number of parts into which you want to divide the problem. If you have a large class, you will be forced to have more than one group work on each part of the problem and to develop some method of pooling results across groups. You might call on one group to report, then ask other groups to add comments or discuss differences in their answers or procedures. Following are some alternative methods for dividing into groups:

- Put colored stickers on the handout packet for today's lecture. Students with the same color work together.

- Hand out colored cards to assign students to groups (very time consuming in a large class).

- Have your lecture assistants (preceptors or graduate teaching assistants) hand out colored cards (quicker).

- Tell the students to form groups of four in the area where they are sitting. If seats are bolted instruct them as follows: "Form two pairs such that two people in one row are directly behind their partners. The pair in the front turns to face the pair in the back." Put this direction on a slide or overhead. Once groups are formed, pass out cards to each formed group. The card should describe in detail the piece of the problem you want them to work on. Color code the cards so that you can call on all groups working on the same piece; for example, "Yellow groups will report first."

For **workshop teams,** members must be assigned by the instructor. This avoids more problems than we have space to enumerate. It is useful to know certain pertinent details about your students before you make group assignments. Have students fill out an information card the first day. Using this information, you might construct teams based on students' skills— GPA, geology background, computer skills, special skills like writing or mathematics. To match students with teammates, limit yourself to only a few criteria and use criteria that may be relevant to the assignment. If, for example, your workshop exercises will require setting up a spreadsheet then it will be important to ask which students already can do that, then assign proficient students to different teams. It is also useful to set up teams as early in the semester as possible, preferably during the first class meeting. You want to set the right tone before students lock in to "business as usual."

Teams will need guidance. At a minimum, provide written guidelines such as the ones shown in Appendix D in this manual. Build in opportunities for the students to give each other feedback. You may even need to provide some basic training on giving constructive feedback. There must be a gradable product for student incentive. Grading group projects is fraught with peril. Think carefully about how to make your grading scheme fair and prevent "freeloading." One approach is to have a balance in grades for individual vs. team work. For example, assign about half the potential points in a lab or workshop to work completed by students individually. The other half of the point total is assigned to team projects. Typically for team projects, each team member is awarded the same number of points. However, if one team member is clearly negligent, the team score may not be awarded equally.

Tips for Running a Cooperative Learning Exercise

Provide clear instructions. Think out the exercise carefully before class. Write careful directions. Put directions on overheads and have them visible at all times (for visual learners). Say the directions out loud (for auditory learners). Ask what questions students have about *specific* aspects of the directions (for kinesthetic learners).

Set short work times and time accurately. Two minutes is about right. If you devise exercises that take a long time, you run the risk of some groups getting way off track and not completing the task. Develop activities students can complete in two to four minutes. Divide more complicated assignments into a series of two-minute segments.

Evaluate. Having students hand in some sort of product that you can grade will encourage attendance. Reading their products will tell you how they are doing with the material. Alternatively, include items on exams that can be answered only by students who completed the exercise.

Preceptors. Preceptors (undergraduate teaching assistants) can be a great help in conducting jigsaw and other group cooperative learning exercises. This is particularly true in a large lecture section where crowd control makes cooperative work challenging.

Preceptors are undergraduate students who volunteer to be members of the instructional team for your course. Some instructors offer preceptorships only to students who have successfully completed the course; others take students who are enrolled in the course during the same semester in which they serve as preceptors. Both models seem to work.

Peter Kresan developed a model for the involvement of undergraduate preceptors in teaching geology. Kresan's model has since been adapted for use in the University of Arizona's new general education curriculum. For information that will help you set up a preceptor course similar to Kresan's, see Appendices A–C in this manual. To learn how the preceptor program works in other courses at the University of Arizona, see the Teaching Teams program Website in Online References.

Team Teach. Cooperation can be just as powerful a motivator for faculty as it is for students. Team teaching is a great way to get moving with cooperative learning if you are feeling reticent.

Online References

These links will help you learn to run efficient cooperative learning exercises.

Johnson, D. W., Johnson, R. T., & Smith, K. A. 1991. Cooperative learning: Increasing college faculty instructional productivity. *ASHE-ERIC Higher Education Report No. 4*. Washington, DC: George Washington University, School of Education and Human Development. [online serial]. *http://www.ed.gov/databases/ERIC_Digests/ed347871.html* (accessed 2003 Feb. 20).

Wilkes, Glenda. *Cooperative learning in the college classroom.* Web site of University Teaching Center, University of Arizona. *http://www.utc.arizona.edu* (accessed 2003 Feb. 20).

Teaching Teams program provides helpful materials and ideas about making use of undergraduates as full partners in your classroom instruction. Many of the ideas involve using preceptors in the implementation of cooperative learning experiences during large lectures. See the instructor section of the site for materials that will help you get started. *http://hal.lpl.arizona.edu/teachingteams/*

References

Note: References marked with a star are references that we think you will find most useful. They are also discussed in the annotated bibliography at the end of the manual.

★ Bonwell, C. C., & Eison, J. 1991. Active learning: Creating excitement in the classroom. *ASHE-ERIC Higher Education Report No. 1*. Washington, DC: George Washington University, School of Education and Human Development.

Chickering, A., & Gamson, Z. 1987. Seven principles for good practice in undergraduate education. *Wingspread, 9:* 1–8.

Larson, H., Mencke, R., Tollefson, S., Harrison, E., & Berman, E. In press. The University of Arizona Teaching Teams Program: A just-in-time model for peer assistance. In Miller, J.E., Groccia, J.E., & Dibasio, D., eds. In press. *Student assisted teaching and learning: Strategies, models, and outcomes.* New York: Anker Publishers.

Stover, L., Story, K., Skousen, A., Jacks, C., Heather Logan, H., & Bush, B. In press. The Teaching Teams program: Empowering undergraduates in student-centered research universities. In Miller, J.E., Groccia, J.E., & Dibasio, D., eds. In press. *Student assisted teaching and learning: Strategies, models, and outcomes.* New York: Anker Publishers.

Wood, D., Hart, J., DeToro, D., Lebowitz, S., & Libarkin, J. In press. The role of graduate teaching assistants in undergraduate education: Embracing a new model of teaching and learning. In Miller, J.E., Groccia, J.E., & Dibasio, D., eds. In press. *Student assisted teaching and learning: Strategies, models, and outcomes.* New York: Anker Publishers.

★ Johnson, David W., & Johnson, R. T. 1989. *Cooperation and competition: Theory and research.* Edina, MN: Interaction Book Company.

McKeachie, W., Pintrich, P., Yi-Guang, L., & Smith, D. 1986. Teaching and learning in the college classroom: A review of the research literature. Ann Arbor: Regents of the University of Michigan.

Whitman, A. 1988. Peer teaching: To teach is to learn twice. *ASHE-ERIC Higher Education Report No. 4.* Washington, DC: Association for the Study of Higher Education. ED 305 016. 103 pp. MF-01; PC-05.

CHAPTER 5

How to Teach Your Students to Study Effectively

We do not believe in ourselves until someone reveals that deep inside us something is valuable, worth listening to, worthy of our trust, sacred to our touch. Once we believe in ourselves, we can risk curiosity, wonder, spontaneous delight, or any experience that reveals the human spirit.

—E. E. CUMMINGS

I would live to study, and not study to live.

—FRANCIS BACON

For the rest of my life I want to reflect on what light is.

—ALBERT EINSTEIN

Ah, to have students like Bacon and Einstein! It has been our experience that students learn and take delight in learning in proportion to the amount of effort they put into application and mastery. But in an introductory course, most students are still learning how to learn. Years of experience working with college freshmen and interviewing them about their preparation have made it clear that many arrive poorly prepared for the challenge of intensive academic effort.

- Many freshmen have studied less than six hours per week in high school.
- Few have learned how to learn science on their own.
- Fewer still know how to preview the textbook in preparation for lecture.
- Almost none have experience taking notes in a large lecture hall.

Instructors control the incentives here. What have you built into your course to assist freshmen who are trying to bridge the (often very wide) gap between expectations at the high school level and what is expected of them in college? We suggest that you review the student Study Guide for *Understanding Earth*. In the guide you will find lots of exercises and questions you can assign that will help students learn the material in *Understanding Earth* chapters. While you are at it be sure to take a look at the introductory chapters to the guide where we provide ideas for students about the text and how to prepare for lecture.

Chapter 3 in Part I of the student Study Guide for *Understanding Earth* outlines a method of study that is lecture centered. Consider reinforcing the activities in the Study Guide by making them credit assignments. Following is a very brief (annotated) outline of that chapter.

- **Customize learning strategies to your learning style** A brief introduction to learning styles. How one can learn more efficiently by customizing one's method of study to one's strengths as a learner.

- **Make geology lecture a high-priority activity.** Here is where we make the case to the students that attending lecture and active participation are the key to success in geology. See what you think of our arguments. The case needs to be made. Failing to attend lecture is almost perfectly correlated with failing the course.

- **Before lecture:** Chapter Preview

    The major strategy for lecture preparation is to preview the chapter. During your review of the Study Guide you will note that preview questions are provided for each textbook chapter at the beginning of the corresponding chapter of the Study Guide. To reinforce the behavior of previewing, we provide an exercise titled Try This Now. Consider assigning the Try This Now exercises for credit.

    If there is any study strategy worth your active encouragement, it is previewing. Imagine what it would be like if large numbers of your students came to lecture already thinking about the material, with questions about the material already on their mind. Would students be more attentive during lecture? We think they would. **Hint:** If you want students to do something, you MUST assign points for credit.

- **During lecture:** Note-taking checklist

    Few freshmen have learned how to take notes in a large lecture hall where interaction with their instructor can be intimidating. We provide a checklist with basic ideas about taking a good set of notes. Then we suggest an exercise where they rate their own notes. This exercise is another possible study skills assignment for credit.

- **After lecture:** Note review and intensive study session

    For note review, we provide a basic checklist students can use to develop the habit of careful review. Any point on this checklist could easily be worked into a two-minute think/pair/share exercise during one of your lectures. Then follow it up with a slide showing the entire checklist. Intensive study session suggestions for each chapter of *Understanding Earth* are provided in the Study Guide. These include helpful Exercises and Review Questions that you can easily use for cooperative learning or five-minute written assignments in class or as homework.

- **Exam preparation**

    We suggest that you review this section of the student Study Guide for *Understanding Earth* shortly before you give your midterm. Students will greatly appreciate any tips you provide for midterm and final preparation. For freshmen, exam preparation is a new skill. Identify tips you want to reinforce by comments during your lecture or review session. Put one or two preparation tips on a slide, which you display during a lecture or review session. You can choose to discuss the slide or just let the students read it while you are reviewing content.

- **Provide post-exam help.** After the exam encourage students to come in for help. For help sessions we recommend that you keep the following close at hand in an exam review folder:
  - ✓ Copy of the exam and answer key
  - ✓ Student Study Guide for *Understanding Earth*
  - ✓ Copy of the visual on the next page
  - ✓ Sample (exemplary) notes by one or two of your preceptors on difficult concepts
  - ✓ *Eight-Day Study Plan* (Appendix A of the Study Guide)
  - ✓ Anything else you find useful

Obviously, the attitude to foster during post-exam help sessions is that anyone willing to work hard can learn to study more effectively and get a better score on the next exam. Try to build a cooperative team of two (the student and you) who are committed to the student's success. First, spend some time thinking and talking *cooperatively* with the student. Then lay out what the student needs to do. Also identify what you are willing to do (it's a team effort, right?). Finish up by scheduling an appointment to review the student's progress.

This is a great opportunity to introduce the student Study Guide for *Understanding Earth* and to use the visual on the next page. Emphasize that it is organizational skill as opposed to intelligence that leads to success. Don't even talk about intelligence. It's a worthless concept in this context. Be alert for students who knew the material but lost points due to poor test-taking skills or test anxiety. (See the box on test-taking skills in Chapter 3 in Part I of the Study Guide.) Point out the Eight-Day Study Plan (Appendix A in the Study Guide). It's a good example of how to organize review time. Be sure to spend some time reviewing students' notes. We find that reviewing students' notes is also very helpful when they come in for special help after an exam. This should be a cooperative effort, where students step back and look objectively at what they did, receiving during the process some gentle but clear constructive feedback from you.

The flowchart on the next page, How to Study Geology, can easily be converted to an overhead slide. Consider showing it in one of your lectures and talking with your students for a few minutes about how they should study for your course.

How to Study Geology

DURING LECTURE

Take an excellent set of notes.
- Note-Taking Checklist in the Study Guide

BEFORE LECTURE

Prepare for lecture: Arrive with an overview in mind.
- Chapter preview
- Vital information from other chapters

RIGHT AFTER LECTURE

- Review notes.
- Fill in what you missed.
- Add visual material.
- Use the "Have You Checked Your Notes?" section of the Study Guide.

AFTER LECTURE

Intensive study session
Master the key concepts.
- Web site activities and tools
- Practice Exercises and Review Questions in the Study Guide

EXAM PREP

Begin review one week before the exam with the following items in the Study Guide.
- Chapter Summaries
- Practice Exercises and Review Questions
- Tips for Preparing for Geology Exams (Appendix B)
- Eight-Day Study Plan (Appendix A)

CHAPTER 6

Control the Incentives: Give Credit for Study Skills Assignments

Give a man a fish and you feed him for a day. Teach a man to fish and you feed him for a lifetime.

—CHINESE PROVERB

Perhaps the most valuable result of all education is the ability to make yourself do the thing you have to do, when it ought to be done, whether you like it or not.

—FRED CROPP

We motivate by inspiration, by example, and by controlling incentives. We hope you will consider building incentives into your course that foster good work habits and encourage students to use the proven study strategies taught in the Study Guide. Following is a sampler of assignments instructors have found useful.

Grading Schemes for Study Skills Assignments

Over the years we have worked with many professors in many disciplines who came to us wanting to do something in their classes that would "teach the students how to study more effectively." Some of these efforts succeeded brilliantly, even producing impressive improvement on exam scores. Others were a dismal failure! What made the difference? Obviously, there are many factors to evaluate and consider. But the one that stands out is this: *If you want students to do something you MUST to assign points.* Grading is the major incentive under your control. Fail to use it and almost certainly students will ignore your good advice, fail to attend that workshop on study skills you set up, and fail to try the strategy you suggest. So assign points.

Don't make the mistake of assuming that just because study skills assignments are good for students they will welcome doing them. Teaching study strategies is like teaching any other content. You need to set up incentives. Grading options vary considerably in effectiveness. The table shows options that have been tested by instructors and that from our observations we know can be effective.

Grading Option	Effectiveness
Voluntary: No credit	Won't work.
Students research a learning strategy on the Web (see recommended sites in Online Resources) or attend a workshop on study skills (many campus learning centers offer such workshops). Students write a summary of a concept they consider helpful for extra credit.	Better. But fails to ensure practice.
Students research a learning strategy on the Web or attend a workshop. They do an oral presentation of a concept they consider useful to the class.	Better yet. Teaching others is a good way to learn. However, you may not have lecture time to spare. Works well if you have a workshop class period where students work in teams. Have the students report to their own team. Team members rate the presentation and the ratings determine how many points are assigned. Students will work hard to do a presentation that will be appreciated by their peers. Be sure to provide clear guidelines for expectations (grading scheme). In terms of effectiveness, this technique does not ensure practice.
Have students write answers to preview questions or hand in a set of notes they consider ideal. Notes are graded using the Note Review Checklist in Part I, Chapter 3, of the student Study Guide for *Understanding Earth*.	Also effective. Ensures practice, and the students receive feedback on the quality of their effort. Easy to grade.
Do the assignment in class as a think/pair/share exercise. Require a product that can be graded.	Also effective. Ensures practice. Provides a quality check. Can be worked into normal lecture activities.
Students sign up to work with a preceptor who has received special training in study skills. They receive extra points for participating and completing specified assignments, which are graded by the instructor or TA. The preceptor should not grade for both legal and ethical reasons.	Possibly best of all. It has produced spectacular improvements in student performance in a planetary sciences course at the University of Arizona. Students volunteered for study skills tutoring after the first exam. The instructor documented notable improvement on the second exam. The approach is currently under study and is especially promising given that peer support leads to significant improvement.

Sample Study Skills Assignment: Preview a Text Chapter*

Before Lecture: Preview the chapter.

Introduction: Introduce the exercise during lecture. Either distribute as a handout or put up as an overhead projection the **Puzzling Paragraph, Assignment,** and **Grading Rubric** box that follows. You may want to cover the assignment and rubric portion of the overhead until students have had time to read and puzzle over the paragraph.

Then say something like the following: "As you read this paragraph, did you understand what the paragraph is about? If you did figure out what it is about, did you do so quickly or well into the paragraph?" (Now uncover the upside-down answer.) "Once you know what subject the paragraph is addressing, the whole paragraph makes much more sense. This illustrates how important previewing can be in adding meaning and organization to text and to lectures."

*See the Try It Now exercise in Part I, Chapter 3 of the Student Study Guide for *Understanding Earth*.

The Puzzling Paragraph

Quickly read the following paragraph.

A newspaper is better than a magazine. A seashore is a better place than the street. At first, it is better to run than to walk. You may have to try several times. It takes some skill, but it's easy to learn. Even young children can enjoy it. Once you are successful, complications are minimal. Birds seldom get too close. Rain, however, soaks in very fast. Too many people doing the same things close together can also cause problems. One needs a lot of room. If there are no complications, it can be very peaceful. A rock will serve as an anchor. If things break loose from it, however, you will not get a second chance!

The paragraph contains information of building ans flying a kite.

Assignment: Read the section on previewing in Chapter 3 of the student Study Guide for *Understanding Earth*. Write a short paragraph summarizing why (not how; your answers below will demonstrate whether you know how) it is important to preview.

Grading rubric: This assignment is worth 10 points:

  2 points for paragraph on previewing

  8 points divided equally for the answers to each preview question

Assign the 8 points for the questions based on the following criteria:

  ✓ Includes the "brief answer" in the Study Guide chapter.

  ✓ Goes beyond the brief answer.

  ✓ Demonstrates that student has examined relevant figures

  ✓ Extra point if student raises a reasonable question about the material.

  ✓ Extra point if student can relate the question to *any* real life experience (or interest).

  ✓ No points for long "snow job" answers. No points for just copying the text.

If you assign this exercise to a TA to grade, be sure that the grader thoroughly understands the preview process as explained in the Study Guide. For example, previewing is not intended to produce mastery of material. The goal is for the student to get a glimpse of what will be covered in lecture and to come to lecture with questions in mind. Hence, a fair approach to grading this exercise is to reward students who have a broad but very general overview of the content in the chapter being covered in lecture.

Online Resources

Lecture Note Taking Helpful one-page handout on note taking issued by Saint John's College Academic Unit.
http://www.csbsju.edu/academicadvising/help/lec-note.html

Editing Lecture Notes Helpful one-page handout explaining how to review and improve notes after lecture issued by Virginia Polytechnic Institute, Division of Student Affairs
http://www.ucc.vt.edu/stdysk/editing.html

How to Study Math and Science Helpful one-page handout concerning how to study math and science issued by University of Texas at Austin Learning Center.
http://www.utexas.edu/student/utlc/handouts/862.html

Online study skill workshops and self-assessments. Produced by University Learning Center, University of Arizona
http://www.ulc.arizona.edu

Study workshops. You can send your students to online workshops that deal with time management, note taking, exam preparation, memory techniques, goal setting, and other study skills. Tell them to go to the University of Arizona home page (listed above), then under "Quick Links" check, take an online workshop.

Self-assessment. Students can take a variety of tests to help them assess their learning style, and academic motivation. On the University of Arizona home page check Assessments.

CHAPTER 7

How to Teach to Student Learning Styles

Abraham Lincoln's biographer notes that at one point some considered him a "slow learner." But his mother described his style more accurately. "He had to understand everything. He would go over and over something, explaining it verbally. But once he got an idea he never lost it."

Lincoln was an auditory learner. He learned by going over challenging material and *listening* to himself run through it out loud. Far from a slow learner, he was an intensive processor, a great thinker, and a fine orator.

There are literally as many learning styles as there are learners. In a way, this makes the message to instructors quite simple: Diversify your presentation. Hit key concepts from multiple angles. Build in elements that tap multiple learning modalities.

- Auditory learners learn by *listening*. Lecture is perfect for an auditory learner.
- Visual learners learn by *seeing*. Employ visual materials in color in your lectures.
- Kinesthetic learners learn by *moving* and *doing*. Encourage drawing and writing during lecture and exams. Teach skills (like mineral identification) that your students can practice.

Good lecturers know all this intuitively. Sometimes accused by colleagues as "mere showmen," what the excellent lecturer really does is stimulate students in ways that activate what Howard Gardner refers to as "the multiple intelligences." The following table lists just a few of the many interesting ways we have seen talented science lecturers activate the intelligence of their learners.

Verbal/ Linguistic	Body/ Kinesthetic	Musical	Interpersonal	Naturalistic	Visual Spatial
Humor Storytelling	Human sculpting of DNA transcription	Geology slides with musical accompaniment. Insect music (physics)	Peer instruction	Grand Canyon field trip Student docents Fibonacci series in pine cone rings	Sketching formations (geology) Color-coded maps Cartoons

The faculty lecturer isn't the only one who profits from learning about learning styles. In a cooperative or team-oriented geology class, everyone, including graduate teaching assistants, undergraduate preceptors, and students on workshop teams are asked to do presentations. In a cooperative environment, everyone needs to know how to activate diverse learning styles.

Pay particular attention to learning style when answering questions and tutoring. When students seem slow to comprehend, try switching to a different presentation mode. For example, if you have been talking, draw a picture. If you are showing a slide, try switching to a verbal mode. Watch the students carefully for clues to their learning styles.

A student in introductory biology told her instructor that she simply could not understand a visual overhead he used to explain DNA replication. Suspecting from her behavior (when asked a question she constantly tapped her foot) that she was a kinesthetic learner, the instructor asked her to answer a series of questions. Each question required her to draw the DNA molecule at different stages of replication. This she did easily. Answering questions and drawing helped her to unlock her knowledge. Having drawn the component stages she could then explain the entire replication Her instructor suggested she use a similar approach during exams when she felt stuck. She tried this out, always sketching out the relevant figure before answering the question. Her test scores improved. Kinesthetic learners can often improve their recall by drawing because they learn by moving. Movement taps kinesthetic memory.

Following are some tips for teaching to specific learning styles.

Learning Style	Learner Characteristics	Teaching Tips
Visual	Learns best by seeing. Responds strongly to flowcharts, finds color useful in note taking. Often mentions the quality of visual material in course evaluations.	• Include visual material in lecture: flowcharts, schematics, cross-sections, concept maps. • Teach students how to construct appropriate visual study aids of their own. • Color-code visuals.
Kinesthetic	Learns best by doing. This learning style is activated by experiences where students get to do something with the material rather than listening or watching passively. Traditionally, kinesthetic learners prefer lab and field experiences to lecture. *Movement* such as writing or sketching facilitates their memory and thought.	• In lecture send around samples so students get to experience directly the rock you are discussing. • Cooperative learning is your best tool for activating this learning style during lecture. • Build frequent field trips into your course. • Teach some skills such as mineral identification. • Employ models, e.g., have students mold layers of clay to teach them about syncline/anticlines.
Auditory	Learns best by listening. Profits from summarizing material out loud. May find note taking interferes with understanding the material.	• Lecture is perfect for auditory learners. • Use collaborative learning exercises that require students to summarize difficult or key concepts out loud. • Don't rely entirely on visuals to make important points. Develop verbal summaries.
Sensor	Prefers facts to theory. (About 75 percent of students in a typical college class are sensors.)	• Employ collaborative learning exercises that help sensors "structure" the theory building.

Learning Style	Learner Characteristics	Tips for Teaching
Intuitive (global)	Loves theory and "big-picture" type material (25% of students in a typical college class are intuitive). Must get the big picture to learn. Has trouble with logical, deductive methods. Often seems lost until suddenly getting the big picture. At this point the intuitive (global) learner may demonstrate impressive creativity.	• Begin and end each lecture with an overview • Use cooperative learning exercises that require students to state the "big picture." • Include projects where synthesis is required.
Sequential	Learns in a logical sequential manner.	• Develop a logical, orderly presentation style.
All learners	Note that any student will exhibit a combination of the styles described. Thus, given three students in the class, John might be a visual-sensor-sequential, Mary an auditory-intuitive-global, and Janice a kinesthetic-sensor-sequential learner.	• Use multiple presentation modes of delivery. • Encourage students to study together and help each other in cooperative learning groups that provide a mix of students with diverse skills.

Online Resource

Learning Style Assessment. University Learning Center, University of Arizona. *http://www.ulc.arizona.edu*

CHAPTER 8

Lesson Design

By Kyla Macario
University Teaching Center
University of Arizona
Tucson, Arizona

What do you want your students to know? How do you want them to know it? **Needs assessment** is an invaluable tool for gaining quick knowledge of your learners. On the first day of class have students supply the following information:

- Name
- Grade level, e.g., freshman, sophomore
- Major area of study
- Is this course taken as an elective or a requirement?
- Current and potential levels of interest in topic
- Previous knowledge of topic
- How will the course be helpful in career aspirations?
- What would each student like to learn from the course as a whole?

Considering your class as a whole, what are the five most important concepts/skills students need to gain from your class?

Instructional objectives are specific, measurable, and absolute statements of what the students will know and/or be able to do at the end of each session of instruction. Using words that are not open to broad interpretation will assist you in writing clear, measurable, and concise objectives. Some cognitive performance words:

Identify	Classify	Distinguish	List
Recognize	Check	Compare	Rectify
Plan	Locate	Contrast	Sort
Interpret	Predict	Sequence	Solve
Select	Offer	Relate	Calculate
Compose	Determine	Compute	Evaluate
Construct	Build	Measure	Generate

Create	Articulate	Apply	Define
Analyze	Discriminate	Demonstrate	Order
Adopt	State	Execute	Establish
Formulates	Encode	Recall	Appraise
Summarize	Represent	Verify	Criticize
Infer	Elaborate	Reconstruct	Establish
Diagram	Convert	Manipulate	Compile
Distinguish	Illustrate	Write	Explain
Justify	Outline	Operate	
Modify	Paraphrase	Produce	

Following is an example of solid lesson design.

Thematic Topic: Using a (Burton) compass

Instructional Objectives: As part of a geoscience course, the students will be able to:

- Compare and contrast the three salient situations where geologists take measurements with a (Burton) compass.
- Demonstrate the use of a compass in a field exercise.

Break the content into thematic chunks of information and supporting activities.

1. *Warm-up:* Begin by asking students what they already know about the thematic topic for that class session and what they would like to learn. Use a newspaper clipping, magazine article, or television video clip to introduce the topic as an element of their everyday lives.

2. *Overview:* Tell students what will be presented and discussed in the class that day.

3. *Present ten- to twelve-minute segments* of information. At the end of each segment, allow students to process and practice what they have just heard. Briefly check in with the students at the end of each practice session to make sure they have learned and practiced the information correctly.

   a. Think/pair/share: Have the students reflect briefly on the information or concept just presented, then turn to the person next to them and say what they have learned.

   b. Write/pair/share: Have the students briefly write their understanding of the information or concept just presented, then turn to the person next to them and share what they have written.

   c. Problem solve: Give the students a map to read, a problem to solve based on what was just presented and discussed.

4. *Summary:* Briefly review the information presented, stressing interconnections of information.

5. *Informal evaluation of learning and teaching effectiveness:* Using small index cards, ask the students to write briefly what they learned in class, what they are still confused about, and any comments they would like to share with you regarding the class. The cards are anonymous, collected at the end of class, and can be easily reviewed to see if instructional objectives were met for that class.

Assess student learning frequently and give feedback promptly. Your instructional objectives allow you to construct the "tests" of knowledge and skills attained as you prepare each class session. The strategy for testing is determined from WHAT you want them to know and HOW they are to know it. Examples:

Instructional Objective 1: The salient uses of a compass could be tested by both subjective (students would be asked to *recall* the correct answer) and objective (they would be asked to *recognize* the correct answer) methods of testing.

Instructional Objective 2: The field exercise itself is a practice for the test as students will need to learn the skills for using a compass first. A second field exercise would easily assess their ability to use the instrument.

CHAPTER 9

Ideas on Grading

Minute by minute, testing is the best of all teaching techniques.

—L. B. MIRRIELEES

Most subjects at universities are taught for no other purpose than that they may be retaught when the students become teachers.

—G. C. LICHTENBERG

Lichtenberg describes education at its worst: a rudderless ship propelled by tradition rather than careful design. Grading can never be meaningful in a course that is not meaningful. Grading begins with setting course objectives that are clear and meaningful and relevant to each segment of your learner population.

What grades should provide:

- Valid measure of success in the course
- Consistent measure of success in the course
- Learning tool
- Manageable grading task for the instructor or graduate teaching assistant who grades it

Valid Measure of Success?

Do your test grades measure what you hope they will? To be valid, the content of a test must reflect both your stated course goals (see Chapter 1, Learning Objectives) and what you actually covered in lecture. To ensure fair coverage, it is a good idea to list *how many test items* you want to allocate to each course objective and/or concept. Then write the items accordingly. Tips for writing objective test items are included in Chapters 10 and 11.

Think about your exam from the point of view of the learner. It is helpful to include some prompts on the exam. (Can we read minds?) I find students have the most problems with fill-in-the-blanks questions. Often the answer is a term that is new and somewhat technical or the question is vague. For fill-in-the-blanks I provide a few choices for them to choose from.

Consistent Measure of Success?

Projects and other substantive written assignments provide one of the best methods we have for testing higher-order thinking skills such as those required for geology field trip reports. However, written assignments bring with them a problem: Is our grading consistent? Would the student whose paper I graded last night at 1 A.M. have received the same grade if it had been at the top of the stack and I had graded the paper three hours earlier? Would this paper receive the same grade if my teaching assistant had graded it? Would the grade be the same no matter which of my three teaching assistants graded it? My preceptors provided feedback on an early version of this paper. Did their intervention lead to a better paper? Or might the preceptor have misled the student about what was expected?

Troubling questions. But there is a tool that can help you avoid these pitfalls: the grading rubric. A grading rubric is a set of criteria you develop to ensure that you grade papers consistently and fairly. Here's how to develop a rubric.

1.   Clearly articulate what you hope to see in the students' work. Make a list.

2.   Read some papers to see what your students actually did with the assignment.

3.   Adjust your expectations.

4.   Develop criteria. How will you know you got what you wanted?

5.   Construct the rubric.

Sample Grading Rubric

Question: Compare and contrast the sediments in the active channel of Baseline Wash with the sediments in the cut bank. How were the sediments in the cut bank deposited? Why are they now exposed in the cut bank? Discuss.

Grading rubric:

✓ Description of active channel sediments
✓ Description of cut bank sediments
✓ Differences and similarities of the two sediments
✓ Origin of cut bank sediments
✓ History of the stream channel
✓ Evidence to back up discussion of topics
✓ Logical organization

It is particularly important to construct a rubric if work is graded by graduate teaching assistants. We also recommend that you and the TAs as a group grade six to eight papers before the grading is divided among teaching assistants.

Learning Tool?

Mirrielees instructs us that we learn by being tested. Indeed, active learning is defined as learning directed toward answering meaningful questions that we want to answer. The frequent, graded, pop quiz is well validated as a teaching strategy that improves students' performance. Consider incorporating a short quiz on the most important concept at the end of every lecture hour. It works!

Quizzes and exam grades reflect only part of what a student may learn in geology. Higher-order thinking, fieldwork skills, and attitudes toward science can often be assessed better by means other than tests. Build in a variety of options for students to demonstrate that they have learned something. A few possibilities:

- Field trip questions (see the sample grading rubric)
- Lab reports
- Projects
- Poster and oral presentations

How important should grades be? From a student point of view, good grades represent a key without which students may be barred from attending graduate school or professional school and from career opportunities. Given the importance some students attach to grades, it is not surprising that a significant minority of students cheat on exams. What is surprising is how far some students will go. A few years ago our testing office staff were cautioned by the Educational Testing Service (ETS) to check student erasers. It seems that some students were bringing hollow erasers with answers written in tiny letters to the Graduate Record Exam!

There is a great deal an instructor can do to prevent cheating:

- Set a collaborative class atmosphere.
- Give fair tests.
- Proctor exams and quizzes carefully.
- State policy regarding cheating clearly.

It is essential that your syllabus include a clear statement about the consequence of cheating on exams. Be familiar with the academic code of conduct on your campus and how it is administered. Most cheating problems can be avoided simply by being clear with your students. Clearly outline your policy before cheating occurs. Be firm and consistent in your approach if cheating does occur.

Easy to Grade?

If you have 150 student in one course, careful design and layout of questions can save significant time grading. Think about the grading process when you format the exam. For exams with all objective questions, use machine scoring if it is available. A mix of question types is desirable (see Chapter 10). Keeping questions of one format together simplifies grading. For open-ended questions, plan the grading rubric at the time you write the question. This will assure that you have constructed a gradable question. Have well-defined spaces for answers. If answers to objective questions are in a column on one side of the exam, the grader can easily construct a key that overlays the answers.

CHAPTER 10

How to Write Good Test Questions

What is a learner-centered exam? Put most simply it is one that puts the learning needs of students first. It is an exam that tests concepts students really need to learn in a manner that maximizes their opportunity for success. To achieve this end, a learner-centered exam should be

- based on course objectives that are clear and comprehensible to the students in the class.
- attuned to the learning needs of student market segments, e.g., majors, non-majors, related majors, that make up the class.
- fair. Items should be unambiguous and clearly worded. Testing methods that are anxiety-provoking for students should not be used.
- takes into account the variety and diversity of student learning styles.

Note that three of the four criteria apply to the entire course. No exam can be truly learner-centered unless it is anchored in a learner-centered design for the entire course. The entire process can be divided into five steps.

Step One: Set Clear Course Goals— Learning Objectives

Ideally, the process of writing a good test should begin with careful review of the learning objectives of the course. Writing good course learning objectives is prerequisite to writing good test items. For ideas on developing clear course learning objectives see Chapter 1. Note also that sample learning objectives are provided for every chapter in **Part II, Chapter Resources** in this manual.

Step Two: Write Criterion Tasks for Each Objective

Before they can be used to develop test items, learning objectives must first be honed into *criterion tasks*: (1) *knowledge* students will be able to demonstrate, (2) *skills* they will be proficient with, and (3) kinds of *problems* they will be able to solve.

At this point the classification of learning objectives in Part I, Chapter 1 in this manual provides a useful tool. Adapted from the Bloom Taxonomy of Educational Objectives

(Bloom, 1956; Crooks, 1988), KASA (knowledge, applications, skills, and attitudes) helps us to sort our course objectives into thinking tasks and to test students on higher-order thinking skills rather than simple recall.

> **K**—Knowledge
> **A**—Applications
> **S**—Skills
> **A**—Attitudes

Here's an example of how this classification scheme can be used in writing a geology test item. Suppose, for example, that *soil formation profiles* is on your list of essential topics for geology students majors who take your class. The KASA model suggests four kinds of learning tasks that you might decide to require of your students:

- **Knowledge.** If you just want your students to know the definition of a *soil*, you could ask them to define *soil* (short answer) or you could use *soil profile* as the stem of a multiple-choice item with three or four alternative definitions to choose from.

- **Applications.** You may want your students to go beyond recognition and definition and do some interpretation. In this case, you could show a labeled soil profile followed by a multiple-choice question that requires students to interpret the climate regime under which the soil formed.

- **Skills.** Making observations of a soil horizon in the field, students could be asked to assign a preliminary soil type.

- **Attitudes.** Our use of soils today is problematic because what could be a renewable resource is becoming a nonrenewable resource. Students could be asked to write on this topic. The learning task might be defined as writing a position paper for a senator or other elected official dealing with soil erosion issues.

It's up to you to decide which learning objectives are appropriate for your students. But generally, it makes sense to reserve higher-order thinking and application items for really important concepts. Note that in geology, visual test items are often required to test for higher level thinking and application. You will find examples of these in the student Study Guide.

Step Three: Teach to the Objectives

In addition to lecture coverage, it is important to build in opportunities to practice the criterion tasks. Practice may take the form of in-class collaborative learning exercises or assigned out-of-class exercises. For an introduction to collaborative learning techniques such as learning groups and study teams, see Part I, Chapter 4 of this manual. You may also wish to contact your campus learning and/or teaching center. The KASA taxonomy is also helpful for developing practice exercises.

Step Four: Derive Test Questions from Course Learning Objectives

Obviously the exam should focus on key learning objectives. To ensure that this happens on your exam, you may find it helpful to write an exam plan. Typically, an exam plan includes a list of key objectives and how many points you want to devote to each.

Step Five: Write Test Questions

- **Cover criterion tasks.** To be fair, an exam should reflect the major emphasis and organization of your course. It is useful to assign the number of exam points you want to devote to each objective. Then write or select test bank items accordingly. Provide a mix of items that takes into account the learning styles of your students (see Part I, see Chapter 11 of this manual) and the kind of skills you want students to master (e.g., geological interpretation, critical thinking, writing).

- **Include visual material in your test items.** Geology is a visual discipline. Do use visual materials in your test items. Graphics encourage students to learn in the mode in which most professional geologists think. The student Study Guide contains many good examples of visual test items.

- **Test critical thinking and higher-order geology skills.** Have students interpret a formation, predict which of several seaside homes will survive a seismic event, or decide what kind of volcano they are seeing given descriptive information that you provide. Obviously, you have to prepare students for higher-order items by providing guided practice. Practice may occur during lecture, cooperative learning exercises, take-home assignments where students receive comments and formative feedback, and field trips.

- **Prepare new exams each time you teach the course.** While it is time consuming to make up exams, a past exam may not reflect how you presented the material this term. The Test Bank provided for *Understanding Earth* may take some of the drudgery out of the procedure. Do revise Test Bank items as needed to fit what you actually taught your students.

- **Prepare clear instructions.** Test them on a colleague or teaching assistants.

- **Use an item analysis to test the accuracy of test items.** Instructors sometimes find it useful to develop their own test item bank. A useful resource is your campus teaching center. Often teaching centers can provide expert advice on construction of exams as well as statistical analysis of test items on your exam.

Item analysis provides a useful means of developing accurate multiple-choice items. In this statistical procedure, each alternative of each multiple-choice question is correlated to the student's total score. Logically, good students should do better than poor students on a good item. Thus, an item where the correct response is highly correlated with the total score and all distracter alternatives show low correlations with the total score is probably rating students fairly. Conversely, a distracter that correlates higher with total score than the correct alternative suggests that there is something wrong with the item. You then have the option of throwing out the bad item or revising it for future use. Ask your campus teaching center about the availability of this kind of service.

References

Bloom, B. S., ed., 1956. *Taxonomy of educational objectives.* Vol. I: *Cognitive domain.* New York: McKay.

Crooks, T. J. 1988. The impact of classroom evaluation practices on students. *Review of Educational Research, 58*(4): 438–481.

CHAPTER 11

How to Minimize Student Test-Taking Problems

I have come to a frightening conclusion. I am the decisive element in the classroom. It is my personal approach that determines the climate. It is my daily mood that makes the weather. As a teacher, I possess tremendous power to make a student's life miserable or joyous. I can be a tool of humor, hurt or healing. My response decides whether a crisis will be escalated or de-escalated, and a [student] humanized or dehumanized. No machine, sophisticated as it may be, can do this job.

—HAIM GINOT, TEACHER, 1972

The tests one gives and the manner with which one gives them are more than simply a way to see what the students know. They are major attributes of the educational climate of your classroom. Consider giving some thought to climate control.

The following Top Ten List comes from our University of Arizona Learning Center. It summarizes the problems college students have with taking tests. Although they are individual learning problems, many are an unnecessary result of the way tests are constructed and administered. Hence, there are many strategies open to the instructor that can help to assure that test takers are successful. Hopefully, you will find them as useful as we and other professors have.

Top Ten Student Test-Taking Problems

Problem 10 "Test-taking anxiety interferes with my performance on exams."

What the instructor can do:

- Keep in mind that for students in their first course in geology, figuring out "what's important" is one of the biggest problems.
- Remember to share some of your reasoning about why key material is important with your students.
- Offer a review session before each exam.

- Consider giving students some of the specific questions ahead of time.
- Address a few specific exam questions during lecture.
- Consider allowing your students to refer to their notes or one page of notes during an exam.
- Teach students how to organize. Give a study skills assignment (see Chapters 5 and 6 in Part I of this Instructor's Manual) that focuses on exam preparation, such as completing an Eight-Day Study Plan (Appendix A of the student Study Guide for *Understanding Earth*).
- Begin each exam with a few easy factual items for warm-up.
- Avoid fast-paced or overly long exams.
- Train your proctors to provide a calming testing situation.

Problem 9 "I misread multiple-choice (or true-false) questions."
What the instructor can do:

- Avoid writing items with double negatives (e.g., "Determine which of the following options is not false.").
- Avoid writing items with confusing formats (e.g., "Which of the following minerals *is not* found in diamond?").
- Proofread each alternative carefully and get rid of confusing or unduly complicated grammatical constructions.
- Get feedback on questions from teaching assistants and preceptors.

Problem 8 "I misread the directions on the test."
What the instructor can do:

- Make your directions clear and simple.
- Test your directions on a colleague.
- Solicit student input about your test directions.
- Do a practice run on reading directions carefully during the review session for the first exam.

Problem 7 "I ran out of time."
What the instructor can do:

- Allow extra time for those who need it. This requires a little organization, particularly when another class immediately follows yours. Encourage students to let you know ahead of time if they need help. Note that for some students with a diagnosed learning disability you are required by law to do this.
- Avoid time-pressed testing situations. Ask yourself whether quick responses really fit the objectives you have laid out for the course.
- If you decide speed is really essential, provide opportunities for students to practice under time-pressed conditions before the test.

Problem 6 "I made a mistake transferring the answer to the answer sheet."
What the instructor can do:

- Have students mark answers beside the questions, not on a separate sheet. If your department uses generic answer sheets that are scanned electronically, inquire whether the benefits gained by using scannable answer sheets really justify the inconvenience to students. This becomes a double whammy if you combine having to copy answers to a second sheet with a time-pressed situation.

Hint: See Part I, Chapter 9 of this manual for some alternative ways of ensuring that exams are not difficult to score.

Problem 5 "I reasoned my way into the wrong answer."

What the instructor can do:

- Keep in mind that studies of college freshmen show that most are just beginning to develop critical thinking skills; indeed, many get stuck at the stage of defining the problem. Set your expectations to provide a reasonable challenge, not "mission impossible."
- Provide in-class practice on key thinking and interpretive skills you want your students to master. See Chapter 4 for ideas about how to provide cooperative learning exercises that will provide students an opportunity to practice skills in class.
- Consider giving students some of the specific questions ahead of time.
- Address a few specific exam questions during lecture. Model the thinking you want the students to master. Then have them practice in groups of two.

Problem 4 "I changed a correct answer to the wrong one."

What the instructor can do:

- Advise students that when they are unsure, their first guess is usually correct. They should beware of changing answers unless they can clearly identify the error. Say it (for auditory learners) and write it into your exam directions (for visual learners). Provide an example (for kinesthetic learners).

Problem 3 "I didn't choose the *one best* multiple-choice answer."

What the instructor can do:

- Teach students how to take a multiple-choice exam.
- Avoid trick questions.
- Use *bold italics* to emphasize key words students should attend to.

Problem 2 "I lack a strategic approach to preparing for multiple midterm and final exams."

What the instructor can do:

- Teach students how to organize. Give a study skills assignment (see Chapters 5 and 6) that focuses on exam preparation such as completing an Eight-Day Study Plan and/or the Final Exam Prep Worksheet (Appendices A and B of the student Study Guide).
- Consider giving students some of the specific questions ahead of time.
- Address a few specific exam questions during lecture.
- Conduct a review session prior to each exam.

Problem 1 "I didn't study."

This is the most common (if students are responding honestly!) and most difficult problem for the instructor to deal with.

What the instructor can do:

We cannot provide motivation (that is the student's job). But we can set up contingencies that encourage and reward desired learning behaviors.

- Keep in mind that for students in their first course in geology, figuring out "what's important" is one of the biggest problems.

- Remember to share with your students some of your reasoning about why key material is important.
- Offer a review session before each exam to help students focus.
- Consider giving students some of the specific questions ahead of time.
- Address a few specific exam questions during lecture.
- Teach students how to study, how to learn. See Chapters 5 and 6 in Part I of the Instructor's Manual for assignments on studying (learning how to learn).
- Teach students how to organize. Give a study skills assignment (see Part I, Chapters 5 and 6 of this manual) that focuses on exam preparation.
- Practice skills in class via cooperative learning exercises.
- Use peer tutors (preceptors) in your class to reinforce studying.
- Provide opportunities for extra credit.
- Provide prompt feedback (reinforces performance).

We do not believe in ourselves until someone reveals that deep inside us something is valuable, worth listening to, worthy of our trust, sacred to our touch. Once we believe in ourselves, we can risk curiosity, wonder, spontaneous delight, or any experience that reveals the human spirit.

—E. E. CUMMINGS

Write Test Items to Diverse Learning Styles

In the typical introductory geology course we are likely to encounter a considerable variety of student learning styles (see the table on the next page). How can all this diversity be accommodated in the tests you write? A simple direct answer is that it cannot be fully accommodated. But building variety into your test questions can help. Types of items that tend to favor each learning style are identified in the last column of the table.

Hint: As in other aspects of teaching, the tendency is to write test items that are advantageous to students fortunate enough to have the same learning style that we do. **Example:** Instructors who are visual-intuitive-sequential learners might tend to favor test items that include flow-charts: a flowchart is a visual aid that provides a "big picture" of a process in a sequential manner. But what about learners that are auditory-sensors? Circle the learning styles in the table that *are not your own*. Then ask yourself what kinds of test items you can write that give such students a fair opportunity to demonstrate their knowledge.

Learning Style	Learner Characteristics	Test Items That Tap Each Learning Style
Visual	Learns best by seeing. Responds strongly to flowcharts, finds color useful in note taking.	Include visual items in your tests: flowcharts, schematics, cross-sections (a good idea anyway, given the highly visual nature of geology concepts).
Kinesthetic	Learns best by doing. Prefers lab and field experiences to lecture. Movement such as pacing and toe tapping facilitates memory and thought.	Include items that test skills such as mineral identification and items based on lab and field experiences. Encourage students to sketch when they get stuck on a test item. Sketching activates kinesthetic memory.
Auditory	Learns best by listening. Profits from summarizing material out loud.	It is very unusual to present test items in the auditory mode, but the computer provides an opportunity to do so. Be aware that talking to themselves is how auditory learners best remember. When you are proctoring an exam, try not to confuse this activity with cheating.
Sensor	Prefers facts to theory. (About 75 percent of students in a typical college class room are sensors.)	Always begin exams with a set of basic fact items in multiple-choice or true/false format.
Intuitive	Loves theory and "big-picture" type material. (Only 25 percent of students in a typical college class room are intuitive.)	Items that test global understanding and theory.

Naturally, any given student will exhibit a combination of the styles described. John might be a visual-sensor-sequential, Mary an auditory-intuitive-global, and Janice a kinesthetic-sensor-sequential learner.

CHAPTER 12

How to Evaluate Your Course[*]

If you don't know where you're going, you're liable to wind up somewhere else.

—DAVID CAMPBELL

Course evaluation may be linked to evaluation of teaching effectiveness. It is important to distinguish clearly between *formative evaluation*, something any instructor can and should initiate, and *summative evaluation,* designed to evaluate teaching for the purposes of granting tenure and promotion.

	Formative Evaluation	Summative Evaluation
Purpose	For course development	For important decisions that involve performance appraisal.
Standard	You (the instructor) set the standard.	Standard must be *explicit* and *normed.*
Data	The more data collected the better.	Data must be *limited* and *targeted* to an audience of reviewers such as your department or college tenure and promotion committee.
End product	When you're satisfied, you're done.	A formal report is crucial.

Ideally, formative evaluation should link to summative. If your college or university is strongly committed to student learning, then you will find that developing an effective course is essential preparation for tenure and promotion review.

---

[*] For this chapter we draw heavily on various workshop materials developed by Elena Berman, Assessment and Enrollment Research, University of Arizona, and Beth Harrison, University Teaching Center, University of Arizona. Thanks to both for their support of this and other teaching projects.

Principles of Evaluation

What does good evaluation look like? Following are nine useful principles paraphrased from the Web site of the American Association for Higher Education (AAHE). A discussion of these principles will be found on the Web site: *http://www.aahe.org/assessment/principl.htm*

1. **Begin with what you value** (see Part I, Chapter 1 in this manual).

2. **Make assessment multidimensional** (see Part I, Chapter 1). Learning is a complex process. To assess your instruction use multiple modes of evaluation and feedback: measures of student performance, course evaluations, campus-wide surveys, instruments that assess student attitudes toward science, focus groups, and so on. For example, many faculty members who utilize undergraduate preceptors in their classes discover that preceptors provide an invaluable source of feedback.

3. **Set clear objectives** (see Part I, Chapter 1).

4. **Assess both outcomes and process.** To improve outcomes, we need to look closely at what students experience along the way. Focus groups (see the next section) can help with this assessment.

5. **Make the process ongoing, not episodic.** The point is to monitor progress in the spirit of continuous improvement. This may be achieved by tracking the progress of individual students or the progress of cohorts. **Example:** Majors who take your course and then go on to other courses.

6. **Represent the entire educational community.** Student learning is a campus-wide responsibility. Think of assessment as collaborative activity. Look for ways to involve staff (in your learning center, teaching center, library, and administration), alumni, and of course students in the assessment of your course. **Hint:** Keep it simple.

7. **Answer questions people really care about.** This is vital in summative evaluation processes dealing with promotion and tenure. But even formative evaluation should include the collection of some information that will interest the decision makers in your life. That is just good reality testing.

8. **Make assessment part of a larger set of conditions that promote change.** Assessment is most important on campuses that deeply value the quality of teaching and learning. On such campuses information about learning outcomes is integral to decision making. It is actively sought.

9. **Address your responsibility to students and the public.** Our deeper obligation is not just to collect and report information about our teaching. It is to improve. This is a two-way street. Those to whom faculty are accountable have an inherent social contract to support efforts to improve.

Focus Groups

Focus groups are an excellent way to learn more about the experience students have in your course as they try to achieve the learning objectives you have set for them. This is the essence of AAHE Principle 4. Focus groups are provided on a growing number of college campuses. Often they are based on a process called small group instructional diagnosis (SIGID). SIGID was developed by D. Joseph Clark at the University of Washington's Biology Learning Center. To use SIGID, you will need an outside observer, typically a staff member from your college teaching or learning center to lead the focus group.

1. The first step is to arrange a meeting between instructor and focus group leader.

2. The focus group leader attends class and is introduced by the instructor, who then leaves for 20 to 30 minutes. Students form groups and answer three questions:

    • What do you like about this course?
    • What do you think needs improvement?
    • What specific suggestions do you have for change?

Responses are discussed and recorded by the focus group leader.

3. The instructor receives a written summary and meets with the focus group leader.

4. The instructor reacts to student feedback at the next class.

Focus groups can have a positive effect on motivation for both instructor and students. Students are motivated by seeing that their feedback is taken seriously. Faculty are motivated and empowered by the positive feedback they receive, which often reveals a simple solution to problems that had previously seemed difficult. Finally, because focus groups are run at midterm, there is time to make changes to improve the learning process that semester for the students who provide the feedback.

Consider asking your campus teaching or learning center to develop a SIGID process for faculty if it is not already available.

References

Bloom, B. S., ed. 1956. *Taxonomy of Educational Objectives. Cognitive domain, 1.* New York: McKay, 1956.

Crooks, T. J. The impact of classroom evaluation practices on students. *Review of Educational Research, 58*(4): 438–481.

Redmond, M., & D. Clark. 1982. Small group instructional diagnosis: A practical approach to improving teaching. *AAHE Bulletin, 34*(6): 8–10.

Internet Source

American Association for Higher Education (AAHE) Assessment Forum
Nine principles of good practice for assessing student learning
http://www.aahe.org/assessment/principl.htm

CHAPTER 1

Building a Planet

Chapter Summary

- The human creative process, field and lab observations, and experiments help geoscientists to formulate testable hypotheses (models) for how the Earth works and its history. A hypothesis is a tentative explanation that can help focus attention on plausible features and relationships of a working model. If a testable hypothesis is eventually confirmed by a large body of data, then it may be elevated to a theory. Theories are abandoned when subsequent investigations show them to be false. Confidence grows in those theories that withstand repeated tests and are able to predict the results of new experiments.

- Our solar system probably formed when a cloud of interstellar gas and dust condensed about 4.5 billion years ago. The planets vary in chemical composition in accordance with their distance from the Sun and with their size.

- Earth probably grew by accretion of colliding chunks of matter. Very early after the Earth formed, it is thought that our Moon formed from material ejected from the Earth by the impact of a giant meteorite. Bolide impacts are rare events now but space is littered with debris that has occasionally hit the Earth and profoundly impacted life.

- Heat generated from the Moon-forming impact and the decay of radioactive elements probably caused much of the Earth to melt. Melting allowed iron and other dense matter to sink toward the Earth's center and form the core. Lower density (lighter) matter floated upward to form the mantle and crust. Release of trapped gases (mostly water) from within the Earth gave rise to the oceans and an early atmosphere. In this way, the Earth was transformed into a differentiated planet with chemically distinct zones: an iron core; a mantle of mostly magnesium, iron, silicon, and oxygen; and a crust rich in oxygen, silicon, aluminum, calcium, potassium, sodium, and radioactive elements.

- As the Earth cooled, an outer relatively rigid shell, called the lithosphere, formed. Dynamic processes driven by heat transfer, density differences, and gravity broke the outer shell into plates that move around the Earth at rates of centimeters per year. Major components (atmosphere, hydrosphere, and biosphere) of Earth's surface systems are driven mostly by solar energy. Earth's internal heat energizes the lithosphere, asthenosphere, deep mantle, outer and inner core.

- The oldest known rocks found on the Earth's surface are about 4 billion years old.

- The composition of Earth's atmosphere and oceans, and life history was profoundly changed by the addition of oxygen when photosynthetic life evolved over 2 billion years ago.

Learning Objectives

Focus your instruction on clear learning objectives. In this section we provide a *sampling* of possible objectives for this chapter. No class could or should try to accomplish all these. Choose based on your analysis of your class. Refer to Chapter 1: *Learning Objectives—How to Define Your Goals for the Class* in the Instructional Design section of this manual for thoughts and ideas about how to go about such an analysis.

Knowledge. At the end of this unit the student should:

- Know the distinction between hypothesis and theory.
- Know the principle of uniformitarianism.
- Know the nebula hypothesis for the evolution of the solar system.
- Know when and how the Earth's interior differentiated.
- Know the modern ideas for the origin of the Earth's Moon.
- Know the role bolide impacts played in Earth and life history.
- Know the basics of plate tectonics.

Skills/Applications/Attitudes

- Discuss the consequences of the early Earth becoming partially molten.
- Appreciate the role of the scientific method in problem solving.
- Appreciate the vastness of the geological time scale in relation to the history of humans.
- Appreciate the idea that Earth is our space ship and therefore it makes sense for us to understand the basics of how the Earth operates.
- Appreciate the concept of earth as a system of interacting surface and internal components, e.g., hydrosphere, atmosphere, biosphere, lithosphere, asthenosphere.

General Education Skills

- Write a summary of the idea that the movement of tectonic plates is the surface manifestation of convection in the mantle from the point of view of a skeptic. (Writing/Critical Thinking)
- Use this exercise to identify questions and confusion students have regarding Earth's internal systems. This will help students assimilate the information on plate tectonics in Chapter 2.

Freshman Survival Skills

- Encourage students to read the three introductory chapters of the *Student Study Guide for Understanding Earth*. These chapters explain how to use the study guide and provide helpful guidelines for reading a science text like *Understanding Earth* and studying geology. The most effective way to encourage this activity is to make it an extra credit assignment. (Textbook reading, note taking, time management, exam preparation.)
- Encourage students to preview Chapter 1 before lecture by awarding credit for restating in their own words acceptable answers to the **Chapter Preview Questions** in the *Student Study Guide for Understanding Earth*. (Previewing/Textbook Reading)

• Distribute a chapter outline and a selection of mixed format study questions before the first lecture on Building a Planet. (Note Taking)

Sample Lecture Outline

Digital copy is available from Instructor's CD and web site.
http://www.whfreeman.com/understandingearth

    Sample lecture outlines highlight the important topics and concepts covered in the text. We suggest that you download a digital copy of this outline from the web site and customize it to your own lecture before handing it out to students. At the end of each chapter outline, consider adding a selection of review questions, representing a range of thinking levels.

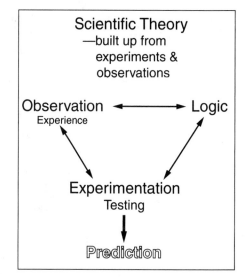

Chapter 1: Building a Planet

The Scientific Method
    Testable hypothesis—working model
    Theory

Brief History of Geology—Principle of
    Uniformitarianism

Origin of Our Solar System
    Nebular hypothesis
    Sun vs. inner planets vs. outer planets
        Inner terrestrial planets
        Giant outer gaseous planets
    Origin of the Earth's Moon

Differentiation of Earth
    Early melting
        Impact event that generates Moon contributes significant heat
        Accretion—heat from smaller impacts
        Radiogenic heat
    Consequence of melting:
        Core, mantle, and early crust form
        Metallic and silicate phases separate
            Metallic core
            Fe, Mg, and Ca rich mantle
            Si, Na, K rich crust
            Early atmosphere and oceans degas from planet's interior by volcanism

Bombardment from space has had profound impact on both Earth and life history.

Earth as a system of interacting components energized by the sun and internal heat
    Atmosphere, hydrosphere, biosphere, lithosphere, asthenosphere, deep mantle, outer and inner core

Plate Tectonics System
    Key components of Plate Tectonic Theory
        Plates = lithosphere moving on soft asthenosphere
        Convection/gravity help to explain how plates move

Geologic Time
    Oldest known rocks are 4 billion
    Chemical and biological evolution of life
    Oxygen becomes a major gas in the atmosphere
    Life's "Big Bang" about 600 million years ago is marked by the appearance of a great diversity of animal life.

CD and Web site Resources

Instructor's CD Highlights

- *Key Textbook Figures and Tables:*

    Figure 1.1: The Scientific Method

    Figure 1.3: Evolution of the solar system

    Figure 1.4: The solar system

    Figure 1.5: The differentiation of early Earth

    Figure 1.8: The evolution of the Earth's atmosphere

    Figure Story 1.10: Major components and subsystems of the Earth system

    Figure 1.11: Convection

    Figure 1.12: Geologic time from the formation of the solar system to the present

- *Photo Gallery:* Includes slide set images from the previous three editions

Web site Highlights

http://www.whfreeman.com/understandingearth

- **Presentation Tools**

    Animations: Visit the web site for animations, including animations of figures from this chapter.

    PowerPoint Presentation

    PowerPoint Presentation with Lecture Notes

    Photo Gallery

- **Course Preparation**

    Instructor's Manual

    Sample Lecture Outline

    Sample Exercises

- **Student Study Resources—Assessable**

    Graded Online Quizzing

    Geology in Practice: A Road Map, Geologic Models and Testable Hypotheses

    This *Geology in Practice* contains the Arctic sea ice model for Earth's active plates animation and the following exercises which can be used for in-class discussion, homework, or extra credit.

    Exercise 1: Geologic Models and Working Hypotheses

    Exercise 2: A Road Map and Testable Hypotheses

    Exercise 3: How Does A Scientific Hypothesis Become A Theory?

- **Student Study Resources—Non-Assessable**

    Online Review Exercises: Identify the Plate Boundary

    Concept Self-Checker

    Flashcards

Teaching Tips

Cooperative/Collaborative Exercises and In-Class Activities

Coop Exercise # 1: Earth is Our Space Ship

by Robert Butler, Department of Geosciences, University of Arizona, Tucson, Arizona.
Students are seated in groups of six. Starting with a short and simple trip across town, student groups are asked to produce a list of items required to accomplish a journey of increasing

duration and complexity. I usually start this exercise by asking groups to list what they would need to consider to make a trip in one afternoon to a local shopping mall. Groups are given a minute to arrive at this list. After that minute has passed, I ask one group at a time to report something from their list and I write these on an overhead for all to see. Obvious things that will show up on this list are: transportation (by car, by bus, by bike, walk?); money; look at the newspaper for sales notices; etc. Depending on the time allowed, the next step can be to consider a trip across state or skip directly to a trip across country. This requires a bit more time for groups to compile their lists. I usually allow two minutes for development of this list and I will go sit with one student group and help them with their list. The question of mode of transportation becomes an important issue of discussion for this trip. Flying is fast but can be expensive; travel by car is slow but provides flexibility; if you travel by car, you need to budget money for gas, etc. Food and lodging become important considerations on a cross-country trip, so student groups begin to deal with the logistics, expense, and questions of creature comfort that surround food and lodging.

The next level of complexity is to ask students to consider a trip to Mars in which they would circle Mars a few times and then return to Earth. Students are usually getting confident by the time the list of necessities for the cross-country trip are listed but they rapidly lose that confidence when asked to design a trip to Mars. You need to provide at least five minutes for construction of the "required" list for this space travel. While students are working on this, I usually jump around among two or three groups in different parts of the room to keep groups on task. With some prodding, the class usually does a credible job developing at least the basic list of requirements. Constructing this list forces students to think about many requirements for human survival that are taken for granted and rarely considered explicitly. The list of items and systems required for a trip to Mars generally will include the obvious space vehicle (we don't get hung up on design), food, water, and air to breath. Deeper thought leads to appreciation for the importance of fuel to propel the spaceship and provide energy for the guidance systems and warmth of the travelers. Generally it will occur to one or more groups that they need to have a waste disposal system. More subtle are considerations of the potentially harmful space environment (UV radiation, cosmic rays, vacuum of space).

This class discussion is concluded by showing a slide of "Mother" Earth taken from space. The point is made that Earth is our space ship. It makes sense for us to understand the basics of how the Earth operates. To do that, we need to consider not just the solid Earth but also the hydrosphere, atmosphere, biosphere, and interactions within the Earth systems and of those systems with our space environment. One can bring in environmental concerns such as floods, earthquakes, and global climatic change. If time permits, I show a graph of world population growth and ask students to ponder the question of how much more complex it is to design a space ship for six billion humans instead of the four or five passengers they were thinking of when they developed their list of requirements for their space ship. If you want to get pointed with this discussion, you can ask students to consider that the United States consumes 40% of the world's resources to support 6% of the world's population. Are we a sustainable society? (A society which can continue without decreasing the options for the next generations)?

This exercise will tie wonderfully with discussions at the end of the semester when Chapter 23: *Earth Systems, Cycles, and Human Impacts* is assigned reading.

Coop Exercise #2: Sense of Scale for Our Solar System— A BB vs. a Basketball

Use this short cooperative exercise to give students a sense of scale for our solar system and space beyond. You will need a BB and a basketball. Holding the BB between your fingers, present it to the class as representing the size of the Earth in a scale model of the solar system. Our sun is about 109 times larger in diameter than the Earth and a basketball is a good representation for the size of our sun in this scale model. Ask a student to stand up and hold the BB (Earth) between their fingers somewhere in front of class. Then give the basketball to

Five-Minute Write

- What questions do you have about lecture?
- What did you find most interesting about lecture?
- How was lecture relevant to you?

another student and ask the class to coach this student where the basketball should be relative to the BB such that their distance would be proportional to the actual distance between Earth and Sun. Essentially the size and distance between the BB and basketball are scaled and consistent with their relative sizes and distances.

In a scale model of our solar system where the sizes and distances between the Sun and Earth are consistent with their relative sizes (a basketball and a BB), the Earth is about 90 feet from the Sun. In a large lecture hall for 150 students, the basketball and BB are located approximately at the opposite corners of the room.

If you maintained the proportionality of this basketball and BB model and showed the closest star, with the Sun in Tucson, Arizona, Alpha Centuri would be a basketball somewhere around Detroit.

Coop Exercise # 3: Five-Minute Write

The Five-Minute Write is done during the last five minutes of lecture. Ask students to put their name on a sheet of paper and then address the three questions on the overhead (see adjacent sample). Start the next lecture by discussing the answers to some of the questions students had about the previous lecture.

Freshman Survival Skills Assignment

In the beginning of your course it is prudent to include a few exercises to help the freshmen in your class learn how to learn and to reinforce mastery of the basics of good preparation for college level lectures. Learning skills are like critical thinking skills. They tend to be mastered slowly, over time with lots of practice: even upper division students and graduate students sometimes need coaching about how to learn. See Part I: *Instructional Design* for a discussion of why this is so and ideas about how to do it. Chapter 1 discusses freshman survival as a national educational priority. Chapters 5 and Chapter 6 discuss how to develop credit assignments to encourage students to learn how to learn.

The assignment to **Preview a Textbook Chapter** is highly recommended. It may help your students develop the good habit of coming to lecture prepared. You will find this assignment in Chapter 6 of the Instructional Design section of this manual (see Part I, Chapter 6: *Control the Incentives: Assign Credit to Study Skill Assignments*. Making this an assignment early in the course will help to set the tone that you expect students to come to lecture prepared.

Topics for Class Discussion

- One page articles listed below provide an excellent basis for class discussion and homework on the scientific method. They are also referred to in the *Geology in Practice* exercises.

  Shermer, M. (February, 2003). Psychic Drift—Why most scientists do not believe in ESP and psi phenomena, *Scientific American*, p. 31.

  Shermer, M. (October, 2002). The Physicist and the Abalone Diver—The difference between the creators of two new theories of science reveals the social nature of the scientific process, *Scientific American*, p. 42.

  Shermer, M. (April, 2002). Skepticism as a Virtue—An inquiry into the original meaning of the word "skeptic," *Scientific American*, p. 37.

  Shermer, M. (April, 2001). Colorful Pebbles and Darwin's Dictum—Science is an exquisite blend of data and theory, *Scientific American*, p. 38.

- A comparison of the relative volume and mass for each of the major layers within the Earth provides a useful perspective.

Volume and Mass of Earth's Layers

Layer	Volume (% of total)	Mass (% of total)
Atmosphere	————	0.02
Continental crust	0.44	0.42 (continental & ocean)
Ocean crust	0.16	
Mantle	83.02	67.77
Outer core	15.68	31.79 (outer and inner core)
Inner core	0.70	

• A comparison of planetary atmospheres. Ask your students to fill in two additional rows to this table: surface temperature range and atmospheric pressure.

The Atmospheric Composition of Earth, Venus, and Mars

Gas	Venus	Earth	Mars
Carbon dioxide (CO_2)	96%	0.03%	95%
Nitrogen (N_2)	3.5%	78%	2.7%
Oxygen (O_2)	0.003%	21%	0.15%
Argon	0.006%	0.9%	1.6%

• Where does matter comes from?
   The heavy elements are created in stars, nova, and supernova by nucleosynthesis.

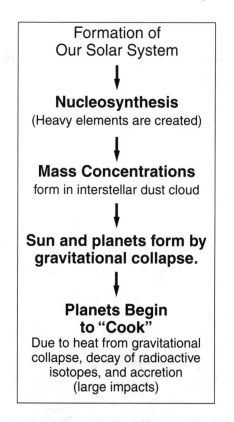

Formation of
Our Solar System
↓
Nucleosynthesis
(Heavy elements are created)
↓
Mass Concentrations
form in interstellar dust cloud
↓
Sun and planets form by gravitational collapse.
↓
Planets Begin to "Cook"
Due to heat from gravitational collapse, decay of radioactive isotopes, and accretion (large impacts)

There is good reason that the Earth's crust and mantle consist primarily of silicate minerals and the core of iron. Silicon and iron are two of the ten most abundant elements in the universe.

Ten Most Abundant Elements in the Universe

Element	Symbol	Atomic number	Number of atoms per million of hydrogen
hydrogen	H	1	1,000,000
helium	He	2	80,000
oxygen	O	8	740
neon	Ne	10	130
nitrogen	N	7	92
carbon	C	6	450
magnesium	Mg	12	40
silicon	Si	14	37
iron	Fe	26	32
sulfur	S	16	19

Teaching Resources

Student Study Guide Highlights

In Part I: Chapters provide strategies for learning geology. Ideally, students would read these chapters early in the course.

Chapter 1   Brief Preview of the *Study Guide for Understanding Earth* by Press, Siever, Grotzinger, and Jordan

Chapter 2   Meet the Authors of *Understanding Earth, 4th Edition*: How to use your geology textbook

Chapter 3   How to Be Successful in Geology (or just about any other challenging course)

Part II. Chapter 1: *Building a Planet*

Before Lecture:

Preview Questions & Brief Answers

During Lecture:

Learning Warm-up Tip

After Lecture:

Check Your Notes

Exam Prep:

Chapter Summary

Practice Exercise: *The Evolving Early Earth*

Review Questions (Answers to all review questions are given at the end of the Study Guide.)

Sample Exercises

Digital copy is available from Instructor's CD and web site.
http://www.whfreeman.com/understandingearth

• Sense of Scale Exercise

This exercise is designed to get students thinking about the scale of major planetary features, a sense for the vastness of geologic time, and a sense for the rates of geologic processes.

Sense of Geologic Time

1. The oldest rock yet to be found on the earth is from Canada and is radiometrically dated at almost four billion years. Radiometric dates usually measure the interval of time that has elapsed since the igneous rock solidified from a molten state. Various lines of evidence, including radiometric dates on meteorites and lunar samples, suggest that the earth and our solar system is about 4.5 to 5 billion years old. Over this interval of time, staggering compared to human standards, the atmosphere and hydrosphere of the earth evolved.

   A billion years is an immense length of time! To gain a sense of the magnitude of geologic time, figure out how many years it would take for you to count to one billion, assuming that each count takes one second. Another words, how many years in one billion seconds?

   Show your work and keep track of the units!

   Answer _____

Sense of Scale

2. Air is our most precious resource. Without food, we can live for weeks and without water, we can live for days. But without air to breathe we survive about four minutes! At the top of Mt. Everest at 29,028 feet, it's hard to walk without a tank of oxygen, even if you are in the world's best physical shape. In a commercial jet, traveling across country at 35,000 feet, you would be dead in minutes without the pressurized cabin and a supply of oxygen to breathe.

   Relative to the planet earth, the atmosphere we survive in is extremely thin. Most people live at or close to sea level because most major cities of the world are along coastlines. Some cities and villages in Mexico, South America, and China, for example, are at higher (8000 to 12,000 feet) elevations. Few people live above 15,000 feet. Mt. McKinley in Alaska is about 20,320 feet high and climbers do get to the top without oxygen tanks but they need tremendous determination due in large part to the thin atmosphere.

   Because most people live below an elevation of 15,000 feet, let's simply say that this is the height or thickness of our atmosphere in which humans effectively live. Sure you can survive at higher elevations but we thrive when we are lower.

   A) Calculate how many miles in 15,000 feet, round off to the nearest tenth of a mile.

   Show all work.

   Answer_____

   B) Ask students to translate the distance they calculate in part A to the distance between their campus and some well-know feature or major intersection.

   Answer_____

"Walking" to the Center of the Earth

3. The earth's interior is composed of three main concentric zones: the crust, the mantle, and the core. The outermost layer, the crust, averages about 40 km thick on the continents and is thinner (average 10 km) under the oceans. The middle layer, the mantle, is

an average of 2900 km thick, and the core, the inner most layer, has an average radius of 3470 km, about the size of the planet Mars.

A) Assuming you can walk 10 miles in a day (and that you can tolerate the tremendous heat and pressure), how many days would it take you to walk to the crust-mantle interface (called the Moho), if you started from the land surface? (**Hint:** 1 mile = 1.6 km).

Show your work and round off to the nearest whole day.

Answer_____

B) How many more days would it take you to get to the center of the Earth?

Answer_____

C) How many months would the whole trek take?

Answer_____

Rates at Which Geologic Processes Operate

4. Some geologic processes like volcanism and earthquakes occur intermittently but can cause significant and sometimes catastrophic change very quickly. Other processes like weathering and erosion tend to act continuously but gradually and may seem to be imperceptibly slow. Regardless of whether we can notice changes or not, geologic processes, acting over long periods of time (thousands and millions of years) produce significant changes to the Earth's surface.

   If you were to visit the Grand Canyon occasionally over a period of many years, you would most likely notice no change. Even the details in the cliffs would probably seem "forever" frozen. Yet the Colorado River is continuously, albeit somewhat slowly, cutting into and eroding the Colorado Plateau. The Grand Canyon is gradually getting deeper and wider.

   Some geologists find evidence to suggest that this mile deep canyon may have formed within the last four million years. Assuming a uniform rate of erosion and without considering canyon widening due to slope retreat, calculate how fast (in millimeters per year) the Colorado River would have to downcut per year to form the mile-deep Grand Canyon in four million years.

   Show all your calculations.

Answer _____

CHAPTER 2

Plate Tectonics: The Unifying Theory

Chapter Summary

- For over the last century some geologists have argued for the concept of continental drift based on:
    - —the jigsaw-puzzle fit of the coasts on both sides of the Atlantic
    - —the geological similarities in rock ages and trends in geologic structures on opposite sides of the Atlantic
    - —fossil evidence suggesting that continents were joined at one time
    - —the distribution of glacial deposits as well as other paleoclimatic evidence

- In the last half of the Twentieth Century the major elements of the plate tectonic theory were formulated. Starting in the 1940s (WWII), ocean floor mapping began to reveal major geologic features on the ocean floor. Then, the match between magnetic anomaly patterns on the seafloor with the paleomagnetic time scale revealed that the ocean floor had a young geologic age and was systematically older away from the oceanic ridge systems. The concepts for seafloor spreading, subduction, and transform faulting evolved out of these and other observations.

- According to the theory of plate tectonics, the Earth's lithosphere is broken into about a dozen moving plates. The plates slide over a partially molten, weak asthenosphere, and the continents, embedded in some of the moving plates, are carried along.

- There are three major types of boundaries between lithospheric plates:
    - —divergent boundaries, where plates move apart
    - —convergent boundaries, where plates move together and one plate often subducts beneath the other
    - —transform boundaries, where plates slide past each other

- Volcanoes, earthquakes, and crustal deformation are concentrated along the active plate boundaries. Mountains typically form along convergent and transform plate boundaries. Where divergent plate boundaries are exposed on land, subsiding basins and mafic volcanism are typical.

- Various methods have been used to estimate and measure the rate and direction of plate movements. Today seafloor-spreading rates vary between a few to 24 cm per year.

- Seafloor isochrons provide the basis for reconstructing plate motions for about the last 200 million years. Distinct assemblages of rocks characterize each type of plate boundary. Using diagnostic rock assemblages embedded in continents and paleoenvironmental data recorded by fossils and sedimentary rocks, geologists have been able to reconstruct ancient plate tectonic events and plate configurations.

- Driven by Earth's internal heat, convection of hot and cold matter within the mantle, the force of gravity, and the existence of an asthenosphere are important factors in any model for the driving mechanism of plate tectonics.

- Currently studies of the plate-driving forces focus on discovering the exact nature of the mantle convection. Questions being addressed include: 1) Where do the plate driving forces originate? 2) At what depth does recycling occur? 3) What is the nature of rising convection currents?

Learning Objectives

Focus your instruction on clear learning objectives. In this section we provide a *sampling* of possible objectives for this chapter. No class could or should try to accomplish all these. Choose based on your analysis of your class. Refer to Chapter 1: *Learning Objectives—How to Define Your Goals for the Class* in the Instructional Design section of this manual for thoughts and ideas about how to go about such an analysis.

Knowledge

- Know the basic components of Plate Tectonics and its history of development.
- Know the geologic characteristics of the different plate boundaries.
- Understand how the age of the seafloor is estimated and measured.

Geology Skills/Applications/Attitudes

- Appreciate the historical development of a major scientific theory.
- Describe how geologists reconstruct the assembly and breakup of continents, like Pangaea.
- Discuss the working hypotheses for the driving mechanism of plate tectonics.

General Education Skills

- Write a summary of the Wegener's version of Plate Tectonics from the point of view of a skeptic (Writing/Critical Thinking).
- Argue for or against Wegener's version during a class debate where students are randomly assigned positions (Speaking/Critical Thinking).

Freshman Survival Skills

- Encourage Students to preview Chapter 2 before the first lecture on Plate Tectonics by awarding credit for restating in their own words acceptable answers to **Chapter Preview Questions.** (Previewing/Textbook Reading)
- Distribute a chapter outline and a selection of mixed format study questions before the first lecture on Plate Tectonics. (Note-Taking)

Sample Lecture Outline

Digital copy is available from Instructor's CD and web site.
http://www.whfreeman.com/understandingearth
Sample lecture outlines highlight the important topics and concepts covered in the text. We suggest that you download a digital copy of this outline from the web site, and customize it to your own lecture before handing it out to students. At the end of each chapter outline, consider adding a selection of review questions, representing a range of thinking levels.

Chapter 2: Plate Tectonics: The Unifying Theory

Continental Drift
    Jigsaw-puzzle fit of continents
    Trends of rock types and structures
    Fossils—*Mesosaurus*
    Glacial deposits
Plate Tectonics
    Global patterns
        Magnetic patterns recorded in rocks—Vine and Matthews
        Topography and symmetry of the ocean floor and continents
        Global distribution of earthquakes
        Global distribution of volcanism and intrusion
        Ages of continents and ocean floor
        Paleoclimates
        Distribution of fossils and modern life
Active Plate Margins
    Divergent—oceanic ridge/continental rift
        Mid-Atlantic Ridge—Iceland
        Gulf of California
        Red Sea
        East Africa Rift Valley
            Rifting of continental crustal
            Beginning of a new ocean basin
    Convergent—subduction & collision zones
        Ocean/ocean crust
            Japan and Philippines
        Ocean/continental crust
            West coast of South America
            Northwest coast of North America
        Continental/continental crust
            Himalayas & Tibetan Plateau
            Collision of India and Asia
        Shear—Transform fault
        Cutting continental crust—San Andreas Fault
Mechanism for Plate Tectonics
    Convection
    Plastic upper mantle— asthenosphere
    Phase changes in crustal rocks
    Gravity
        Ridge push
        Slab pull

CD and Web site Resources

Instructor's CD Highlights

- *Key Textbook Figures and Tables:*

    Figure 2.1: The jigsaw-puzzle fit of continents bordering the Atlantic Ocean

    Figure 2.2: Fossils of the late Paleozoic reptile *Mesosaurus*

    Figure 2.5: Earth's plates today

    Figures 2.6 a & b: Rifting and seafloor spreading along the Mid-Atlantic Ridge and early stages of rifting within eastern Africa

    Figure 2.9 a, b, & c: Three types of convergent boundaries

    Figure Story 2.11: Magnetic mapping can measure the rate of seafloor spreading

    Figure 2.14: Age of seafloor crust

    Figure 2.15: Assembly and breakup of Pangaea

    Figure 2.16: Factors thought to be important in driving plate tectonics

    Figure 2.17: Competing hypotheses for mantle convection

    Figure 1.11: Convection currents in Earth's interior

- *Photo Gallery:* Includes slide set images from the previous three editions

Web site Highlights

http://www.whfreeman.com/understandingearth

- **Presentation Tools**

    Animations: Visit the web site for animations, including animations of figures from this chapter.
    PowerPoint Presentation
    PowerPoint Presentation with Lecture Notes
    Photo Gallery

- **Course Preparation**

    Instructor's Manual
    Sample Lecture Outline
    Sample Exercises

- **Student Study Resources—Assessable**

    Graded Online Quizzing
    Geology in Practice: New Neighbors
    The following *Geology in Practice* exercises on the San Andreas fault can be used for in-class discussion, homework, or extra credit.

    Exercise 1: When will Los Angeles and San Francisco slide next to each other?

    Exercise 2: What is the average rate of motion along the San Andreas fault over its geologic history?

    Exercise 3: How might you explain the "San Andreas fault discrepancy?"

- **Student Study Resources—Non-Assessable**

    Online Review Exercises: Identify the Earth's Plates
    Identify the Plate Boundaries
    Plate Boundaries in Motion
    Plate Tectonics Field Trip

    Concept Self-Checker
    Flashcards

Teaching Tips

Cooperative/Collaborative Exercises and In-Class Activities

Refer to Chapter 4: *Cooperative Learning Teaching Strategies* in the Instructional Design section of this manual for general ideas about conducting cooperative learning exercises in your classroom.

Coop Exercise #1: Characteristics of Active Plate Boundaries

The material for this exercise is the chart in Practice Exercises and Review Question, Exercise #1 at the end of Chapter 2 of the *Student Study Guide for Understanding Earth*. A copy is provided below.

Practice Exercises

Exercise 1: Characteristics of active tectonic plate boundaries. Complete the table below by filling in the blank spaces.

| | Divergent See Figures 2.5, | Convergent See Figures 2.5 and 2.9. | | | Transform See Figures |
Characteristics	2.6, 2.7, and 2.8.	Ocean/ ocean	Ocean/ continental	Collision	2.5 and 2.10.
Examples		Japanese Islands Marinas Trench Aleutian Trench		Himalayas and Tibetan Plateau	
Topography	oceanic ridge, rift valley, ocean basins, ocean floor features offset by transforms, seamounts	trench, island arc			offset of creek beds and other topographic features that cross the fault
Volcanism		present			not characteristic

Lecture on the types of plates and then have students team up and complete as much of the chart as they can in five minutes. This provides a check on their note-taking and general understanding of diverging and converging plate movement. Afterward call on teams for answers.

Tips for running this exercise. Limit the time to five minutes. Limit the exercise to only one column of the table. Assign the remainder of the table as a take home exercise they complete outside of class. Explain how the exercise will help them remember the material of this chapter. To be sure students stay on task, move about the room and visit teams during this exercise. Be sure to allow the opportunity for students to ask questions as they are working on the problem. It helps if you know the names of the students you call on. (Refer to IRM Chapter 3: *How to Encourage Discussion* if you would like some tricks for learning student names.)

Coop Exercise #2: Stripes on the Sea Floor

by Randall Richardson, Department of Geosciences, University of Arizona, Tucson, Arizona

Students often have trouble understanding the origin of magnetic stripes on the sea floor associated with spreading at mid-ocean ridges. We have already discussed that the Earth's magnetic field reverses polarity from time to time.

I have the class assemble into a large mass at one end of the classroom. I tell them that they are the magma chamber beneath a divergent plate boundary (an oceanic ridge) and that for the purpose of this demonstration the magma chamber has been rotated on its side. I pick two students to stand in front of the other students and mention that these two students represent ocean crust above the magma chamber and the spreading center. I have the ocean crust rift apart by asking the two students to each take one step apart sideways and allow two students from the magma chamber to join the line in front of the chamber. These two new students face forward (away from the magma chamber) because they formed when the Earth's magnetic field is in its normal polarity. Now all four students outside the magma chamber again take a step sideways letting two more students out. Because I haven't reversed the polarity of the Earth's magnetic field, these students also face forward.

All six students take a step sideways and let two more students out. This time, however, I tell them that the Earth's magnetic field has reversed, and these two new students come out facing backward. Typically, the four students representing oceanic crust already out try to turn and face the other direction, but I tell them that they have already cooled and are locked in the Earth's normal polarity. Only the new ones face backward.

I let the process continue, sometimes reversing the magnetic field, but in the end producing "stripes" of students facing opposite directions, representing crust that was created during normal and reversed polarity times.

We continue until the students run into a wall or until I feel that they understand the process.

If you begin this demonstration with the initial two students representing continental crust above the magma chamber, the formation of a continental rift can be illustrated and discussed. Students can see why the oldest sea floor is next to the continents and farthest from the mid-ocean ridge (they were the first ones out). Be careful about the use of terminology, though, because this is only Chapter 2 in the text and the students are just beginning to expand their knowledge of geology.

Coop Exercise # 3: Five-Minute Write

The Five-Minute Write is done during the last five minutes of lecture. Ask students to put their name on a sheet of paper and then address the three questions on the overhead (see adjacent sample). Start the next lecture by discussing the answers to some of the questions students had about the previous lecture.

Freshman Survival Skills Assignment

In the beginning of your course it is prudent to include a few exercises to help the freshmen in your class learn how to learn and to reinforce mastery of the basics of good preparation for college level lectures. Learning skills are like critical thinking skills. They tend to be mastered slowly, over time with lots of practice: even upper division students and graduate students sometimes need coaching about how to learn. See the Design Section of this manual for a discussion of why this is true and ideas about how to do it. Chapter 1 discusses freshman survival as a national educational priority. Chapters 5 and 6 discuss how to develop credit assignments to encourage students to learn how to learn.

The Plate Tectonics lecture is early in the course and presents challenging material. The assignment **Preview a Text Chapter** is highly recommended for this chapter. It may help your students develop the good habit of coming to lecture prepared. You will find this assignment in Chapter 6 of the Instructional Design section of this manual (see Part I, Chapter 6: *Control the Incentives: Assign Credit to Study Skill Assignments*).

Topics for Class Discussion

- Describe the processes that could someday make Baja and southern California a part of southern Alaska.
- How does the asthenosphere fit into the plate tectonic theory?

Five-Minute Write

- What questions do you have about lecture?
- What did you find most interesting about lecture?
- How was lecture relevant to you?

- How are paleomagnetic properties of rocks on the continents used to reconstruct the positions of the continents through time?
- Explain three ways the approximate rate of sea-floor spreading can be determined.
- How can ancient plate boundaries be recognized in the geologic record?
- Do continents get subducted? Discuss.

Plate Tectonic Web site

http://www.ucmp.berkeley.edu/geology/tectonics.html

This web site includes information on the history and the mechanisms driving plate tectonics, plus plate tectonics animations.

Teaching Resources

Student Study Guide Highlights

In Part I: Chapters provide strategies for learning geology. Ideally, students would read these chapters early in the course.

Chapter 1   Brief Preview of the *Study Guide for Understanding Earth* by Press, Siever, Grotzinger, and Jordan

Chapter 2   Meet the Authors of *Understanding Earth, 4th Edition:* How to use your geology textbook

Chapter 3   How to Be Successful in Geology (or just about any other challenging course)

Part II. Chapter 2: *Plate Tectonics: The Unifying Theory*

Before Lecture:

Preview Questions & Brief Answers

During Lecture:

Learning Warm-up Tip

After Lecture:

Check Your Notes

Exam Prep:

Chapter Summary

Practice Exercises: *Characteristics of active tectonic plate boundaries*
Construct a conceptual flow chart or a diagram that illustrates modern ideas on how plate tectonics works.

Review Questions (Answers to all review questions are given at the end of the Study Guide.)

Minerals: Building Blocks of Rocks

Chapter Summary

- Minerals are natural inorganic solids with a specific crystal structure and chemical composition.
- Minerals form when atoms or ions chemically bond and come together in an orderly, three-dimensional geometric array—a crystal structure.
- The strength of the chemical bonds in the crystalline structure determine many of the physical properties, e.g., hardness, cleavage of minerals.
- Silicate minerals are the most abundant class of minerals in the Earth's crust and mantle.
- There are three important groups of silicates:

  ferromagnesium silicates, e.g., olivine and pyroxene—common in the mantle

  feldspar and quartz—common in the crust

  clay mineral—commonly produced by chemical weathering
- Other common mineral classes include carbonates, oxides, sulfates, sulfides, halides, and native metals.
- Diagnostic physical properties of minerals include hardness, cleavage, fracture, luster, color, specific gravity (density), and crystal habit.
- Why study minerals?

  One can deduce the composition of rocks because minerals have a definite composition.

  One can infer the environment in which the rock formed because most minerals are stable only under certain conditions of temperature and pressure.

  For fun and profit. Gemstones are treasured for their beauty, color, and rarity. Many minerals are used in industrial processes and manufacturing.

Learning Objectives

Focus your instruction on clear learning objectives. In this section we provide a *sampling* of possible objectives for this chapter. No class could or should try to accomplish all these. Choose based on your analysis of your class. Refer to Chapter 1: *Learning Objectives—How to Define Your Goals for the Class* in the Instructional Design section (Part I) of this manual for thoughts and ideas about how to go about such an analysis.

Knowledge

- Know what defines a mineral.
- Know the building blocks of matter and how they chemically bond.
- Know how atoms combine to form the crystal structures of minerals.
- Know some basic atomic structures for common rock-forming minerals.
- Know the major rock-forming minerals and their physical properties.

Skills/Applications/Attitudes

- Know how the physical properties of minerals are linked to the mineral's atomic (crystal) structure and chemical bonds.
- Identify common rock-forming minerals based on field and hand specimen observations.

General Education Skills

- Write a one-page position paper on asbestos that incorporates the key points in *Earth Issues* box 3-2: *Asbestos: Health Hazard, Overreaction, or Both.* (Writing/Critical Thinking)

Freshman Survival Skills

- Encourage Students to preview Chapter 3 before the first lecture on minerals by awarding credit for restating in their own words acceptable answers to Chapter Preview Questions. (Previewing/Textbook Reading)
- Distribute a chapter outline and a selection of mixed format study questions before the lecture on Minerals. (Note Taking)

Sample Lecture Outline

Digital copy is available from Instructor's CD and web site.
http://www.whfreeman.com/understandingearth
Sample lecture outlines highlight the important topics and concepts covered in the text. We suggest that you download a digital copy of this outline from the web site, and customize it to your own lecture before handing it out to students. At the end of each chapter outline, consider adding a selection of review questions, representing a range of thinking levels.

Chapter 3:
Minerals: Building Blocks of Rocks

Mineral—Building Blocks of Rocks
    Naturally occurring
    Inorganic
    Specific chemical composition
    Crystalline
Matter
    Atoms/ions/molecules
    Periodic Table of the Elements
    Chemical reactions
    Bonding—covalent vs. ionic
Mineral Formation
    Crystallization
    Availability and mobility of constituents

Composition of the Crust

By volume ≈ 99% of the Earth's crust consists of only 8 elements:

OXYGEN—O
SILICON—Si
ALUMINUM—Al
IRON—Fe
CALCIUM—Ca
SODIUM—Na
POTASSIUM—K
MAGNESIUM—Mg

Silicates Minerals

Major Rock-Forming Minerals
Three important groups of silicates

• Ferromagnesium,
     e.g., olivine, pyroxene
     Fe & Mg silicates

• Feldspars and quartz
     Ca, Na, & K silicates
     Quartz is pure silica

• Clay minerals
     K, Al, Mg, Fe silicates

Conceptual flowchart illustrating the factors
that influence the physical properties of minerals

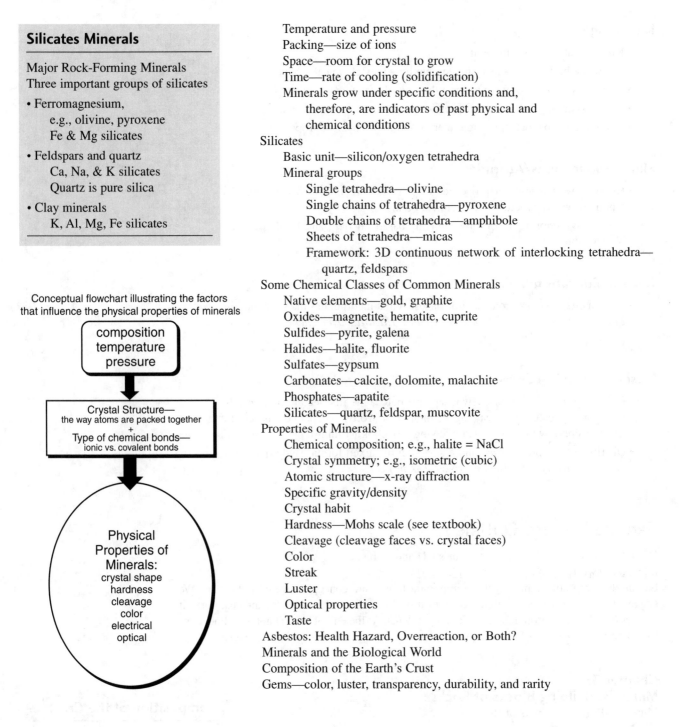

composition
temperature
pressure

Crystal Structure—
the way atoms are packed together
+
Type of chemical bonds—
ionic vs. covalent bonds

Physical
Properties of
Minerals:
crystal shape
hardness
cleavage
color
electrical
optical

Temperature and pressure
Packing—size of ions
Space—room for crystal to grow
Time—rate of cooling (solidification)
Minerals grow under specific conditions and,
     therefore, are indicators of past physical and
     chemical conditions
Silicates
     Basic unit—silicon/oxygen tetrahedra
     Mineral groups
          Single tetrahedra—olivine
          Single chains of tetrahedra—pyroxene
          Double chains of tetrahedra—amphibole
          Sheets of tetrahedra—micas
          Framework: 3D continuous network of interlocking tetrahedra—
               quartz, feldspars
Some Chemical Classes of Common Minerals
     Native elements—gold, graphite
     Oxides—magnetite, hematite, cuprite
     Sulfides—pyrite, galena
     Halides—halite, fluorite
     Sulfates—gypsum
     Carbonates—calcite, dolomite, malachite
     Phosphates—apatite
     Silicates—quartz, feldspar, muscovite
Properties of Minerals
     Chemical composition; e.g., halite = NaCl
     Crystal symmetry; e.g., isometric (cubic)
     Atomic structure—x-ray diffraction
     Specific gravity/density
     Crystal habit
     Hardness—Mohs scale (see textbook)
     Cleavage (cleavage faces vs. crystal faces)
     Color
     Streak
     Luster
     Optical properties
     Taste
Asbestos: Health Hazard, Overreaction, or Both?
Minerals and the Biological World
Composition of the Earth's Crust
Gems—color, luster, transparency, durability, and rarity

CD and Web site Resources

Instructor's CD Highlights

• *Key Textbook Figures and Tables:*
     Figure 3.2: Electron structure of the carbon atom
     Figure 3.3: The Periodic Table of Elements
     Figure 3.6: Structure of sodium chloride
     Figure 3.7: Sizes of ions

  • *Photo Gallery:* Includes slide set images from the previous three editions

Web site Highlights
http://www.whfreeman.com/understandingearth

  • **Presentation Tools**

   Animation: Visit the web site for animations, including animations of figures from this chapter.
   PowerPoint Presentation
   PowerPoint Presentation with Lecture Notes
   Photo Gallery

  • **Course Preparation**

   Instructor's Manual
   Sample Lecture Outline
   Sample Exercises

  • **Student Study Resources—Assessable**

   Graded Online Quizzing
   Geology in Practice: Why Is the Hope Diamond Blue?
   The following *Geology in Practice* exercises can be used for in-class discussion, homework, or extra credit.
       Exercise 1: *Why is the Hope Diamond Blue?*
       Exercise 2: *Why are rubies red and sapphires blue?*
   The *Geology in Practice* site also provides information on the characteristics of gemstones, cubic zirconia, carat vs. karat, and common causes of color in minerals.

  • **Student Study Resources—Non-Assessable**

   Online Review Exercises: Chemistry Review
                 Understanding Minerals

   Concept Self-Checker
   Flashcards

Teaching Tips

Cooperative/Collaborative Exercises and In-Class Activities
Refer to Chapter 4: *Cooperative Learning Teaching Strategies* in the Instructional Design section of this manual for general ideas about conducting cooperative learning exercises in your classroom.

Coop Exercise #1: Identifying Minerals
The worksheet for this exercise is Exercise 3: *Identifying Minerals Using Their Physical Properties* (in Practice Exercises and Review Questions, *Student Study Guide for Understanding Earth*, Chapter 3: *Minerals*. For Exercise 3 pick one of the five descriptions and work through it in class. A good way to do this is to divide students into pairs and give each team two minutes to come up with a correct answer. Then call on one of the teams to

Five-Minute Write

- What questions do you have about lecture?
- What did you find most interesting about lecture?
- How was lecture relevant to you?

give their answer and explain how they arrived at that answer. Another option is to have students write their answers on a slip of paper with their name. Collect the slips for possible grading or use it to take attendance.

Coop Exercise # 2: Five-Minute Write

The Five-Minute Write is done during the last five minutes of lecture. Ask students to put their name on a sheet of paper and then address the three questions on the overhead (see adjacent sample). Start the next lecture by discussing the answers to some of the questions students had about the previous lecture.

Topics for Class Discussion

- Why are the physical properties of diamond and graphite so different?
- Why does a mineral have a definite chemical composition?
- What is the difference between crystal faces and cleavage faces?
- Why does quartz exhibit no cleavage?
- What test would you do to distinguish a real quartz crystal from a piece of glass cut and polished to look like a quartz crystal. Refer to x-ray films of quartz available in the *Photo Gallery*.
- Karat is a measure of purity, expressed in 24ths. 24 karat gold is 100% pure. 14 karat gold is 14/24 = 58.3% gold. The difference between karat, a measure of purity, and carat, a measure of the mass of a gem stone, often confuses people. For centuries the mass (weight) of gems was compared to weight of local seeds, e.g., carob beans. Carat is derived from a Greek word (keration) for carob bean. A one-carat diamond weighs 0.20 (1/5) grams.

  Here is a question for an in-class discussion.

  You make gold jewelry and you are in the market for some 12-karat gold wire. Pure gold sells for $300 per ounce. You want to pay strictly for the gold in the wire (no fabrication fee, etc.), so how much do you offer to pay for one ounce of 12-karat gold?

  A. $300
  B. $200
  C. $150
  D. $100

- Precious and semiprecious gems are always a topic of interest among students. A table of the chemical compositions of familiar precious and semiprecious gems is included in the section titled "Interesting Information About Minerals" at the end of this chapter.

Teaching Resources

Student Study Guide Highlights

In Part I: Chapters provide strategies for learning geology. Ideally, students would read these chapters early in the course.

Chapter 1   Brief Preview of the *Study Guide for Understanding Earth* by Press, Siever, Grotzinger, and Jordan

Interesting Information About Minerals

The Elements

In 1661 Robert Boyle, a British physicist, defined a chemical element as a substance that could not be chemically broken down into simpler substances. Oxygen, hydrogen, and mercury were among the first to be identified. Oxygen was identified by Joseph Priestly in 1774.

Cubic Zirconia

Cubic zirconia (ZrO_2) was introduced as a synthetic gemstone in 1976. It has a hardness of 8, takes a good polish, and resists scratching. Cubic zirconia is an attractive simulate for diamond because of its hardness and especially because of its high refractive index which produces brilliant colors. Its melting point is 2750°C.

Color in Minerals

Color is the response of the eye to electromagnetic radiation. When all the wavelengths in the visible spectra are present, the eye perceives white. When some wavelengths are removed, the eye detects color. All colors come from the differential absorption and transmission of certain wavelengths of light. Basically there is no color without light.

When light interacts with a mineral, those wavelengths with energies corresponding exactly to the energy differences between the energy levels of electrons within atoms will be absorbed, as electrons are excited from one energy level to another. Such selective absorption produces the color of the mineral.

Trace amounts of transition elements, e.g., Ti, V, Cr, Mn, Fe, Co, Ni, Cu, within the atomic structure of minerals are a common cause of color. Substitution of these elements within the crystal structure give rise to various crystal field and charge transfer transitions that absorb various wavelengths of visual light. For example, the green color of peridot (gem quality olivine) is due to the absorption of light with a wavelength that corresponds exactly to the energy difference between the electrons in the *d*-orbital levels in Fe^{2+}. Refer to the Geology In Practice Exercise: *Why Is the Hope Diamond Blue?*

Chemical composition of principle types of precious and semiprecious gems.

Name	Composition
Amber	Hydrocarbon (fossil resin)
Beryl	$Be_3Al_2Si_4O_{18}$
Aquamarine	"
Emerald	"
Chrysoceryl	$BeAl_2O_4$
Catseve	"
Corundum	Al_2O_3
Ruby	" (with trace of Cr)
Sapphire	" (with trace of Ti)
Diamond	C
Feldspar	$KAlSi_3O_4$
Amazonstone	"
Garnet	$(Ca,Mg,Fe)_3(Al,Fe,Cr)_2(SiO_4)_3$
Jadeite	$Na(Al,Fe)Si_2O_4$
Peridot	Mg_2SiO_4
Opal	Hydrous silica
Pearl	$CaCO_3$
Quartz	SiO_2
Agate	"
Amethyst	"
Jasper	"
Onyx	"
Spinel	$MgAl_2O_4$
Topaz	$Al_2SiO_4(F,OH)_2$
Turquoise	$CuAl_4(PO_4)_4(OH)_8 \cdot 5H_2O$

Diamonds and Diamond Cutting

The largest diamond was found in 1905 at the Premier Mine in South Africa. It is called the Callinam or Star of Africa and weighed 3025 carats, approximately 1.3 pounds. It was cut into 105 separate gems. The two largest are 516 and 509 carats and are the largest cut diamonds.

During the early days of making synthetic diamonds, all kinds of carbon-bearing matter was being used. The motivation for experimenting with all kinds of materials was sparked by the very broad patent filed to protect the synthetic diamond-making process. Some of the earliest synthetic diamonds were made from peanut butter taken off a cracker that the scientist was eating. It produced a green diamond due to the high nitrogen content.

Diamonds cleave in four directions, parallel to the faces of the octahedron. Jewelers take advantage of these planes of cleavage to alter the shape of the diamond. A scratch is made on the surface of the diamond, using the only substance that will scratch a diamond—another diamond. Then a sharp blade is inserted in the scratch and oriented parallel to the cleavage plane. The blade is tapped sharply with a mallet. If all goes well, the diamond crystal splits smoothly along a cleavage plane. If not, the diamond may shatter into tiny pieces. Irregularly shaped diamonds can be shaped in this way once the cleavage directions are located with x-ray analysis.

Graphite Tennis Rackets

Graphite used in tennis rackets begins as a powder. The powder is extruded as thin filaments under conditions that promote crystal growth. The crystalline fibers are then woven and combined with other fibers of plastic, fiberglass, and ceramics.

Rocks: Records of Geologic Processes

Chapter Summary

- The properties of rocks and rock names are determined by mineral content (the kinds and proportions of minerals that make up the rock) and texture (the size, shapes, and spatial arrangement of its crystals or grains).
- There are three major rock types. Igneous rocks solidify from molten liquid (magma). Crystal size within igneous rocks is largely determined by the cooling rate of the magma body. Sedimentary rocks are made of sediments formed from the weathering and erosion of any pre-existing rock. Deposition, burial, and lithification (compaction and cementation) transform loose sediments into sedimentary rocks. Metamorphic rocks are formed by an alteration in the solid state of any pre-existing rock by high temperatures and pressure.
- The Rock Cycle is a useful flow chart describing the relationships between geologic processes and the major rock types. Plate tectonics is our model for how the rock cycle operates on Earth today.

Learning Objectives

Focus your instruction on clear learning objectives. In this section we provide a *sampling* of possible objectives for this chapter. No class could or should try to accomplish all these. Choose based on your analysis of your class. Refer to Chapter 1: *Learning Objectives—How to Define Your Goals for the Class* in the Instructional Design section of this manual for thoughts and ideas about how to go about such an analysis.

Knowledge

- Know that rocks are classified based on their mineral content and texture.
- Know the three major types of rocks and how they are formed.
- Understand how the rock cycle is linked to plate tectonics.

Skills/Applications/Attitudes

- Use the rock cycle to describe relationships between different rock types.
- Interpret the basic geologic history represented by an outcrop of rocks.

General Education Skills

• Write a one-page newspaper article interpreting an interesting local rock out-crop to an audience of citizens of your community. (Writing/Critical Thinking)

Freshman Survival Skills

• Encourage Students to preview Chapter 4 by means announcing ahead of time that there will be a quiz on the preview questions at the beginning of this lecture. See **Teaching Tips**.

Sample Lecture Outline

Digital copy is available from Instructor's CD and web site.
http://www.whfreeman.com/understandingearth
Sample lecture outlines highlight the important topics and concepts covered in the text. We suggest that you download a digital copy of this outline from the web site, and customize it to your own lecture before handing it out to students. At the end of each chapter outline, consider adding a selection of review questions, representing a range of thinking levels.

Chapter 4: Rocks: Records of Geologic Processes

Rocks are defined by their mineralogy and texture.

Major rock type	Igneous	Sedimentary	Metamorphic
Source of materials	Melting of rocks in crust and mantle	Weathering and erosion of rocks exposed at the surface	Rocks under high temperatures and pressures in deep crust and upper mantle. Plus rocks near the surface that are broken by faulting or impact.
Rock-forming process	Crystallization (solidification of melt)	Sedimentation, burial, and lithification (compaction and cementation)	Shearing and recrystallization in the solid state.
Textures	**intrusive** (plutonic)—large interlocking crystals **extrusive** (volcanic)—glassy and/or fine-grained texture	**clastic**—grains of rocks and minerals **chemical and biochemical**—precipitates, evaporites, seashells, plant matter	**non-foliated**—minerals randomly oriented **foliated**—alignment of minerals within rock
Some common minerals	Quartz Feldspar Mica Pyroxene Amphibole Olivine	Quartz Clay minerals Feldspars Calcite Dolomite Gypsum Halite	Quartz Feldspar Mica Garnet Pyroxene Staurolite Kyanite

Rock Outcrops—bedrock
Rock Cycle: Interactions between the Plate Tectonic and Climate Systems
    Flow chart describes the relationships between geologic processes and the major rock types.

CD and Web site Resources

Instructor's CD Highlights

• *Key Textbook Figures and Tables:*

Figure 4.2: The three different types of rocks

Figure 4.3: Extrusive igneous rocks

Figure 4.4: Weathering breaks down rock into smaller particles that are then carried downhill and downstream by erosion to be deposited as layers of sediment.

Figure 4.6: Metamorphic rocks form under four main conditions

Figure Story 4.9: The rock cycle

• *Photo Gallery:* Includes slide set images from the previous three editions

Web site Highlights

http://www.whfreeman.com/understandingearth

• **Presentation Tools**

Animations: Visit the web site for animations, including animations of figures from this chapter.

PowerPoint Presentation

PowerPoint Presentation with Lecture Notes

Photo Gallery

• **Course Preparation**

Instructor's Manual

Sample Lecture Outline

Sample Exercises

• **Student Study Resources—Assessable**

Graded Online Quizzing

Geology in Practice: Finding the Meaning to Patterns in Nature: Minerals are the Alphabet and Rocks Are the Words.

Geology in Practice exercises provide students with images, field and lab observations, and ask students to identify the rock type, rock name, and common minerals within the rock. *Geology in Practice* exercises can be used for in-class discussion, homework, or extra credit.

Exercise 1: Rock 1

Exercise 2: Rock 2

Exercise 3: Rock 3

• **Student Study Resources—Non-Assessable**

Online Review Exercises: Rock Cycle Review

Understanding the Rock Cycle

How did that happen?

Concept Self-Checker

Flashcards

Teaching Tips

Cooperative/Collaborative Exercises and In-Class Activities

Coop Exercise #1: Cooling Rates of Igneous Rocks

This is Part B of Exercise 1: *Rock Cycle Review* in Chapter 4 of the *Student Study Guide for Understanding Earth.*

Exhibit an overhead transparency of the following table.

Types of igneous rocks	Cooling rates	Textures
Extrusive		
Intrusive		

Have students pair up with the person sitting next to them. Ask each team to fill in the chart, sign their names, and turn in the completed chart to you. Allow three minutes to complete the task. Let students know ahead that you will call on them to report so they need to memorize their answers. Call on one of the teams to give their answer and explain their thinking. If you wish, you can grade this exercise or use it to take attendance.

A good follow-up would be to suggest that students work through the remaining parts of Exercise 1 and other study questions in their Student Study Guide.

Coop Exercise #2: Five-Minute Write

Five-Minute Write

- What questions do you have about lecture?
- What did you find most interesting about lecture?
- How was lecture relevant to you?

The Five-Minute Write is done during the last five minutes of lecture. Ask students to put their name on a sheet of paper and then address the three questions on the overhead (see adjacent sample). Start the next lecture by discussing the answers to some of the questions students had about the previous lecture.

Freshman Survival Skills Assignment

In the beginning of your course it is prudent to include a few exercises to help the freshmen in your class learn how to learn and to reinforce mastery of the basics of good preparation for college level lectures. Learning skills are like critical thinking skills. They tend to be mastered slowly, over time with lots of practice: even upper-division students and graduate students sometimes need coaching about how to learn. See Part I of this manual for a discussion of why this is true and ideas about how to do it. Chapter 1 discusses freshman survival as a national educational priority. Chapters 5 and 6 in Part I discuss how to develop credit assignments to encourage students to learn how to learn.

Chapter Preview Quiz

Encourage students to preview Chapter 4 by announcing ahead of time that there will be a quiz on the preview questions at the beginning of this lecture. Grade this quiz using the brief answers in the student study guide chapter as a key. The idea is to reward rapid previewing *not* mastery of all the content in the chapter. It may be helpful to explain to the students that what you are teaching them is a method that will help them get more from lecture by establishing a framework or overview of the material. Explain the difference between *before lecture, rapid preparation,* and the more time consuming *intensive study* that will be required to master the material and prepare for exams. Tell them the goal of previewing is to get more from lecture, i.e., a better set of notes. If you made a previewing assignment as suggested in Chapters 1–3 of this manual, you can explain that this is really just that same assignment over again. Only this time they will write it out in class, from memory. It may motivate the students to point out how previewing is faster, more efficient than trying to read the entire chapter before lecture. If you use similar methods in your own technical reading, let them know that, too.

Sample Exercise

Digital copy is available from the Instructor's CD and web site.
http://www.whfreeman.com/understandingearth

Adopt a mineral, rock, and fossil exercise for lecture and lab. Pass around a paper or cloth bag containing samples of minerals and/or rocks in lecture or lab. Each student or student team takes a sample out of the bag. This is the sample that students "adopt" for this exercise. They have one week to complete a one to two page paper about the specimen. Teaching assistants and undergraduate preceptors assist students with identification in the learning center, lab, or workshop over the week that they are working on the assignment. If the course has a lab or workshop, we require students to present an oral report and turn in an essay about the sample. If the student is not participating in a lab or workshop, they turn in their essay for a grade in lecture. We also post a selection of web sites about rocks and minerals to help students with their identification and in finding out more about the sample for the essay.

Topics for Class Discussion
Cooling rates and igneous rock textures. Refer to Figure 4.3.

Additional Tips and Information
It is very important for many learners that they see many examples illustrating the basic types of textures in igneous, sedimentary, and metamorphic rocks. Rock texture and composition does not need to be emphasized here because each major rock type will be treated by a whole chapter and series of lectures. Nevertheless, now is the time to start showing students examples of rock textures using slides, photomicrographs, and actual specimens. The *Geology in Practice* exercises for this chapter involve students with interpreting visual and field observations of rock outcrops and samples.

Teaching Resources
Student Study Guide Highlights
In Part I: Chapters provide strategies for learning geology. Ideally, students would read these chapters early in the course.

> Chapter 1   Brief Preview of the *Study Guide for Understanding Earth* by Press, Siever, Grotzinger, and Jordan

> Chapter 2   Meet the Authors of *Understanding Earth, 4th Edition:* How to use your geology textbook

> Chapter 3   How to Be Successful in Geology (or just about any other challenging course)

Part II. Chapter 4: *Rocks: Records of Geologic Processes*

> Before Lecture:

>> Preview Questions & Brief Answers

> During Lecture:

>> Learning Warm-up Tip

> After Lecture:

>> Check Your Notes

> Exam Prep:

>> Chapter Summary

>> Practice Exercises: *Rock Cycle Review*
>>> *Understanding the Rock Cycle*
>>> *How did that happen? Geologic Processes in the Rock Cycle*

Review Questions (Answers to all review questions are given at the end of the Study Guide.)

CHAPTER 5

Igneous Rocks: Solids from Melts

Chapter Summary

- Igneous rocks can be divided into two broad textual classes: 1) coarsely crystalline rocks, which are intrusive (plutonic) and therefore cooled slowly, and 2) finely crystalline rocks, which are extrusive (volcanic) and cooled rapidly. Within each of these broad textual classes, the rocks are subdivided according to their composition. General compositional classes of igneous rocks are felsic, intermediate, mafic, and ultramafic, in decreasing silica and increasing iron and magnesium content. Tables 5.1, 5.2, and Figure 5.4 summarize common minerals and composition of igneous rocks.

- The lower crust and upper mantle are typical places where physical conditions induce rock to melt. Temperature, pressure, rock composition and the presence of water all affect the melting temperature of the rock.

How to Melt a Rock: The Generation of Magma

- Increase temperature.
  Not all minerals melt at the same temperature. Refer to Figure Story 5.5: Bowen's Reaction Series. So the mineral composition of the rock affects the melting temperature. Felsic rocks with higher silica content melt at lower temperatures than mafic rocks, which contain less silica and more iron/magnesium.

- Lower the confining pressure.
  A reduction in pressure can induce a hot rock to melt. A reduction in confining pressure on the hot upper mantle is thought to generate the basaltic magmas that intrude into the oceanic ridge system to form ocean crust. Refer to Figure 5.13.

- Add water.
  The presence of water in a rock can lower its melting temperatures up to a few hundred degrees.
  Water released from rocks subducting into the mantle along convergent plate boundaries is thought to be an important factor in magma generation at convergent plate boundaries. Refer to Figures 5.14 and 5.15.

- There is an amazing variety of igneous rocks on Earth. Two processes help to explain how the composition of igneous rocks can be so variable – how magmas differentiate. They are partial melting and fractional crystallization.

- Most rocks probably melt only partially. Then, due to differences in density and mobility (viscosity), the melt can collect into larger bodies. Because iron, magnesium, and calcium are concentrated in silicate minerals with high melting temperatures and silica, sodium, and potassium are concentrated in silicate minerals with low melting temperatures, the degree to which the rock melts will influence the bulk chemical composition of the melt and remaining solids. For example, as more of the rock melts, the melt typically becomes enriched in iron, magnesium, and calcium because minerals with high melting temperatures and high iron content contribute increasingly more to the melt.

- Fractional crystallization simply involves the separation of a fraction of the early formed crystals from the melt. Segregation of the melt and solids from each other may be a result of the melt migrating upwards, leaving the solids behind, or the settling of early formed, iron-rich, heavy minerals, leaving a pool of magma depleted in iron and enriched in silica relative to the bulk composition of the original magma body. In this way, fractional crystallization can enhance compositional differences between the parent magma and the rock that eventually crystallizes from the magma. Refer to Figure Story 5.5.

- The Bowen's Reaction Series in Figure Story 5.5 is a flow chart describing how the very general bulk composition of a magma can change as the magma solidifies or as a rock melts.

- Names are given to igneous rock bodies based on their size and shape. Figure 5.7 summarizes the common igneous rock bodies, such as batholith, pluton, dike, and sill.

- In the context of plate tectonics, it is believed that mafic magmas are generated by partial melting of the upper mantle along divergent plate boundaries and beneath hotspots. Felsic and intermediate magmas are commonly associated with convergent plate boundaries and are thought to be generated by partial melting induced by the release of water from subducting slabs of crust.

Learning Objectives

Focus your instruction on clear learning objectives. In this section we provide a *sampling* of possible objectives for this chapter. No class could or should try to accomplish all of these. Choose based on your analysis of your class. Refer to Chapter 1: *Learning Objectives—How to Define Your Goals for the Class* in the Instructional Design section (Part I) of this manual for thoughts and ideas about how to go about such an analysis.

Knowledge

- Know how igneous rocks are classified.
- Know how and where magmas form.
- Know the forms of intrusive and extrusive igneous rock bodies.
- Know the order of mineral crystallization (Bowen's Reaction Series).
- Know how the formation of igneous rocks is linked to plate tectonics.

Applications

- How does magmatic differentiation and the Bowen's Reaction Series account for the great variety of igneous rocks?
- Can students recognize volcanic and plutonic rocks by their differing textures?

General Education Skills

- Write a summary of James Hutton's reasoning concerning the texture of igneous rocks. (Writing/Critical Thinking)

Freshman Survival Skills

- Encourage students to study geology strategically with a five-minute lecture on "How to Study Geology." See **Teaching Tips** for ideas about how to do this.

Sample Lecture Outline

Digital copy is available from Instructor's CD and web site.
http://www.whfreeman.com/understandingearth
Sample lecture outlines highlight the important topics and concepts covered in the text. We suggest that you download a digital copy of this outline from the web site, and customize it to your own lecture before handing it out to students. At the end of each chapter outline, consider adding a selection of review questions, representing a range of thinking levels.

Chapter 5: Igneous Rocks: Solids from Melts

Igneous Rock Classification
    Texture
    Mineral and chemical composition

Type	Texture	Rock name			
Volcanic extrusive	Aphanitic	Rhyolite	Dacite	Andesite	Basalt
Plutonic intrusive	Phaneritic	Granite	Granodiorite	Diorite	Gabbro
Composition		Felsic—enriched in Si, Na, and K	Intermediate	Intermediate	Mafic—enriched in Fe, Mg, and Ca

Ultramafic rock—peridotite
The composition of an igneous rock depends on:
    —the initial bulk composition of the magma
    —the fate of the early formed crystals
    —the fate of the remaining melt
To melt a rock:
    —increase temperature (i.e., add extra heat)
    —reduce confining pressure
    —add water
Partial melting—produces magma mainly from minerals with the *lowest* melting temperatures. Compared to the bulk composition of the melting rock, the minerals with the lower melting temperatures are:
    —lower in the Bowen's Series
    —depleted in Mg, Fe, and Ca
    —enriched in Si, Na, K
Origins of magmas
    Melting depends on the:
        —temperature
        —pressure
        —composition of rock
        —amount of water
    Basalt/Gabbro
        Mafic magma
        Forms crust of ocean basin
        Source—partial melting of upper mantle
        Ophiolite Suite—seafloor rock assemblage
    Andesite/Diorite
        Intermediate magma
        Associated with subduction zones
        Source—partial melting of subducting ocean crust

Origin of Basalt

BASALTIC MAGMA
(mostly a pyroxene melt)

↓ Pressure release partial melting

PERIDOTITE
(olivine + pyroxene in upper mantle)

Granite/Rhyolite
>   Felsic magma
>   Abundant in continental crust

Forms of Magmatic Intrusions
>   Dike
>   Sill
>   Stock
>   Pluton
>   Batholith
>   Veins/Pegmatite veins

Why is there such a great variety of igneous rocks in the Earth's crust?

- Rocks formed by the freezing of the last part of a silicate magma may have compositions quite different from rocks made up of the early crystals that have settled out. So, igneous rocks with different compositions *can* be generated from the same original (parent) magma.
- Magmatic differentiation
- Separation of the solid (crystals) and liquid (melt/magma) phases during crystallization results in irreversible changes in the bulk composition of the solid and the remaining melt.
- Mechanisms

>   Fractional crystallization—separation of crystals from melt

>   Partial melting—subduction zone

- Implications

>   Compositions of solid and liquid phases are continuously changing as the silicate magma crystallizes.

>   Early formed crystals are enriched in Fe, Mg, and Ca and depleted in Si, Na, and K.

>   Melt becomes progressively enriched in Si, Na, and K.

Distribution of Igneous Rocks within the Earth

Continental Crust—Felsic and intermediate rocks

Ocean Crust—Mafic rocks

Mantle—Ultramafic rocks

Major Zones of Igneous Activity

Major Zone of Igneous Activity

Plate tectonic setting (examples)	Magma type (example rock type)
Spreading centers	
• oceanic ridge (Mid-Atlantic Ridge)	• mafic (basalt/gabbro)
• continental rift (East Africa Rift)	• mafic to felsic (silicic)—more variable because some continental crust may melt.
Subduction zones	
• Oceanic Island Arc (Japan)	• mafic to intermediate
• Continental volcanic arc (Cascade Range, Mt. Saint Helens and Rainier, Andes in South America)	• mafic to felsic (silicic)—more variable because some continental crust may melt.
Intraplate mantle plumes ("hotspots")	
• Oceanic hotspots (Hawaii)	• mafic (basalt)
• Continental hotspots (Yellowstone)	• mafic to felsic (silicic)—more variable because some continental crust may melt.

CD and Web site Resources

Instructor's CD Highlights

- *Key Textbook Figures and Tables:*

    Figure 5.3: Formation of intrusive and extrusive igneous rocks
    Figure 5.4: Classification of igneous rocks
    Figure Story 5.5: Fractional crystallization
    Figure 5.13: Magmatic spreading at seafloor spreading
    Figure 5.14: Rock formation at subduction zones
    Table 5.1: Changes in Some Major Chemical Elements from Felsic to Mafic Rocks
    Table 5.2: Factors Affecting Melting Temperatures

- *Photo Gallery:* Includes slide set images from the previous three editions

Web site Highlights

http://www.whfreeman.com/understandingearth

- **Presentation Tools**

    Animations: Visit the web site for animations, including animations of figures from this chapter.
    PowerPoint Presentation
    PowerPoint Presentation with Lecture Notes
    Photo Gallery

- **Course Preparation**

    Instructor's Manual
    Sample Lecture Outline
    Sample Exercises

- **Student Study Resources—Assessable**

    Graded Online Quizzing
    Geology in Practice: Reading the Geologic Story of Igneous Rocks: Solids from Melts
    This *Geology in Practice* gives students photomicrographs, views of outcrops, and other background information and asks them to identify and interpret igneous rocks. The *Geology in Practice* exercises can be used for in-class discussion, homework, or extra credit.
    Exercise 1: Mineral grain size in igneous rocks
    Exercise 2: Textures of Volcanic Rocks
    Exercise 3: Igneous Activity and Plate Tectonics
    Exercise 4: Carbonatite Lavas and Magmas on Other Planets

    Student Study Resources—Non-Assessable

    Online Review Exercises: Igneous Rocks Review
    Identify the Igneous Rocks
    Before & After: Magmas and Rock Types

    Concept Self-Checker
    Flashcards
    Online Review Exercises for Chapter 4: Bowen's Reaction Series Review

Teaching Tips

A Tool to Help Your Students Learn from Rock Samples

Many instructors bring in interesting samples of igneous rocks. Telling an interesting story about the particular sample (the interesting place you found it, the eruption that produced it, etc.) is a method for catching your students' interest and helping relate to the subject.

One problem introductory students have with samples is that, lacking field and lab experience, they have no good mental framework to tie the sample to. All too often they look and, lacking a framework in their mind, promptly forget the rock that you show them. You can help them learn by providing the needed framework, an organizing tool. One simple method is to show them a simple chart like the one below. Show them a slide of the chart at the beginning of the lecture. Announce that you will be passing around a lot of igneous rock samples today and talking about them. Tell the students to copy the chart onto one full page of notebook paper and keep it handy throughout the lecture. Urge them to try to fill out *all categories* of the chart *for every rock sample* you show them. **Hint:** Announcing there will be a quiz on the chart at the beginning of the next lecture will greatly increase the incentive for students to work hard at following your suggestion! Doing this once early in the course will set an example for how students can take and organize notes about samples for the entire semester.

Note also that we include this suggestion in Part II, Chapter 5 of the Study Guide in a section titled: During Lecture. This is a good time to "plug" the usefulness of the Study Guide.

Example: Rock Sample Note-Taking Chart
Set up this table on one __full page__ of your notebook.

Rock name	Texture clues (coarse, fine, etc.)	Composition clues (mineral clues, color, dark/light, etc.)	Story about the rock to help you remember it	Other notes and comments
Example: ***Granite***	Coarse	I could make out crystals of a black mineral (hornblende), white to tan grains (feldspars), and thin silvery sheets (mica), in a light gray matrix (quartz).	"Came from a local mountain near our campus. I slipped and fell just before I found this sample." (Humor never hurts when you are trying to get and keep your students attention!)	Showed a slide (thin section) in which the crystals were clearly visible. Crystals were mostly feldspar and quartz! What I thought was mica turned out to be the rock with a penny, no muscovite mica. I tried to scratch it with a penny, no luck, must be kind of hard (above 3 on the Mohs scale). Granite rocks average greater than 5.

Sample # 1

.

.

.

Sample #X

Cooperative/Collaborative Exercises and In-Class Activities

Coop Exercise #1: Partial Melting
Use the questions below as a basis for a Think/Pair/Share collaborative exercise in lecture. Present the class with the question and illustration on an overhead. Give students two minutes to discuss the correct answer with another student—sitting to their left or right. Choose

a pair of students to present their answer and an explanation. Ask other pairs if they agree and if not to explain why. Allocate about five minutes for this exercise.

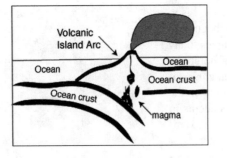

Question (Circle best answer for A–C.)

Compared to the basaltic ocean crust, the magma generated by partial melting of the subducting slab will have

A. more/less Si
B. more/less Fe and Mg
C. more/less Na and K

Refer students to Figure Story 5.5 and Figures 5.14 and 5.15.

Multiple choice questions that require analysis or interpretation work great for a short Think/Pair/Share in lecture. For example, Review Questions 10, 18, 22, 24 in the *Student Study Guide* are all good for brief in-class collaborative exercises.

Five-Minute Write

- What questions do you have about lecture?
- What did you find most interesting about lecture?
- How was lecture relevant to you?

Coop Exercise # 2: Five-Minute Write

The Five-Minute Write is done during the last five minutes of lecture. Ask students to put their name on a sheet of paper and then address the three questions on the overhead (see adjacent sample). Start the next lecture by discussing the answers to some of the questions students had about the previous lecture.

Freshman Survival Skills Assignment

In the beginning of your course it is prudent to include a few exercises to help the freshmen in your class learn how to learn and to reinforce mastery of the basics of good preparation for college level lectures. Learning skills are like critical thinking skills. They tend to be mastered slowly, over time with lots of practice: even upper division students and graduate students sometimes need coaching about how to learn. See Part I: *Instructional Design* for a discussion of why this is so and ideas about how to do it. In Part I of this manual, Chapter 1 discusses freshman survival as a national educational priority. Chapters 5 and 6 discuss how to develop credit assignments to encourage students to learn how to learn.

How to Study Geology: Brief Lecture

Use the overhead **How to Study Geology** as the basis of a five-minute lecture in which you provide your students with some tips on how to study for your particular geology course. You may want to review the *Student Study Guide for Understanding Earth* for specific examples to present to the students.

Each chapter of the Study Guide is organized like the overhead with ideas about what to do to prepare **before lecture,** how to take a good set of notes **during lecture,** how to study **after lecture,** and review questions to use during **exam prep.** The **How to Study Geology** flow chart comes from Part I Instructional Design, Chapter 5: *How to Teach Your Students to Study Effectively.* Possible points to cover include:

- The importance of previewing the chapter before lecture and how this improves learning.
- How to take a good set of notes in your lecture.
- How to use you and your office hours.
- The best way to learn is by answering questions.
- Your thoughts about web site exercises, Study Guide exercises, or other question sets you want the students to use.
- The value of using the Study Guide.

How to Study Geology

DURING LECTURE

Take an excellent set of notes.
- Note-taking Checklist in the Study Guide

BEFORE LECTURE

Prepare for lecture: Arrive with an overview in mind.
- Chapter preview
- Vital information from other chapters

RIGHT AFTER LECTURE

- Review notes.
- Fill in what you missed.
- Add visual material.
- Use the "Have You Checked Your Notes?" section of the Study Guide.

AFTER LECTURE

Intensive study session
Master the key concepts.
- Web site activities and tools
- Practice Exercises and Review Questions in the Study Guide

EXAM PREP

Begin review one week before the exam with the following items in the Study Guide.
- Chapter Summaries
- Practice Exercises and Review Questions
- Tips for Preparing for Geology Exams (Appendix B)
- Eight-Day Study Plan (Appendix A)

Topics for Class Discussion

- How does a porphyritic texture form?
- Why is it very unlikely that olivine and quartz would occur in the same igneous rock?
- How do magmas move through the crust? **Note:** Use a lava lamp.
- How fluid is a silicate magma?

    Note: A Hawaiian Island basaltic lava at 1100°C is about 1 million times more viscous than water (0°C, 1 atm). Felsic magmas at 800°C and with 6% (by weight) of water are about 10 to 100 times more viscous than the dry basalt. Dry felsic magmas at 800°C can be one hundred thousand times more viscous than wet felsic magmas or 14 orders of magnitude more viscous than water.

- Olivine is the first silicate mineral to crystallize out of mafic magmas at high temperatures. As the temperature of the melt lowers, the olivine reacts with the melt to form pyroxene. How is it that olivine can be found in igneous rocks at all?
- A geochemist and petrologist have just finished studying a volcanic field. Here is what they found. The field consists of a high, rather irregular central peak, surrounded by a large, flat expanse, dimpled with cinder cones, and associated flows. The peak is made out of a series of flows and pyroclastic debris of varying thickness and composition. In general, the flows on the peak showed a systematic trend in composition. The younger flows were enriched in sodium, potassium, and silica, compared to the older flows. In contrast, the cinder cones and associated lava flows were all basaltic with only minor variation in composition. Based on these findings, the geologists concluded that the lavas, which construct the peak, were derived from a single, probably relatively large, magma chamber. Whereas, the cinder cones and associated basaltic flows came from small, separate magma bodies. Do you agree with their conclusions? Explain.
- Many students have problems understanding Bowen's Reaction Series. Once students work through it with their instructor, they realize that it is a very effective flow chart with information on:
- the crystallization sequence of silicate minerals in a cooling magma
- which minerals melt first and last within a rock
- the composition of igneous rocks—which minerals commonly occur together
- why there is such a great variety of igneous rocks—how the composition of magmas evolve
- the silicate crystal structure of minerals
- the susceptibility of silicate minerals to chemical weathering
- models for the origin and evolution of the ocean and continental crusts
- Basalt/gabbro and rhyolite/granite have the same compositions, respectively. Why are they given different rock names?
- The *Photo Gallery* has a good selection of photomicrographs and close-ups of hand specimens illustrating igneous rock textures. Use the images as a basis for in-class discussion, exercise, or a quiz.
- The origin of granite:
    —melting of pre-existing rocks, e.g., shales, gneiss, granite
    —differentiation by fractional crystallization from an initially less felsic magma or a partial melt derived from a less felsic rock.

- In a mafic magma, both olivine, built with single silica tetrahedra, and plagioclase, built with a framework structure of silica tetrahedra, can crystallize simultaneously. How can this be possible?

Notes: Essentially the iron and magnesium act to "poison" the polymerization reaction that forms more complex silicate crystal structures. As iron and magnesium are incorporated into the early formed ferromagnesium minerals, the remaining magma becomes depleted in iron and magnesium. This allows more complex silicate minerals to "polymerize," e.g., to form chains, double chains, and framework structures. Even at the highest temperatures of crystallization for a mafic magma within the crust, framework silicates can form because the magma does not have enough iron and magnesium to completely "poison" their formation.

• The very coarse-grained pegmatites and the very fine-grained aplite dikes can form within the same granitic body. How can such different grain-sizes develop within the same magma body?

Both pegmatites and aplites form within a vapor-rich phase. In the case of pegmatites, the high vapor (water and carbon dioxide) content facilitates ion mobility, which speeds up the rate of crystallization. So, big crystals can grow rapidly. The very fine-grained aplites typically occur as fracture-fillings precipitated from water-rich phases in the later stages of the crystallization of a granitic body. Very rapid changes in pressure within the magma chamber induce the rapid crystallization of the aplite and its very fine-grained texture.

Teaching Resources

Student Study Guide Highlights

In Part I. Chapters provide strategies for learning geology. Ideally, students would read these chapters early in the course.

Chapter 1   Brief Preview of the *Study Guide for Understanding Earth* by Press, Siever, Grotzinger, and Jordan

Chapter 2   Meet the Authors of *Understanding Earth, 4th Edition:* How to use your geology textbook

Chapter 3   How to Be Successful in Geology (or just about any other challenging course)

Part II. Chapter 5: *Igneous Rocks: Solids from Melts*

Before Lecture:

Preview Questions & Brief Answers

During Lecture:

Learning Warm-up Tip

After Lecture:

Check Your Notes

Exam Prep:

Chapter Summary

Practice Exercises: *Igneous rock textures*
Distribution of igneous rocks within the earth
Predicting the change in composition in a crystallizing magma
Partial melting and magma composition
Predicting the composition of magma generated in subduction zones

Review Questions (Answers to all review questions are given at the end of the Study Guide.)

CHAPTER 6

Volcanism

Chapter Summary

- Volcanism occurs when molten rock inside the Earth rises buoyantly to the surface because it is less dense than the surrounding rock. Volcanism is a surface expression of magma generation within the Earth.

- Silicate lavas can be classified into three major types, felsic (rhyolite), intermediate (andesite), and mafic (basalt), respectively, based on decreasing amount of silica and increasing amounts of iron and magnesium.

- Eruption styles, volcanic deposits, landforms, and potential hazards are strongly linked to the chemical composition and gas content of the lava. Because basaltic lavas are relatively fluid and dry, they typically exhibit less explosive eruptions and erupt as lava flows. Rhyolite lavas are very viscous and usually wet. Therefore, they typically erupt very explosively as pyroclastic flows or, if dry, form domes.

- There is a strong connection between major types of volcanism and crustal plate boundaries. Basaltic lavas are associated with divergent plate boundaries and hot spots. The ocean crust is created by basaltic volcanism at the ocean ridge system. Basalt is thought to be generated by decompression melting of the ultramafic upper mantle. Basaltic, andesitic, and rhyolitic lavas erupt at convergent zones. The lavas generated along any particular convergent zone will depend in large part on what rocks are being subducted and the amount of melting of the overriding crust.

- There are both benefits and hazards associated with volcanism. Geothermal heat is growing in importance for electric energy generation. Earth's oceans and atmosphere are thought to have condensed from volcanic degassing of our planet's interior. Volcanic dust and gases can impact global climate. Volcanic eruptions and associated mudflows can have disastrous impacts on a region and it people. Important ore-forming processes occur when groundwater circulates around the magma chamber and through hot rock beneath a volcano, or seawater circulates through ocean-floor rifts.

Learning Objectives

In this section we provide a *sampling* of possible objectives for this chapter. No class could or should try to accomplish all these. Choose based on your analysis of your class. Refer to Chapter 1: *Learning Objectives—How to Define Your Goals for the Class* in the Instructional Design section of this manual for thoughts and ideas about how to go about such an analysis.

Knowledge

- Know what kinds of rock materials erupt from a volcano.
- Know why volcanism occurs.
- Know the three major lava types and how they relate to eruptive style and volcanic landforms.
- Know the global pattern of volcanic activity and how it relates to plate tectonics.
- Know how geologists monitor and predict volcanic activity.

Skills/Applications/Attitudes

- Given a field description of the landforms and volcanic deposits, interpret the styles of past eruptions and the magma type(s).
- Discuss important considerations for how risks from a hazardous volcano can be reduced.
- The section *Volcanism and Human Affairs* offers some fine opportunities for teaching students a balanced approach in regard to using scientific data for responsible decision making.

General Education Skills

- Write a one-page **volcanism hazard position paper** for the city planning & zoning department of one of the communities listed in Figure 6.25. Assume you are working this up for presentation to a county board of supervisors. Defend your statement with relevant information from Chapter 6. (Writing/Critical Thinking)
- Write an interesting one-page hypothetical "newspaper account" of the eruption of Thera in 1623 B.C. Assume that you lived to tell about the eruption and tsunami.

Freshman Survival Skills

- Encourage freshmen to develop exam preparation skills by requiring them to make use of the Eight-Day Study Plan. See Teaching Tips.
- Teach your students how to develop a visual summary of this chapter. See Teaching Tips.

Sample Lecture Outline

Digital copy is available from Instructor's CD and web site.
http://www.whfreeman.com/understandingearth
Sample lecture outlines highlight the important topics and concepts covered in the text. We suggest that you download a digital copy of this outline from the CD and web site, and customize it to your own lecture before handing it out to students. At the end of each chapter outline, consider adding a selection of review questions, representing a range of thinking levels.

Chapter 6: Volcanism

What Comes Out of a Volcano?
    Lava
    Cinders
    Ash/pyroclastic deposits
    Gases (mostly water)

Factors Influencing Eruptive Style
    Lava composition—amount of SiO_2
    Lava temperature
    Amount of gas
Kinds of Eruptions/Types of Volcanoes
    Central vent or cone eruptions
        Shield volcano—Hawaii
        Cinder cone—Sunset Crater, Arizona
        Composite (strato) volcano—Mount Saint Helens, Washington
    Ash flow/pyroclastic flow—Pompeii/Vesuvius
    Fissure flows—Columbia Plateau/Laki Fissure, Iceland
    Lava domes—Mammoth, California
    Oceanic spreading center—vent and fissure flows
        —pillow lavas
    Calderas—Crater Lake, Oregon
    Phreatic—Krakatoa, Indonesia
    Diatremes—Shiprock, New Mexico
Other Volcanic Deposits and Features
    Lahars (mudflows)
    Geysers, fumaroles, and hot springs
        —Yellowstone
Volcanism and Climate
Global Patterns
    Convergent and divergent plate boundaries
    Hot spots
    Hydrothermal deposits
Volcanic Hazards
    Eruptions
    Earthquakes
    Mud flows
    Air fall ash
    Pyroclastic flows
    Volcanic gases
Geothermal energy

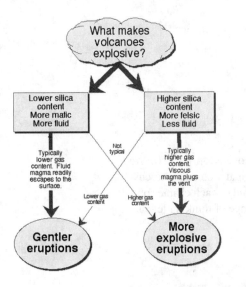

Lava / Magma Characteristics

Lava/Magma Composition	Mafic	Intermediate	Felsic
Volcanic rock	Basalt	Andesite	Dacite and Rhyolite
Typical eruptive temperature	1000° to 1200°C		800° to 1000°C
Viscosity	Highly fluid		Highly viscous
Explosiveness	Low ("quiet")		Highly explosive
Typical flow velocity	0.7 to 13 m/min.	13 m/day	less than 13 m/day
Typical flow length	15 to 150 km	8/km	less than 1.5 km
Typical flow thickness	5 to 15 m	30 m	215 m

CD and Web site Resources

Instructor's CD Highlights

    • *Key Textbook Figures and Tables*
        Figure 6.1: Simplified diagram of a volcanic geosystem

- *Photo Gallery:* Includes slide set images from the previous three editions.

Web site Highlights

http://www.whfreeman.com/understandingearth

• Presentation Tools

Animations: Visit the web site for animations, including animations of figures from this chapter.
PowerPoint Presentation
PowerPoint Presentation with Lecture Notes
Photo Gallery

• Course Preparation

Instructor's Manual
Sample Lecture Outline
Sample Exercises

• Student Study Resources—Assessable

Graded Online Quizzing
Geology in Practice: Tracking Tectonic Plate Motions with Hot Spots
This *Geology in Practice* illustrates how the Hawaii and Yellowstone hotspots may be used as an internal frame of reference for the movement of tectonic plates. Exercises can be used for class discussion, homework, or extra credit.

> Exercise 1: Absolute Motion of the Pacific Plate
> Exercise 2: Absolute Motion of the North American Plate

• Student Study Resources—Non-Assessable

Online Review Exercises: The Volcanic Plumbing System
Where do volcanoes occur?
Find the Volcanic Hot Spots

Concept Self-Checker
Flashcards

Teaching Tips

Cooperative/Collaborative Exercises and In-Class Activities

Coop Exercise #1: Interpretation of Volcanic Deposits and Landforms

The questions below appear in Chapter 6 of the Student Study Guide and require students to interpret volcanic deposits and landforms. These questions make good brief in-class Think/Pair/Share exercises. Present one of the questions on the overhead to the class. Give students one minute to THINK about the best answer for the multiple-choice question. Ask students to discuss their answer and reasons for it with the student sitting next to them. Allow about two minutes for discussion. You can judge the time needed for PAIRING by the amount of discussion going on. Then ask one pair of students to SHARE their answer and reasons why they chose their answer over the other alternatives. Consider soliciting different pairs of students for their reasons why the alternative answers were not the best answer. If students put their answers and a brief discussion for their choice on a piece of paper with their name, you can grade it or use it to take attendance. A strategic application of this exercise is to use it to break up your lecture. Student attention span is short. Exercises like this allow them to think about what they have heard and check their understanding. Note also that answers and additional material for these questions will be found at the end of the Study Guide.

Sample Overhead for Coop Exercise #1
Digital copy available from the Instructor's CD or Web site.

Interpretation of Volcanic Deposits and Landforms

- On a recent three-day hike up a gently sloping mountain, your friends describe to you features they encountered. Frequently they crossed lava flows and fissures, and occasionally they had to detour around large cinder cones. Based on your friends' description, you tell them they were hiking on a

  A. caldera.
  B. composite volcano.
  C. gabbro pluton.
  D. shield volcano.

- Your friends have described to you an eruption that took place at an undisclosed location. The lava they described merely flowed out of a fissure and spread rapidly over a large area. You would inform them that the rock type being formed would most likely be

  A. granite.
  B. andesite.
  C. basalt.
  D. rhyolite.

- A large resort located on a beautiful lake and known for its hot springs, is experiencing a drop in business due to publicity about the recent swarm of small earthquakes in the area. The lake is actually located within a caldera, and beautiful rock towers and spires of weathered volcanic tuff are found all along the edge of the lake. As the director of the resort, you're concerned about the change in business and the potential risk to your guests. What should you do?

  A. You cannot be worried because you know a volcano can't blow up on you.
  B. You know that earthquake swarms can be a precursor to volcanic eruptions, and that very explosive eruptions have happened at the place in the recent geologic past, so you decide that the resort should close until the situation is safe.
  C. Advertise the resort as the best place to see beautiful basalt lava fountains.
  D. Earthquakes have occurred occasionally along a nearby known fault, and there have been no historic volcanic eruptions, so you're not concerned.

- If lava flows of progressively younger ages all erupted from a single large magma chamber, how would you expect their composition to have systematically changed?

  A. The lava flows will be progressively enriched in iron as they get younger.
  B. The lava flows will be progressively enriched in silica as they get younger.
  C. The lava flows will be progressively more mafic as they get younger.
  D. The lava flows will be progressively more fluid as they get younger.

Five-Minute Write

- What questions do you have about lecture?
- What did you find most interesting about lecture?
- How was lecture relevant to you?

Coop Exercise #2: Five-Minute Write
The Five-Minute Write is done during the last five minutes of lecture. Ask students to put their name on a sheet of paper and then address the three questions on the overhead (see adjacent sample). Start the next lecture by discussing the answers to some of the questions students had about the previous lecture.

Freshman Survival Skills Assignments
In the beginning of your course it is prudent to include a few exercises to help the freshmen in your class learn how to learn and to reinforce mastery of the basics of good preparation for

college level lectures. Learning skills are like critical thinking skills. They tend to be mastered slowly, over time, with lots of practice. Even upper division students and graduate students sometimes need coaching about how to learn. See Part I: *Instructional Design* for a discussion of why this is true and ideas about how to do it. Chapter 1 discusses freshman survival as a national educational priority. Chapters 5 and 6 discuss how to develop credit assignments to encourage students to learn how to learn

Homework: Visual Summary of Lava Types
The following Practice Exercise 1 in Chapter 6 of the *Student Study Guide for Understanding Earth* makes a great homework assignment. Constructing visual summaries like this will prove useful later in the course. Note that the Study Guide frequently recommends this kind of exercise to students as a means of getting ready for exams. So, you will find similar exercises in later chapters.

Lava Types—Their properties, eruption styles, deposits, landforms, association with plate tectonics, and hazards. This table will provide you with a very useful study guide for much of Chapter 6. Indeed, the finished table makes an ideal summary of the chapter that should be very useful when you return to this unit in preparation for an exam.

Fill in the blanks with the typical characteristics of each lava type. Keep in mind that different lavas exhibit a range of properties and behaviors. Give the best answer that generally characterizes each. Some answers have been provided as guidelines. Bullets mark information to fill in.

Lava Types	Basalt (mafic)	Andesite (intermediate)	Rhyolite (felsic)
Properties			
eruption temperature	•	intermediate	•
silica content	•	intermediate	high (≈70%)
gas content	low, up to a few percent	variable	high (up to ≈15%)
viscosity	low-fluid magma	intermediate	•
typical flow velocity	0.7 to 30 m/minute	9 m/day	less than 9 m/day
typical flow length	10 to 160 km	8 km	less than 1.5 km
typical flow thickness	5 to 15 m	30 m	200 m
Eruption styles	Typically not very explosive	•	•
Deposits	Flood basalt • • • •	Lava flow Dome Pyroclastic flow— tuff and welded tuff	Obsidian dome • •
Landforms	• • Cinder cone Small caldera	Composite volcano Summit crater Caldera Cinder cone	• • •
Association with plate tectonics	Hot spots •	•	•
Hazards	• •	Lava flow Pyroclastic/ash flow Explosive blast Hot gases Mudflow	Explosive blast Hot gases • •

Midterm Exam Prep

Many freshmen have not had to face the organizational challenges associated with taking two, three, or even four comprehensive exams in one week. You can help them improve their exam-taking skills by encouraging students to use the **Eight-Day Study Plan** provided below. Consider passing it out as a handout or even as an assignment for credit or extra credit. Also consider assessing the effectiveness of this assignment by tracking the exam grade for students who complete an **Eight-Day Study Plan** and those who do not.

Also give serious consideration to providing an exam review session a night or two before the exam or inviting your undergraduate preceptors or graduate teaching assistants to conduct such a review.

Eight-Day Study Plan*

(Make additional copies. Use for every exam you take.)
Here is a guide you can use to prepare for your exam. Everyone develops their own approach to preparing for exams, so feel free to adapt these ideas to your particular needs and situation. The basic idea is to conduct your preparation in a systematic fashion with focus on the most important material. Our plan accomplishes this by dividing the material equally and suggesting how to incorporate the exam prep materials provided in this study guide for each text chapter. You begin the plan eight days prior to the exam.

8 Days Before the Exam: Get organized!

Step 1: Clarify the task. Determine what sort of exam you will take by briefly answering the following questions:

1. This exam will cover (list each chapter to be covered):

    _____

    _____

    _____

    _____

    _____

2. Material and kinds of skills to be particularly emphasized (list chapters/ideas/skills your instructor said would be particularly important):

    _____

    _____

    _____

    _____

    _____

3. Question format will be (check one that applies):
    - ☐ Multiple choice
    - ☐ True/False
    - ☐ Essay
    - ☐ Thought problems
    - ☐ Other (specify) _____

4. Review session is scheduled for (enter date here and be sure to attend):

    _____

Step 2: Divide the material you must review into four equal Parts: A, B, C, D.

---

* Adapted with permission from the University Learning Center, University of Arizona.

7 Days Before the Exam: Begin your review. Review all material in Part A.
Do the following for <u>each</u> chapter you review.

1. **Chapter Summary.** To get yourself started read the chapter summary (Exam Prep section of this guide) for the chapter you want to review.

2. **Practice Exam Questions** Answer Practice Exam Questions (Exam Prep section of this guide) to see where you are with the material. Force yourself to answer all questions for the chapter without referring to the answer key. Correct only after you have tried all items. Be sure to review carefully any items you missed. Correct the misconception that resulted in the error.

3. **Class Notes.** Review your class notes and annotations you made in the text margin by asking yourself questions.

4. **Focus on visual materials and key figures.** This may also be a good time to redo some of the Practice Exercises in this study guide. Many Practice Exercises are designed to help you master the visual concepts of geology. Review visual material in your notes. Test yourself by seeing if you can reconstruct key figures from memory.

5. **Self-Test.** Spend as high a proportion of your study time as possible quizzing yourself.

6 Days Before the Exam: Review Part B. Repeat instructions for Day 7, this time reviewing Part B. *If you have problems with material see your instructor at the next open office hour.*

5 Days Before the Exam: Review Part C. Repeat instructions for Day 7, this time reviewing Part C. *If you have problems with material see your instructor at the next open office hour.*

4 Days Before the Exam: Review Part D. Repeat instructions for Day 7, this time reviewing Part D. *If you have problems with material see your instructor at the next open office hour.*

3 Days Before the Exam: Review All. Review all parts–A, B, C, D fully. Prioritize your time. Focus on important material that will be covered. Work hardest where you are least sure of your self. *If you have problems with material see your instructor at the next open office hour.*

2 Days Before the Exam: Review All. Review all parts–A, B, C, D fully. Prioritize your time. *If you have problems with material see your instructor at the next open office hour.*

Night Before the Exam: Be sure you get the amount of sleep you need to be alert and perform at your best. You don't need to cram. Just stay focused.

Zero Hour: You have prepared well. Allow yourself to be confident. Stay focused and confident during the exam. Use your best test-taking strategies.

Topics for Class Discussion

- How can volcanism have an impact on global climate?
- Compare and contrast basaltic and rhyolitic lavas.
- How is volcanism related to crustal plate boundaries?
- Volcanism on the moon and other planets.
- Hydrothermal ore deposits, e.g., copper porphyry, skarn.

Teaching Resources

Student Study Guide Highlights

In Part I: Chapters provide strategies for learning geology. Ideally, students would read these chapters early in the course.

Chapter 1   Brief Preview of the *Study Guide for Understanding Earth* by Press, Siever, Grotzinger, and Jordan

Chapter 2   Meet the Authors of *Understanding Earth, 4th Edition:* How to use your geology textbook

Chapter 3   How to Be Successful in Geology (or just about any other challenging course)

Part II. Chapter 6: *Volcanism*

Before Lecture:

Preview Questions & Brief Answers

During Lecture:

Note-Taking Tip: Useful abbreviations for volcanism terms

After Lecture:

Check Your Notes

Intensive Study Session

Motivation Tip

Exam Prep:

Chapter Summary

Practice Exercises: *Lava Types— Their properties, eruption styles, deposits, landforms, association with plate tectonics, and hazards. Volcanoes at Plate Tectonic Boundaries*

Review Questions (Answers to all review questions are given at the end of the Study Guide.)

CHAPTER 7

Weathering and Erosion

Chapter Summary

- Physical weathering breaks rock into smaller pieces and chemical weathering alters and dissolves the minerals within the rock. The principal factors that influence weathering are the composition of the parent rock, topography (stability of the land surface), and climate. Typically, there is a positive feedback between physical and chemical weathering, where one enhances the other if conditions are favorable. A good example of this positive feedback is soil formation. As physical and chemical weathering proceeds to alter a stable surface of rock material, a soil forms. The formation of soil promotes weathering by increasing the availability of moisture and producing acidic chemical conditions. Soils also promote plant growth and other organisms which aid both physical and chemical weathering.

- How chemical weathering works is well illustrated by three examples. First, the chemical weathering of feldspars, which are the most abundant silicate mineral in the Earth's crust, illustrates how water with the help of carbonic acid can transform feldspars into clay minerals and dissolve silica and salts (cations). Second, the reaction of calcite and other carbonate minerals that make up limestone exemplifies the role naturally acidic water plays in dissolving rock. Third, the reaction of oxygen with the iron in ferromagnesium minerals like pyroxene illustrates oxidation.

- Physical weathering involves a variety of processes that break rock into fragments. Physical weathering is promoted by chemical weathering, which weakens grain boundaries within the rock. Physical weathering also promotes chemical weathering by increasing the surface area of the broken rock fragments. Frost wedging, crystallization of minerals like salts, and life processes play a major role in breaking rock apart.

- Soils are a product of chemical weathering of rock that has remained in place for a period of time. Soil formation is most affected by climate. The composition of the parent rock, life processes, and topography are also important factors in soil formation. The three most general types of soils are pedalfers (temperate climates), laterites (tropical climates), and pedocals (arid climates). Soils, water, and the air we breathe are the three most basic natural resources.

Learning Objectives

Focus your instruction on clear learning objectives. In this section we provide a *sampling* of possible objectives for this chapter. No class could or should try to accomplish all these. Choose based on your analysis of your class. Refer to Chapter 1: *Learning Objectives—How to Define Your Goals for the Class* in the Instructional Design section of this manual for thoughts and ideas about how to go about such an analysis.

Knowledge

- Know how weathering fits into the rock cycle.
- Know how physical and chemical weathering work.
- Know how soils form as products of chemical weathering.

Skills/Applications/Attitudes

- Be able to link a silicate mineral's susceptibility to chemical weathering to its atomic structure and position in the Bowen's Reaction Series. Refer to Table 7.1, Figure Stories 5.5 and 3.11.
- Be able to discuss how soil formation is closely linked to climate.
- Be able to reconstruct ancient climatic conditions from paleosols.
- Appreciate why soil erosion is a worldwide environmental problem.
- The Earth Policy unit on soil erosion offers an opportunity to foster scientifically responsible attitudes in regard to decision making.

General Education Skills

- Write a scientifically responsible one-page editorial on soil erosion for the local newspaper of a farming community somewhere in the midwestern United States. (Writing/Critical Thinking)

Freshman Survival Skills

- Include a slide on test-taking skills in your next test review session. (See Teaching Tips)
- Encourage learning by providing prompt and detailed feedback to students on their incorrect responses to exam and quiz questions. (See Teaching Tips)
- Provide individual help sessions for students after the first exam. (See Teaching Tips)

Sample Lecture Outline

Digital copy is available from Instructor's CD and web site.
http://www.whfreeman.com/understandingearth
Sample lecture outlines highlight the important topics and concepts covered in the text. We suggest that you download a digital copy of this outline from the CD and web site and customize it to your own lecture before handing it out to students. At the end of each chapter outline, consider adding a selection of review questions, representing a range of thinking levels.

Chapter 7: Weathering and Erosion

Major Factors Controlling Rates of Weathering
    Properties of parent rock
        mineral stability
        rock structure

Climate
>   rainfall
>   temperature

Presence or absence of soil and vegetation
>   thickness of soil layer
>   organic activity

Length of exposure

Chemical Weathering
>   Hydration
>   Role of carbon dioxide
>   Dissolution
>   Oxidation

Products of Chemical Weathering
>   Clays
>   Oxides
>   Salts
>   Silica and quartz sand

Factors Controlling Weathering Rates
>   Chemical stability
>   Solubility
>   Rate of dissolution
>   Relative stability of common rock-forming minerals
>   Positive feedback between physical and chemical weathering

Physical Weathering
>   Plants and burrowing animals
>   Frost action—heat and cold
>   Mineral crystallization
>   Alternating head and cold
>   Exfoliation and spheroidal weathering

Formation of Soils
>   Stability
>   Time
>   Chemical weathering
>   Additions/changes/subtractions

Soil Profiles
>   Pedalfer
>   Laterite
>   Pedocal

Soil Erosion

CD and Web site Resources

Instructor's CD Highlights

- *Key Textbook Figures and Tables*

>   Figure 7.4: The process by which feldspar decays is analogous to the brewing of coffee.
>   Figure 7.5: As a rock mass breaks into smaller pieces
>   Figure Story 7.6: Atmospheric carbon dioxide influences weathering and climate.
>   Figure 7.8: Weathering of iron-rich minerals
>   Figure 7.15: Summary chart of weathering
>   Figure 7.16: Soil profile
>   Table 7.1: Relative Stabilities of Common Minerals Under Weathering
>   Table 7.2: Major Factors Controlling Rates of Weathering

- *Photo Gallery:* Includes slide set images from the previous three editions.

Web site Highlights

http://www.whfreeman.com/understandingearth

- **Presentation Tools**

   Animations: Visit the web site for animations, including animations of
      figures from this chapter.
   PowerPoint Presentation
   PowerPoint Presentation with Lecture Notes
   Photo Gallery

- **Course Preparation**

   Instructor's Manual
   Sample Lecture Outline
   Sample Exercises

- **Student Study Resources—Assessable**

   Graded Online Quizzing
   Geology in Practice: How Do Hoodoos Form?
      This *Geology in Practice* involves students with the relationship
      between physical and chemical weathering. The exercises also
      explore various other factors, like exposed surface area and pre-
      existing characteristics of rock that enhance weathering processes.

- **Student Study Resources—Non-Assessable**

   Online Review Exercises:
      Weathering the Storm
      Understanding Soils
   Concept Self-Checker
   Flashcards

Teaching Tips

Cooperative/Collaborative Exercises and In-Class Activities

Coop Exercise #1: Factors in Rock Weathering

The following review question from Chapter 7 in the Student Study Guide can be used as a
basis for a Think/Pair/Share, group discussion, or case study.

In the days of the Pharaohs of Egypt a cherished status symbol was the obelisk, a stone
column decorated with hieroglyphs (designs carved into the stone—usually sandstone). In
1879 the obelisk of Thothmes III from the temple of Heliopolis, Egypt, was moved to Central
Park in New York City. Within about sixty years the hieroglyphs were barely visible on the
obelisk, while its counterpart still standing in Egypt remains in nearly perfect condition in the
desert sun for almost 4000 years. Why did the stone obelisk deteriorate "so quickly" when it
was moved to New York City?

Coop Exercise #2: Five-Minute Write

The Five-Minute Write is done during the last five minutes of lecture. Ask students to put
their name on a sheet of paper and then address the three questions on the overhead (see adja-

Five-Minute Write

- What questions
  do you have about
  lecture?
- What did you find
  most interesting
  about lecture?
- How was lecture
  relevant to you?

cent sample). Start the next lecture by discussing the answers to some of the questions students had about the previous lecture.

Freshman Survival Skills: Suggestions to Help Freshmen Improve Their Test-Taking Skills

Students often miss points on exams simply because they are disorganized and nervous. Here are three things you can do to alleviate exam anxiety and mentor students on how to prepare for and take exams.

1. Provide a review session before every exam.

2. During your exam review session put up the slide below and spend a few minutes discussing "strategic test taking." **Tip:** Strategic Test Taking is discussed in the *Student Study Guide for Understanding Earth*. See Chapter 3 in Part I of the Study Guide: *How to Be Successful in Geology.*

3. Provide individual help sessions after exams for students who need them. **Tip:** There are lots of helpful ideas concerning how to provide such individual help in Chapter 11 in Part I of this manual.

Test-Taking Tips
Test Taking and Learning Style

Visual Learners:
- ☐ Pay particular attention to written directions.
- ☐ When you get stuck on an item, close your eyes and picture flow charts, pictures, field experiences, or text.

Auditory Learners:
- ☐ Pay particular attention to verbal directions.
- ☐ Repeat written directions quietly to yourself (moving your lips should be enough).
- ☐ When you get stuck remember your lecturer's voice covering this section.

Kinesthetic Learners:
There are a variety of things kinesthetic learners find helpful when they get stuck on a test item. Try some of these:
- ☐ When you get stuck, move in your chair or tap your foot to trigger memory.
- ☐ Feel yourself actually doing a lab procedure related to the test item you are stuck on.
- ☐ Sketch a flow chart to unlock the memory of a process.

Homework: Visual Summary Exercises for Weathering

Practice Exercises 1 and 2 from the Chapter 7 in Student Study Guide will help students develop a useful visual summary of information on physical and chemical weathering and soil profiles. The exercises provided below are also available on the Instructor's web site or CD where they can be easily downloaded.

Remember that "it is better to teach a person to fish than to just give them a fish." Be sure to model and discuss the kind of thinking that allows one to construct such charts.

Exercise 1: Physical and Chemical Weathering

Fill in the blanks in the flowchart below.

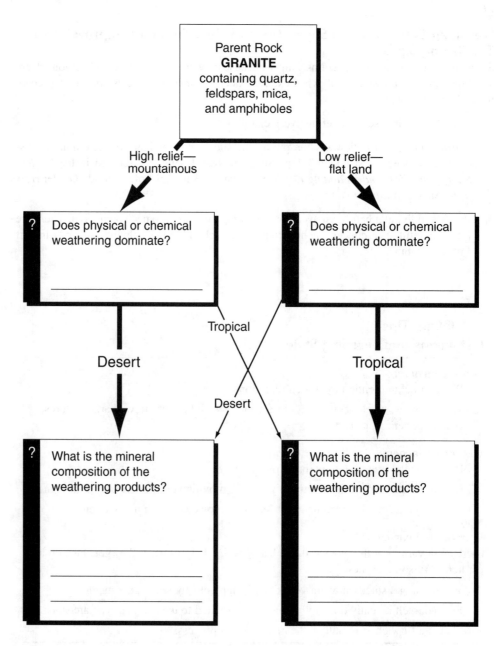

Exercise 2: Soil Types

Fill in the blanks in the table below.

Climate	Soil type	Soil characteristics	Agricultural potential
Desert—warm and dry	*pedocal*		
Temperate—moderate		*variable—clay rich*	
Tropical—warm and wet			*Lush vegetation is supported by an organic-rich top soil. Crops can be grown for only a few years before nutrients are depleted.*

Topics for Class Discussion

- How does physical weathering aid chemical weathering?
  Note: The relationship between physical and chemical weathering is a great example of a positive feedback.

- How is carbonic acid produced and how does it affect weathering?

- A granite contains much more feldspar than quartz. How is it that sand derived from the weathering of granite may be composed mostly of quartz?

- The Chemical Weathering of Minerals in the Bowen's Reaction Series Generally, minerals that crystallized at higher temperature are less stable on the Earth's surface than minerals that formed at lower temperatures. For example, the ferromagnesium minerals tend to chemically weather the fastest.

- Seawater contains 2.20 pounds of dissolved solids per cubic foot. Freshwater lake water contains about 0.01 pounds of dissolved solids per cubic foot. Where do the dissolved solids in seawater come from?

> **Weathering of silicate rocks + volcanic volatiles → source of salt (dissolved solids) in the oceans**

- Clay minerals/Ion Exchange/Soil Fertility
  Soil fertility results from a delicate balance between weathering processes, which release mineral nutrients and intense weathering that can wash the nutrients away. Clay minerals and organic matter help to hold nutrients in soils so that they are not easily washed away but at the same time easy for plant roots to extract.

CLAY MINERALS, ION EXCHANGE, AND SOIL FERTILITY

Nutrients and water are held in the soil by electrostatically charged clays and organic matter.

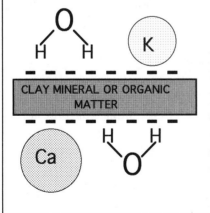

Polar water molecules and cations form weak electrostatic bonds with the negative charge on surface of clays and organic matter.

- When water freezes, it expands 9% and exerts about 15 tons per square inch of force.

- Water molecules in their crystal form have an open-structured hexagonal arrangement that results in the expansion of water upon freezing. Ice is therefore less dense than water.

- Bauxite–Aluminum Ore–mostly $Al(OH)_3 + AlO \cdot OH$

  Bauxite is an uncommon mineral formed by the breakdown of aluminum-bearing rocks under special conditions of intense chemical weathering, typical of tropical climates. Special conditions for the formation of bauxite include:

      abundant rainfall
      ground water that is neither acidic nor alkaline
      aluminum-rich parent rocks
      subsurface drainage, e.g., no swamps
      low relief
      erosion is slow relative to chemical weathering

- Aluminum is the second most abundant metallic element (after silicon) in the Earth's crust, where it averages 8.3%. Aluminum has been produced commercially for only about 100 years. Refining aluminum is very energy intensive. The energy it takes to produce the aluminum in a soda can is equivalent to the energy used by a 100-watt light bulb over a period of 100 hours. Gem quality crystals of aluminum oxide include rubies and sapphires. Corundum, a very hard mineral, is made from aluminum oxide.

- Chromium, manganese, cobalt, copper, zinc, selenium, molybdenum, and iodine are trace elements within soils and important trace nutrients for human health. Recently glaciated lands are typically deficient in iodine because the glacial melt waters leached the iodine from the soil. Because iodine is vital for the healthy operation of the thyroid gland, iodine is added to table-salt to prevent goiter—the enlargement of the thyroid gland due to an iodine deficient diet.

Teaching Resources

Student Study Guide Highlights

In Part I: Chapters provide strategies for learning geology. Ideally, students would read these chapters early in the course.

    Chapter 1   Brief Preview of the *Study Guide for Understanding Earth* by Press, Siever, Grotzinger, and Jordan

    Chapter 2   Meet the Authors of *Understanding Earth, 4th Edition:* How to use your geology textbook.

    Chapter 3   How to Be Successful in Geology (or just about any other challenging course)

Part II. Chapter 7: *Weathering and Erosion*

    Before Lecture:

        Preview Questions & Brief Answers

        Learning Warm-up Tip

    During Lecture:

        Note-Taking Tip: Add visual material to help distinguish between chemical and physical weathering

    After Lecture:

        Check Your Notes

        Intensive Study Session

    Exam Prep:

        Tips for Preparing for Exams

        Chapter Summary

        Practice Exercises: *Physical and Chemical Weathering*
                            Soil Types
                            Soil Formation in Different Regions

Review Questions (Answers to all review questions are given at the end of the Study Guide.)

CHAPTER 8

Sediments and Sedimentary Rocks

Chapter Summary

- Weathering and erosion produce the clastic particles and dissolved ions that compose sediment. Water, wind, and ice transport the sediment to where it is deposited. Burial and diagenesis harden sediments into sedimentary rocks.

- The two major types of sediments are clastic and chemical/biochemical. Clastic sediments are formed from rock particles and mineral fragments. Chemical and biochemical sediments originate from the ions dissolved in water. Chemical and biochemical reactions precipitate these dissolved ions from solution.

- Understanding the characteristics of sediments and modern sedimentary environments provides a basis for reconstructing past environmental conditions, using the rock record. Sedimentary structures, like bedding, ripple marks, and mud cracks, provide important clues about the sedimentary environment.

- Diagenesis transforms sediment into sedimentary rock. Burial promotes this transformation by subjecting sediments to increasing heat and pressure. Cementation is especially important in the lithification of clastic sediments.

- The classification of clastic sediments and sedimentary rocks is based primarily on the size of the grains within the rock. The name of chemical and biochemical sediments and sedimentary rock is based primarily on their composition.

- Plate tectonic processes play an important role in producing depressions (basins) in which sediments accumulate. Sedimentary basins result from rifting, thermal sag, and flexure of the lithosphere.

Learning Objectives

Focus your instruction on clear learning objectives. In this section we provide a *sampling* of possible objectives for this chapter. No class could or should try to accomplish all these. Choose based on your analysis of your class. Refer to Chapter 1: *Learning Objectives—How to Define Your Goals for the Class* in the Instructional Design section of this manual for thoughts and ideas about how to go about such an analysis.

Knowledge

- Understand how sediments are produced, transported, deposited, and transformed into rock.
- Know the major types of sediments and sedimentary rocks, and how they are classified.
- Know common characteristics of sediments, sedimentary rocks, and sedimentary environments.
- Understand how the accumulation of sediments is linked to plate tectonics.

Geology Skills/Applications/Attitudes

- Given a description of sedimentary rock(s) and associated sedimentary structures and fossils, reconstruct characteristics of the source region, agent of transport, distance of transport, and environment of deposition.

General Education Skills

- Write a one-page paper interpreting a local sedimentary rock formation that contains some interesting sedimentary structures and fossils. Write the paper as though it was to be published in a local newspaper for citizens of your community to read. (Writing/Critical Thinking)

Freshman Survival Skills

- Right after the first exam is a make-or-break time for students who received low scores. Given proper assistance, most students are capable of dramatic improvement. This is a good time to make interventions with students who come in for help and to emphasize freshman survival skills. For example, repeat the freshman survival skills information presented earlier in the course.
- Provide individual help sessions for students after the first exam (see Teaching Tips). Encourage students to bring their notes to help sessions.
- Encourage students who want to improve their scores to begin using the *Student Study Guide for Understanding Earth*. Recommend relevant sections in introductory chapters but focus on the importance of their starting to answer the preview questions before lecture and working on review questions after lecture.

Sample Lecture Outline

Digital copy is available from Instructor's CD and web site.
http://www.whfreeman.com/understandingearth
Sample lecture outlines highlight the important topics and concepts covered in the text. We suggest that you download a digital copy of this outline from the CD and web site, and customize it to your own lecture before handing it out to students. At the end of each chapter outline, consider adding a selection of review questions, representing a range of thinking levels.

Chapter 8: Sediments and Sedimentary Rocks

Sedimentary Rocks and the Rock Cycle
    Weathering/erosion/transportation/deposition/burial/diagenesis
Classification (based on composition and texture)
    Clastic
    Chemical and biochemical

Sedimentary Environments
    Continental
    Shoreline
    Marine
    Clastic vs. chemical and biochemical environments
Sedimentary Structures
    Stratification/bedding
    Mud cracks, ripples, cross-bedding, graded bedding
    Bioturbation
    Bedding sequences
Burial and Diagenesis
Diagenesis: Sediments → Sedimentary Rocks
    Heat, pressure, chemical alteration
    Compaction
    Cementation
Types of Sedimentary Rocks
    Conglomerate
    Sandstones
        arkoses
        lithic
        quartz arenites
        graywacke
    Siltstone
    Claystone/Shale
    Limestone
    Dolostone
    Evaporites
    Phosphorite
    Iron formations
    Coal
Sedimentary Rocks Are a Product of
    Parent rock
    Climate
    Agent and distance of transport
    Environment of deposition
Plate Tectonics and Sedimentary Basins
    Subsidence due to rifting, thermal sag, flexure → sedimentary basins

CD and Web site Resources

Instructor's CD Highlights

    • *Key Textbook Figures and Tables*
        Figure 8.1: The sedimentary stages of the rock cycle embrace overlapping processes.
        Figure Story 8.4: A sedimentary environment is characterized by a particular set of environmental conditions and geologic processes.
        Figure 8.10: Typical alluvial cycle
        Figure 8.11: Diagenetic processes produce changes in composition and texture.
        Figure 8.15: The mineralogy of four major groups of sandstones
        Figure Story 8.16: The growth of a carbonate platform
        Figure 8.20: The development of sedimentary basins on a rifted continental margin
        Table 8.1: Minerals Remaining in Clastic Sediments

Table 8.2: Major Chemical and Biochemical Sedimentary Environments

Table 8.3: Major Classes of Clastic Sediments and Sedimentary Rocks

Table 8.4: Classification of Biochemical and Chemical Sediments and Sedimentary Rocks

- *Photo Gallery:* Includes slide set images from the previous three editions.

Web site Highlights

http://www.whfreeman.com/understandingearth

- **Presentation Tools**

    Animations: Visit the web site for animations, including animations of figures from this chapter.

    PowerPoint Presentation

    PowerPoint Presentation with Lecture Notes

    Photo Gallery

- **Course Preparation**

    Instructor's Manual

    Sample Lecture Outline

    Sample Exercises

- **Student Study Resources—Assessable**

    Graded Online Quizzing

    Geology in Practice: Reading the Geologic Story of Sedimentary Rocks: Cutting Through the Layers.

    > The exercises in this *Geology in Practice* can be used for class discussion, homework, or extra credit. Based on outcrop descriptions, images, and photomicrographs, students are asked to interpret different sedimentary rocks, such as the Navajo, Coconino, and Saint Peters Sandstone, plus others.

- **Student Study Resources—Non-Assessable**

    Online Review Exercise

    > Identify the Sedimentary Environment

    > Identify the Common Sedimentary Environment

    > Identify the Depositional Environment

    Concept Self-Checker

    Flashcards

Teaching Tips

Collaborative Exercises and In-Class Activities

Refer to Chapter 4: See *Collaborative Teaching Strategies* in the Instructional Design section of this manual for suggestions about how to set up and run this type of exercise in your classroom.

Coop Exercise #1: Interpreting Sedimentary Rocks

The question below can be the basis for a JIGSAW. Have students team-up in groups of two or three. Post the question on the board or overhead for the whole class to see. Assign just one of the four parts of the question to each student team. Give teams 3–5 minutes to write down a few sentences for an answer. Then review the answers for each part by calling on a member of a team to read the answer the team formulated. Discuss the answers with the whole class by complimenting the teams for their good answers, correcting any misconceptions, and reviewing questions students may have.

What geologic history might be inferred from each of the following rocks:

    A. feldspar-rich sandstone?

    B. well-rounded conglomerate?

    C. sandstone composed almost entirely of quartz?

    D. limestone with abundant fossils?

Coop Exercise #2: Five-Minute Write

The Five-Minute Write is done during the last five minutes of lecture. Ask students to put their name on a sheet of paper and then address the three questions on the overhead (see adjacent sample). Start the next lecture by discussing the answers to some of the questions students had about the previous lecture.

Sample Exercises

Digital copy is available from Instructor's CD and web site.
http://www.whfreeman.com/understandingearth

Essay on Sand

In the spaces provided below (1-5), indicate five erroneous statements in the following paragraph, an *Essay on Sand*.

An Essay on Sand

Nearly all naturally occurring sand on the continents is composed entirely of quartz grains because feldspar, which is the most voluminous mineral group in crustal rocks, is converted entirely to clays by chemical weathering, even in arid to semiarid environments. Sands deposited by rivers are the best sorted and best rounded of all sands because little abrasion or winnowing occurs during eolian and beach transport. In general, coarser grained river sands are better rounded than finer grained river sands because more abrasion occurs during bedload transport than during suspension transport. Sandstone beds are generally interpreted as terrestrial (river, dune, etc.), strand line (beach, tidal bar, etc.), or shallow-marine (shelf, etc.) deposits because not even turbidity currents can transport sediment as coarse as sand to the deep ocean floor. Moreover, the white sands of atolls and small islets built on coral reefs are composed chiefly of grains of calcium carbonate, whereas the black sands of beaches on volcanic islands like Hawaii are composed largely of detritus eroded from lavas like basalt. Buried layers of sand make very poor aquifers, even though they are porous, because their pore spaces are not interconnected and their permeability is thus typically too low to allow ground water to flow through them at a suitable rate. On the other hand, quartz is readily soluble during diagenesis, so that tightly cemented sandstone beds commonly develop large caverns that serve as vast subterranean reservoirs of ground water. Durable sand eroded from bedrock, however, is used by streams as a major abrasive tool for eroding their beds.

Answers to an Essay on Sand

1. By no means is all sand composed entirely of quartz, and feldspar is a common constituent of many sands, especially in arid to semiarid climates where breakdown of feldspar to clays is quite incomplete during weathering and erosion.

2. Eolian and beach sands are commonly better sorted and rounded than river sands because winnowing is quite effective and abrasion intense in dunes and on beaches.

3. Turbidity currents do transport immense volumes of sand from shelves and deltas to the deep sea floor, typically via submarine canyons cutting into continental slopes.

4. Sand layers are commonly excellent aquifers because their pore space forms a superbly interconnected network between the sand grains.

5. Quartz dissolves slowly and with difficulty and caverns form much more readily in limestone.

Sand Properties and Their Geological Influence

Draw connecting lines to match the various attributes of sand (left column) with the geologic influences (right column) that tend to control each of the attributes listed.

1. mineralogical composition

2. degree of sorting

3. degree of rounding

4. degree of lithification

• nature of transporting agent and distance of transport

• compaction and cementation

• nature of depositional environment

• nature of source rock from which sand was eroded.

Interpretation of a Sandstone (Quartz Arenite/Orthoquartzite)

Discuss the paleo-environmental-geographic-tectonic implications of the sandstone described below. Your discussion should include generalized characterizations of the:

a) source area

b) agent of transport

c) distance of transport

d) environment of deposition

e) tectonic stability of region

f) geological age (Geologic Period[s])

Based on the information given below, be sure to provide one or more reasons for your interpretation of the above characteristics. Illustrate your discussion with a diagram.

Description of Sandstone

Exposed in Kansas, Nebraska, Wyoming, and Colorado, the medium-grained and moderately sorted sandstone is very widespread but occurs in a relatively thin sheet with a thickness of 25 to 80 meters. This quartz arenite grades into clay-rich facies to the east, which are interbedded with thinly stratified mudstones and lignite (low-grade coal) seams. The quartz arenite facies contains trough cross-bedding and asymmetric ripple marks but lacks fossils. The lignite beds contain imprints of ferns, tree bark, and leaves of flowering plants. The mudstone facies contains some dinosaur bones.

Note: Facies is a body of rock representing a particular local environment. It implies coexistence with other bodies of rock, representing other local environs, which coexist during a particular period of time.

Note to Instructor:

Students will find a historical geology textbook a helpful reference for the successful completion of this exercise.

Answers to Interpretation of a Sandstone
Grading Guidelines

Although there may be an overall best answer to this exercise, many factors influence the characteristics of sedimentary rocks. If a well-supported discussion is provided by a student, then more than one answer may be acceptable for significant partial to full credit.

Source area (rock type, climate, relief)

Quartz arenites are typically generated from pre-existing sandstones (refer to the *Major Kinds of Sandstone* section of your textbook). It usually requires more than one cycle of weathering, erosion, deposition, and lithification to produce a pure quartz sand. Granite and gneiss are good sources for sand-size grains of quartz. Relatively intense weathering and long distances of transport help to weather away the less stable mineral and rock grains.

Quartz arenites can be generated from a source region of low relief. To form an extensive deposit of sand then requires a long period of time to supply the quantity of sand and/or relatively intense weathering conditions. A high relief in the source region typically generates a large amount of sand. One could argue for high relief source region if the source rock was a pre-existing sandstone and/or there was a long distance of transport and/or there was intense weathering (due to a warm and wet climate) that would result in the destruction of the unstable mineral grains.

In summary, given the compositional maturity of the sandstone (pure quartz), either the source region is dominated by pre-existing sandstones or a relatively wet/warm climate facilitated the decomposition of other silicate minerals, thereby leaving quartz sand as a residual.

Agent and Distance of Transport

The trough cross-bedding and asymmetric ripples are sedimentary structures typically found in water deposited sands. River or tidal currents could produce these structures. The medium grain-size and moderate sorting is consistent with transport and deposition by rivers. Wind and waves usually generate the best-sorted sands. Wind deposited sand is fine-grained. If the source rock is a pre-existing sandstone, the distance of transport may be moderately short. If the source rock were granite or gneiss, then a long distance of transport would help weather away the unstable minerals.

Environment of Deposition

The sedimentary structures, lack of fossils in the sandstone, and terrestrial plant fossils in the associated mudstone and lignite beds to the east all suggest that the sand was deposited on land. River channel deposits would be a responsible environment of deposition if relief were low.

The clay-rich and lignite facies to the east are indicative of a coastal swamp environment, which would be consistent with the sands being deposited by low-gradient rivers just inland from the swamps.

Tectonic Stability of Environment of Deposition

A rapidly subsiding environment of deposition would produce a thick and more localized deposit of sand. The thin and very widespread sheet of this quartz arenite sand is indicative of a tectonically stable environment of deposition, such as a coastal plain along a stable continental margin.

Geologic Age

Although the sandstone contains no fossils, the mudstone and lignite beds do. The assemblage of fossils found in the mudstone and lignite beds are consistent with a Mesozoic (Jurassic–Cretaceous) age. Since the fossil-bearing layers are interbedded in (facies of) the sandstone, their age is approximately the same as the sandstone. Therefore, the approximate age of the sandstone is Jurassic–Cretaceous.

Freshman Survival Skills Assignment
Visual Summary of Sedimentary Rocks

The following exercises from *Student Study Guide for Understanding Earth* provide a good visual summary. You might assign all three exercises for credit. Exercise 1 deals with sedimentary environments. Exercise 2 will help students learn to classify sedimentary rocks according to grain size. Exercise 3 links characteristics of sediments with sedimentary rocks.

Homework Exercise 1: Common Sedimentary Environments

Using Figure 8.1 and Figure Story 8.4 as a guide, fill in the blanks in the table below with the clastic or chemical sediment (e.g., sand, silt, mud, salts, carbonate, peat) that best matches the following environment of deposition.

Environment of deposition	Fill in the blank
Alpine or glacial river channel	
Dunes in a desert	
Flood plain along a broad meander bend	
River delta along a marine shoreline	
Continental shelf	
Deep sea adjacent to a continental shelf	
Shoreline beach dunes	
Tidal flats	
Organic reef	

Homework Exercise 2: Grain-sizes for Clastic Sedimentary Rocks

Using the terms for *sediments* and *rocks* listed in Table 8.3, fill in the blanks with the appropriate name of the sediment and rock that matches the typical particle size of the *Common Object* given in the table below. **Hint:** A few answers have been filled out as a reference.

Grain size	Common object	Sediment	Rock type
Coarse ↑ ↓ Fine	Football to bus	*boulder gravel*	
	Plum or lime		*conglomerate*
	Pea or bean		
	Coarse-ground pepper or salt		*sandstone*
	Fine-ground pepper or salt		
	Talcum powder or baby powder		

Homework Exercise 3: Clastic and Chemical Sediments and Sedimentary Rocks

Given the descriptive statements on the left side, fill in the blanks with the appropriate sediment type and rock type in the table below. A list of common sediment types are provided below for your reference. Use the following terms for *sediment type* and *sedimentary rock* to fill in the table below.

Sediment types	Sedimentary rocks			
biochemical	arkose	dolostone	limestone	sandstone
clastic	chert	evaporite	peat	shale
chemical	conglomerate	graywacke	phosphorite	siltstone

Statement	Sediment type	Sedimentary rock example
Composed largely of rock fragments		
Precipitated in the environment of deposition		
Important source of coal		
Often formed by diagenesis	*chemical*	*dolostone and phosphorite*
Formed from abundant skeleton fragments of marine or lake organisms, such as coral, seashells, foraminifers		
Produced by physical weathering		
Produced from rapidly eroding granitic and gneissic terrains in an arid or semiarid climate		

Pass around examples of the major types of sedimentary rocks during lecture.

Topics for class discussion

- Why is quartz a common mineral in sandstones?
- Why is shale the most common sedimentary rock?

Teaching Resources

Student Study Guide Highlights

In Part I: Chapters provide strategies for learning geology. Ideally, students would read these chapters early in the course.

Chapter 1   Brief Preview of the *Study Guide for Understanding Earth* by Press, Siever, Grotzinger, and Jordan

Chapter 2   Meet the Authors of *Understanding Earth, 4th Edition:* How to use your geology textbook

Chapter 3   How to Be Successful in Geology (or just about any other challenging course)

Part II. Chapter 8: *Sediments and Sedimentary Rocks*

Before Lecture:

Preview Questions & Brief Answers

During Lecture:

Note-Taking Tip

After Lecture:

Check Your Notes

Intensive Study Session

Memory & Learning Tip–Chunking

Exam Prep:

Chapter Summary

Practice Exercises: *Common Sedimentary Environments*
Grain-sizes for Clastic Sedimentary Rocks
Clastic and Chemical Sediments and Sedimentary Rocks

Review Questions (Answers to all review questions are given at the end of the Study Guide.)

CHAPTER 9

Metamorphic Rocks

Chapter Summary

- Metamorphism is the alteration in the solid state of preexisting rocks, including older metamorphic rocks. Increases in temperature and pressure, and reactions with chemical-bearing fluids cause metamorphism. Metamorphism typically involves a rearrangement (recrystallization) of the chemical components within the parent rock. Rearrangement of components within minerals is facilitated by the following: higher temperatures increase ion mobility within the solid state; higher confining pressure compacts the rock; directed pressure associated with tectonic activity can cause the rock to shear (smear), which orients mineral grains and generates a foliation; and chemical reactions with migrating fluids may remove or add materials and induce the growth of new minerals.

- The three major types of metamorphism are: regional metamorphism, associated with orogenic processes that build mountains; contact metamorphism, caused by the heat from an intruding body of magma; and seafloor metamorphism, also known as metasomatism. Other less common kinds of metamorphism are: burial metamorphism, associated with subsiding regions on continents; high-pressure metamorphism, occurring deep within subduction zones and upper mantle; and shock metamorphism due to meteor impact. Refer to Figure 9.3.

- Metamorphic rocks fall into two major textural classes: the foliated (displaying a preferred orientation of minerals, analogous to the grain within wood) and granoblastic (granular). The composition of the parent rock and the grade of metamorphism are the most important factors controlling the mineralogy of the metamorphic rock. Metamorphism usually causes little or no change in the bulk composition of the rock. The kinds of minerals and their orientation do change. Mineral assemblages within metamorphic rocks are used by geoscientists as a guide to the original composition of the parent rock and the conditions during metamorphism.

- Metamorphic rocks are characteristically formed in subduction zones, continental collisions, oceanic spreading centers, and deeply subsiding regions on the continents.

Learning Objectives

In this section we provide a *sampling* of possible objectives for this chapter. No class could or should try to accomplish all these. Choose based on your analysis of your class. Refer to Chapter 1: *Learning Objectives—How to Define Your Goals for the Class* in the Instructional Design section of this manual for thoughts and ideas about how to go about such an analysis.

Knowledge

- Know and understand the causes of metamorphism.
- Know the various kinds of metamorphism.
- Understand how metamorphic rocks can be used to reconstruct past geologic events.
- Understand how metamorphic rocks can be used as geothermometers and geobarometers.
- Know the chief types of metamorphic rocks and how they are classified.
- Understand how metamorphism is linked to plate tectonics.
- Understand how metamorphism is associated with the formation of mineral deposits.

Geology Skills/Applications/Attitudes

- Given a suite of metamorphic rocks exposed on the Earth's surface today, interpret possible associations with ancient plate boundaries.

General Education Skills

- Using web sites as resources, write a short and interesting newspaper article on one of the gemstones, such as garnets, emeralds, or diamonds, that result from metamorphic processes.

Freshman Survival Skills

- Reinforce the importance of promptly filling in gaps in your notes by stopping about halfway through the lecture on metamorphic rocks and telling students to check their notes with the student sitting next to them.

Sample Lecture Outline

Digital copy is available from Instructor's CD and web site.
http://www.whfreeman.com/understandingearth
Sample lecture outlines highlight the important topics and concepts covered in the text. We suggest that you download a digital copy of this outline from the CD and web site, and customize it to your own lecture before handing it out to students. At the end of each chapter outline, consider adding a selection of review questions, representing a range of thinking levels.

Chapter 9: Metamorphic Rocks

Causes of Metamorphism
 Heat
 Confining pressure due to burial
 Directed pressure due to tectonics
 Fluids—chemical alteration
Kinds of Metamorphism
 Regional
 Contact
 Seafloor (metasomatism)
 Burial
 High-pressure and ultra-high-pressure
 Shock

Textures and Types
    Foliation
        preferred orientation of crystals
        slaty cleavage
        slate, phyllite, schist, gneiss, migmatite
    Granoblastic (non-foliated)
        granular
        no preferred orientation of crystals
        hornfels, marble, greenstone, amphibolite
        porphyroblasts, e.g., garnet and staurolite
Metamorphic Grade—Regional Metamorphism
    Temperature and pressure
    Parent rock composition
    Metamorphic facies
Plate Tectonics and Metamorphism
    Metamorphic P-T paths
        prograde
        retrograde
    Spreading centers—meta-basalts
    Subduction zones—mélange and blue schists
    Continent-ocean convergence
    Continent-continent collision—ophiolites
        Exhumation—links between the plate tectonic and climate

CD and Web site Resources

Instructor's CD Highlights

- *Key Textbook Figures and Tables*
  - Figure 9.2: Temperatures, pressures, and depths at which low- and high-grade metamorphic rocks form
  - Figure 9.3: The main types of metamorphism and where they occur.
  - Figure Story 9.4: Slaty cleavage
  - Figure Story 9.7: Index minerals used to determine isograds
  - Figure 9.8: Changes in mineral composition
  - Figure 9.9: Metamorphic pressure-temperature paths
  - Figure 9.10: P-T paths and rock assemblages
  - Table 9.1: Classification of Metamorphic Rocks on Texture
  - Table 9.2: Major Minerals of Metamorphic Facies Produced from Parent Rocks of Different Composition

- *Photo Gallery:* Includes slide set images from the previous three editions.

Web site Highlights

http://www.whfreeman.com/understandingearth

- **Presentation Tools**

  Animations: Visit the web site for animations, including animations of figures from this chapter.
  PowerPoint Presentation
  PowerPoint Presentation with Lecture Notes
  Photo Gallery

- **Course Preparation**

  Instructor's Manual

Sample Lecture Outline
Sample Exercises

• **Student Study Resources—Assessable**

Graded Online Quizzing
Geology in Practice: Reading the Geologic Story of Metamorphic Rocks
This *Geology in Practice* contains exercises that can be used for class discussion, homework, or extra credit. Descriptions and images of outcrops and hand specimens provide the basis for interpretations of metamorphic rocks.

• **Student Study Resources—Non-Assessable**

Online Review Exercises
What happen where? Metamorphism & Plate Tectonics
Create a Metamorphic Rock
Before & After: Metamorphic Rocks
Concept Self-Checker
Flashcards

Teaching Tips

Collaborative Exercises and In-Class Activities

Refer to Chapter 4: *Collaborative Teaching Strategies* in the Instructional Design section of this manual.

Coop Exercise #1: Classification of Metamorphic Rocks Based on Texture

Practice Exercise 1 from the Student Study Guide is good for a brief Think/Pair/Share activity in lecture. Students often do not realize that metamorphism affects ALL rock types including preexisting metamorphic rocks. It seems a common misconception is that metamorphic rocks are somehow immune from further metamorphism. Review retrograde metamorphism and metamorphic facies when you do this exercise.

Directions: Fill in the table below. Bullets mark where to write your answers.

Hint: Refer to *Metamorphic Textures* section of your textbook and Table 9.1.

Parent rock	Metamorphic rock	Texture (foliated/granoblastic)
Shale		*foliated*
Quartz-rich sandstone		
	Granulite	
Granite		
Limestone		
	Hornfels	
	Amphibolites and greenstones	
	Migmatite	

Coop Exercise #2: Five-Minute Write

The Five-Minute Write is done during the last five minutes of lecture. Ask students to put their name on a sheet of paper and then address the three questions on the overhead (see adjacent sample). Start the next lecture by discussing the answers to some of the questions students had about the previous lecture.

Sample Exercises

Digital copy is available from Instructor's CD and web site.
http://www.whfreeman.com/understandingearth

Making comparisons and contrasts between things can enhance learning. With the completion of Chapter 9: Metamorphic Rocks, your students can now compare and contrast the characteristics of the three major rock types: igneous, sedimentary, and metamorphic. A sample exercise involving students with making comparisons between the major rock types is provided below (**Homework/Exercise 2**).

Homework (Exercise 2): Comparing igneous, sedimentary, and metamorphic rocks

(From the *Student Study Guide for Understanding Earth*, Chapter 9, Practice Exercises and Review Questions)

Complete the table by filling in the blank spaces.

Note that there may be more than one reasonable answer for some blanks. Some answers are provided as examples.

Major mineral composition	Texture	Rock type (igneous, sedimentary, metamorphic)	Rock name (granite, sandstone, marble)
calcium carbonate	granoblastic		
quartz, K & Na feldspar, mica, and amphibole	phaneritic		
clay	fine-grained clastic		
pyroxene, calcium feldspar, and olivine			basalt
quartz	granoblastic		
pebbles and cobbles of a variety of rock types			
fragments of seashells and fine mud		sedimentary	
quartz, muscovite, chlorite, and garnet			schist

Freshman Survival Skills Assignment

Reinforce the importance of promptly filling in gaps in lecture notes by stopping about half way through the lecture on metamorphic rocks and telling students to check their notes with the student sitting next to them.

Topics for Class Discussion

- Patterned fabrics in cloth like corduroy are a good analog for foliated fabrics in metamorphic rocks. Use a paper towel as a quick lecture demonstration to illustrate a preferred orientation within a material. Most paper towels will tear apart much easier in one direction than the other. Ask students to come up with an explanation for this characteristic of paper towels. Then ask them to compare how the towel rips with how a foliated metamorphic rock will break.

- Because marble is commonly used as a facing stone for buildings and for tombstones, I find students think it is a tough rock that will last for a long time. Because marble is made of calcite with a hardness of 3 on the Mohs hardness scale, it is easily sculptured, reacts with acid, and is susceptible to weathering (dissolution) especially in regions where the acidity of rainfall is enhanced by pollution.

- Some students find the concept of metamorphic facies difficult. Consider a careful review of this topic and assign exercises, such as *Thought Questions 5, 6, and 8,* that require students to use Figure Story 9.7 and Figures 9.8, 9.9, and 9.10.

- **Deformation and metamorphism**
  Rock deformation and metamorphism are closely linked. The following conceptual graph illustrates the relationship between rate of strain (deformation) and rate of (re-)crystallization (metamorphism). How a rock behaves (brittlely or plastically) under stress will depend in part on how quickly minerals within the rock can recrystallize, which depends on temperature, pressure, and the rock's composition. As temperature increases, ion mobility increases, and rates of recrystallization increase.

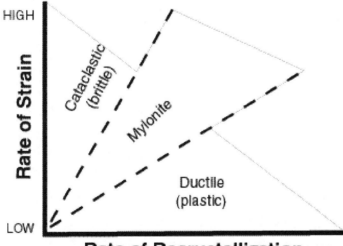

Brittle <= high rate of strain, low T & P

Ductile <= low rate of strain, high T & P

Teaching Resources

Student Study Guide Highlights

In Part I: Chapters provide strategies for learning geology. Ideally, students would read these chapters early in the course.

Chapter 1   Brief Preview of the *Study Guide for Understanding Earth* by Press, Siever, Grotzinger, and Jordan

Chapter 2   Meet the Authors of *Understanding Earth, 4th Edition:* How to use your geology textbook

Chapter   3 How to Be Successful in Geology (or just about any other challenging course)

Part II. Chapter 9: *Metamorphic Rocks*

Before Lecture:

Preview Questions & Brief Answers

During Lecture:

Note-Taking Tip–Abbreviations

After Lecture:

Check Your Notes

Intensive Study Session

Exam Prep:

Chapter Summary

Practice Exercises: *Classification of metamorphic rocks based on texture
Comparing igneous, sedimentary, and metamorphic rocks*

Review Questions (Answers to all review questions are given at the end of the Study Guide.)

CHAPTER 10

The Rock Record and the Geologic Time Scale

Chapter Summary

- The principles of superposition and crosscutting relationships provide a basis for establishing the relative age of a sequence of rocks at an outcrop. Using these two principles, geologists can order (what happened first, second, third, and so on) the geologic events represented by the rocks and geologic features in one outcrop. The principle of original horizontality for sedimentary layers provides a basis for identifying sequences of sedimentary rocks affected by tectonic forces after they were deposited.

- To reconstruct the geologic history of the Earth, geologists also need to correlate the geologic events represented by rocks at one locality with the geologic events represented by rocks at other localities. The principles of superposition, stratigraphic succession, fossils, and radiometric dates of rock units provide a basis for establishing how rock outcrops at different localities may be related to each other, even if they are 100s or 1000s of miles apart.

- The Geologic Time Scale is the internationally accepted reference for the sequence of events represented by Earth's rock record. It was constructed over about the last 200 years by geologists using mainly fossils, superposition, and cross-cutting relationships to establish the relative ages for thousands of rock outcrops around the world. In about the last 50 years, the Geologic Time Scale has been calibrated using radiometric methods.

- We understand Earth's history to the degree to which we can place the record of geologic events in time. The Geologic Time Scale is the accepted standard for how geologic time is subdivided.

Learning Objectives

In this section we provide a *sampling* of possible objectives for this chapter. No class could or should try to accomplish all these. Choose based on your analysis of your class. Refer to Chapter 1: *Learning Objectives—How to Define Your Goals for the Class* in the Instructional Design section (Part I) of this manual for thoughts and ideas about how to go about such an analysis.

Knowledge

- Understand that the relative ages of rocks can be determined from an outcrop using superposition, cross-cutting relationships, fossil succession, and included fragments.
- Know how the relative ages for rock outcrops at two or more locations can be determined using fossils and stratigraphic relationships. Refer to Figure 10.5.
- Know the major divisions of the Geologic Time Scale.
- Understand the importance of the Geologic Time Scale.
- Know how radiometric dating works.

Skills/Applications/Attitudes

- Be able to infer age limits for rock units in a formation using the principles of superposition and cross-cutting relationships.
- Understand how the Geologic Time Scale is calibrated using radiometric dating.
- Be able to use geochronological information like radiometric dates to reconstruct the geologic history represented by a simple stratigraphic sequence.
- Appreciate some of the challenges of interpreting Earth's history given the vastness of geologic time.

General Education Skills

- Write a brief one-page essay titled: Implications of the Geological Time Scale for Human Thought. (Writing/Critical Thinking)

Freshman Survival Skills

- The Geological Time Scale offers a great opportunity for students to learn and practice a variety of memorization strategies such as the ones described in the Student Study Guide.

Sample Lecture Outline

Digital copy is available from Instructor's CD and web site.
http://www.whfreeman.com/understandingearth
Sample lecture outlines highlight the important topics and concepts covered in the text. We suggest that you download a digital copy of this outline from the CD and web site, and customize it to your own lecture before handing it out to students. At the end of each chapter outline, consider adding a selection of review questions, representing a range of thinking levels.

Chapter 10: The Rock Record and the Geologic Time Scale

Relative vs. Radiometric Ages
    Ordering geologic events
    Calibrating with radiometric dates
The Stratigraphic Record
    Principle of original horizontality
    Principle of superposition
    Stratigraphic succession

Fossils
Formation
Unconformities
    Disconformity
    Nonconformity
    Angular unconformity
Cross-cutting relationships
Sequence stratigraphy
The Geologic Time Scale
    Phanerozoic Eon = interval of well-displayed life
    Eras = stages in the development of life
    Epochs of the Tertiary and Quaternary = % of modern species of mollusks
Correlation—establishing the time-equivalence of rocks at different locations
    Sequence stratigraphy
    Seismic stratigraphy
Ordering geologic events is not enough!—the need for calibration and "Absolute Time"
Calibration of the Geologic Time Scale with "Absolute Time" Methods
Radiometric Time: Adding Dates to the Time Scale
    Parent vs. daughter atoms
    Exponential decay
    Half-life/rate of decay
    Decay schemes
        Uranium/lead
        Potassium/argon
        Rubidium/strontium
        Carbon-14
    Major assumptions
        Decay rate is constant and accurately known.
        Rock or mineral has remained a "closed" system.
        Daughter is solely a product of the radioactive decay of the parent.
Estimating Rates of Geologic Processes

CD and Web site Resources

Instructor's CD Highlights

- *Key Textbook Figures and Tables*

    Figure 10.1: The amount of time required for some common processes and events

    Figure 10.5: William Smith could piece together the sequence of rock layers of different ages containing different fossils by correlating outcrops...

    Figure 10.8: An angular unconformity is an erosion surface...

    Figure 10.9: Cross-cutting relations of igneous intrusions and deformation allow us to place geologic events with the relative time frames given by stratigraphic succession.

    Figure 10.10: Comparison of seismic profiles

    Figure Story 10.11: A cross-section of four formations enables geologists to reconstruct the stages of an area's geologic history.

    Figure 10.12: The Geologic Time Scale

    Figure 10.17: Geologic timeline of Earth's history.

    Table 10.1: Major Radioactive Elements Used in Radiometric Dating

- *Photo Gallery:* Includes slide set images from the previous three editions

Web site Highlights
http://www.whfreeman.com/understandingearth

- **Presentation Tools**

    Animations: Visit the web site for animations, including animations of
    figures in this chapter.
    PowerPoint Presentation
    PowerPoint Presentation with Lecture Notes
    Photo Gallery

- **Course Preparation**

    Instructor's Manual
    Sample Lecture Outline
    Sample Exercises

- **Student Study Resources—Assessable**

    Graded Online Quizzing
    Geology in Practice: Reconstructing Geologic History
    This *Geology in Practice* contains exercises that can be used for
    in-class discussion, homework, or extra credit. Exercises require
    students to order geologic events and interpret the geologic histo-
    ry for sequences of rock units.

- **Student Study Resources—Non-Assessable**

    Online Review Exercises:
    Field Relationships for Relative Time Dating
    Geologic Time Scale Review
    Which rock layer is the oldest?
    Identify the Rock Layers
    Before & After: Evidence of Geologic Time
    Concept Self-Checker
    Flashcards

Teaching Tips

Collaborative Exercises and In-Class Activities
Refer to Chapter 4: *Collaborative Teaching Strategies* in the Instructional Design section of
this manual.

Coop Exercise #1: Hypothesis Testing, a Sense of Time, and Conversion of Units
by Randall Richardson, Department of Geosciences, University of Arizona, Tucson, Arizona
Students gain valuable experience working with large numbers, significant digits, hypothesis
testing, and data quality.

I break the class into groups of about 15. I have them calculate their ages in seconds,
write it down on a piece of paper, and put it in a bag. I add my own age in seconds to the bag.
We hypothesize that they can tell when my age is drawn from the bag. We pull one out. It may
be some number like 599,184,000 seconds. I ask them, "When you tell someone hold old you
are, how many significant digits do you use?" The typical response is something like, "two"
(in this case, the student was 19). We talk about giving your age as 19.4397 (also six significant digits), and they typically laugh. Then, why is the answer given to six significant digits?
"Because that's what the calculator said when I took 60*60*24*365*19." Thus, we learn
about significant digits. Then I ask if the number drawn is mine. Most say it is not. I ask,
"How come?" "Because it's too small." I use this to help them see that they have an expected result in mind when they collect the data. Then we continue pulling numbers until mine is

pulled. They are all very happy when they can distinguish mine (it is at least a factor of two bigger in a first year class; if there are older students in the class we sometimes modify the hypothesis). Then, we draw the rest and in most cases there is at least one mistake. Sometimes the mistake is enough to make it difficult to distinguish the 'noisy data' from my age. We then talk about the quality of data, and how noise in data can lead to erroneous conclusions.

Coop Exercise #2: Building a Concrete Sense of Geologic Time

by Randall Richardson, Department of Geosciences, University of Arizona, Tucson, Arizona
This is an effective way to help elementary school to college-level students learn about geologic time.

One goal is for students to be able to visualize events that happened an incredibly long time ago, such as the extinction of the dinosaurs 65 million years ago, and to realize that the event occurred within less than 2% of Earth's entire history.

After having talked about the geologic time scale (Precambrian: prior to 570 Ma; Paleozoic: 570–245 Ma; Mesozoic: 245–65 Ma; Cenozoic: 65 Ma–Present), I ask for two volunteers from the class to hold a rope that is 50 feet long. I say that one end is the beginning of the Earth (4.6 billion years ago), and the other is today. Then, I give out about 14 clothespins and ask various students to put a clothespin on the "time line" at various "geologic times." For example, I ask them to put one where the dinosaurs died out (end of the Mesozoic). They almost invariably put it much too old (65 Ma is less than 2% of Earth history!). Then, I ask them to put one on their birthday (they now laugh). Then I ask them to put one where we think hominoids (humans) evolved (~3–4 Ma), and they realize that we have not been here very long geologically. Then I ask them to put one at the end of the Precambrian, where life took off in terms of the numbers of species, etc. They are amazed that this only represents less than 15% of Earth history. Finally, I ask them to think of the time line as their own age, and think about how long ago, on a comparable time scale, the dinosaurs died. It is only about two months ago! The exercise is very effective at letting them get a sense of how long geologic time is, and how "recently" some major geologic events happened when you consider a time scale that is the age of the earth.

Geologic Time Rope Table for Faculty Reference

Event	Age (MA)	% Geo time	Distance
#1 Formation of Earth	4600	100.00	50.00 ft
#2 Oldest rock	4100	89.00	44.57 ft
#3 Earliest fossil record: algae	3500	76.09	38.54 ft
#4 Earliest shelled animals (marine)	600	13.04	6.52 ft
#5 Primitive fishes: First vertebrates	500	10.87	5.43 ft
#6 First land plants	425	9.24	4.62 ft
#7 First amphibians	380	8.20	4.13 ft
#8 First dinosaurs	245	5.33	2.66 ft
#9 First mammals	245	5.33	2.66 ft
#10 Flowering plants and hardwoods	120	2.61	1.30 ft
#11 Extinction of the dinosaurs	65	1.41	0.71 ft
#12 Abundant placental mammals	62	1.40	0.70 ft
#13 Grazing mammals diversify	35	0.76	0.38 ft
#14 Australopithecus appears	5	0.11	0.02 ft
#15 Ice Ages begin	1.6	0.03	0.01 ft
#16 Last Ice Age ends	0.01	0.0002	0.0001

Sample GeoTime Cards for students involved in Geo Rope Coop exercise

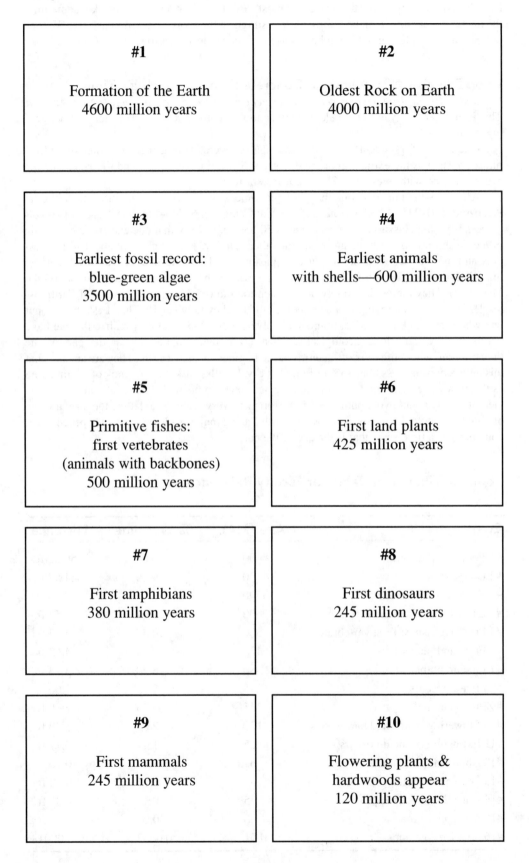

#1

Formation of the Earth
4600 million years

#2

Oldest Rock on Earth
4000 million years

#3

Earliest fossil record:
blue-green algae
3500 million years

#4

Earliest animals
with shells—600 million years

#5

Primitive fishes:
first vertebrates
(animals with backbones)
500 million years

#6

First land plants
425 million years

#7

First amphibians
380 million years

#8

First dinosaurs
245 million years

#9

First mammals
245 million years

#10

Flowering plants &
hardwoods appear
120 million years

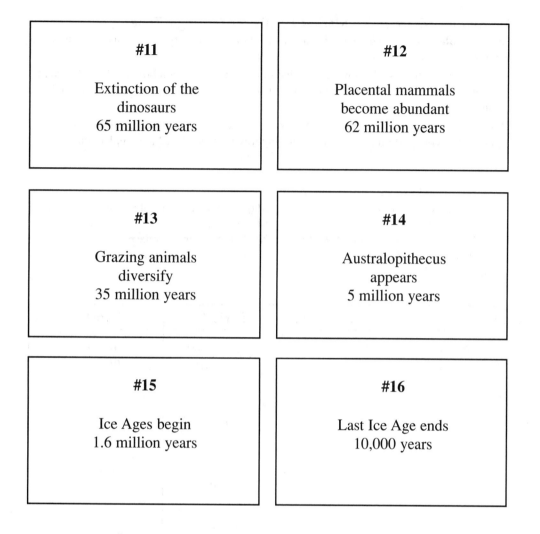

#11

Extinction of the
dinosaurs
65 million years

#12

Placental mammals
become abundant
62 million years

#13

Grazing animals
diversify
35 million years

#14

Australopithecus
appears
5 million years

#15

Ice Ages begin
1.6 million years

#16

Last Ice Age ends
10,000 years

Coop Exercise #3: Five-Minute Write

The Five-Minute Write is done during the last five minutes of lecture. Ask students to put their name on a sheet of paper and then address the three questions on the overhead (see adjacent sample). Start the next lecture by discussing the answers to some of the questions students had about the previous lecture.

Additional Ideas for Coop Exercises

Review Questions 6, 13, 17, 18, 19, and 21 in the *Student Study Guide* require students to interpret or evaluate radiometrically dated samples and can be used in lecture as a basis for a short Think/Pair/Share.

Freshman Survival Skills Assignment

The geological time scale offers a great opportunity for students to learn and practice a variety of memorization strategies such as Practice Exercises 3 and 4, provided in the Student Study Guide. First talk to the students a bit about memory strategies you consider useful. You can supplement this discussion if you like with the material from the Study Guide and information provided below. Then, assign Exercise 3 or 4 in the Study Guide as an extra credit assignment. Let the students know you will include some items on the exam that will require them to know the geologic time scale.

Five-Minute Write

- What questions do you have about lecture?
- What did you find most interesting about lecture?
- How was lecture relevant to you?

Homework (Exercise 3): Marker Events for Geologic Time.

(From the *Student Study Guide for Understanding Earth*, Chapter 10, Practice Exercises and Review Questions.)

A. Enter each event, listed below, on the line in the appropriate eon box in which the event happened. When possible order your listing so that the oldest is at the bottom of the list and the youngest is on top.

B. Fill in the names of eras, periods, and epochs in the correct sequence from oldest at the bottom to youngest on top. Refer to both Figures 1.12 and 10.12 to complete this exercise.

Significant (Marker) Events in Earth History

Dinosaur extinction event   Major phase of continent formation completed
Earliest evidence of life   Moon forms
End of heavy bombardment of the Earth   Nucleus-bearing cells develop
Evolutionary Big Bang   Oxygen build up in atmosphere
Humans evolve

Eon	Era	Period	Epoch
Phanerozoic *Humans evolve* _____		*Quaternary* _____ *Tertiary*	*Holocene* *Pleistocene* _____ _____ _____ _____
	Mesozoic	*Jurassic* _____	
	_____	_____ *Pennsylvanian* _____ _____ *Ordovician*	
_____			
Proterozoic _____ *First nucleus-bearing cells develop*			
Archeon _____ _____ _____			
Hadean _____ _____ *Earth accretion begins*			

Notes to Students from Student Study Guide
Strategies to help you learn the Geological Time Scale

1. **Marker Events** are simply interesting things that happened: animals or plants that evolved, creatures that dominated the earth, large extinction events. Look at Figure 10.12. Select some **marker events** you already know about. Example: Can you guess one of the Periods during which dinosaurs were dominant? The movie *Jurassic Park* has made this an easy question. When did complex life begin? Find some other marker events of particular interest to you. Maybe you are surprised at how early some events occurred; e.g., the "earliest evidence of life." Marker events will help you remember the Geology Time Scale.

2. **Logical Chunks.** Group the information into short lists you can remember. Study the groupings of the time scale with Figure 10.12 in front of you. Learn it as a series of short lists. Understand the following logic:

   • **Eons** are the biggest time chunks. There are only four (Hadean, Archean, Proterozoic, Phanerozoic) to remember. Only the most recent (Phanerozoic eon) is broken down further. Hadean sound like Hades (hell), not a bad description of the young planet with its molten surface and asteroids crashing into it.

   • **Eras** are next biggest. You only have to learn eras for the Phanerozoic. There are only Phanerozoic eras to remember: Old Life, Middle Life, and New Life. Think of it that way first, you can tack on the Greek stems later (see #3 below).

   • **Periods** are next. **All** three eras are further divided into periods.

   • **Epochs** are the smallest divisions of geologic time. You only have to learn epochs for the most recent era (Cenozoic or New Life). All epochs of the Cenozoic end in "cene" (for Cenozoic).

3. **Word Stems** Word stems are clues to meaning. Greek and Latin Stems are used a great deal by scientists. You can look them up in any good dictionary. A few helpful stems for the geological time scale include:

   Eras:

   Paleo- = Greek: "old"

   Meso- = Gk: "middle"

   Ceno- = Gk: "new"

   -zoic = Gk: "life"

Homework (Exercise 4): Geologic Time Scale Mnemonic

Construct a mnemonic device for remembering the geologic time scale names. The first letter of each word must match the first letter of the corresponding period or epoch in the proper order. You may use your native language, but be careful not to mix up the words when you do so.

Examples (refer to Figure 10.12 for the Geologic Time Scale):

   Here's a good mnemonic for the Periods of the Geologic Time Scale:

   Chronically Overworked Student Decks Monotonous Physics Professor To Justify Contradictory Test Questions.

   Here's a good mnemonic for the Epochs of the Cenozoic:

   Please Eat Our Mushroom Pot Pie Hot.

Topics for Class Discussion

- How are the rates of radiometric decay measured?
- How do geologists determine a radiometric age? **Note:** See slide sets for images and additional explanations.
- How is the Geologic Time Scale calibrated by radiometric dates?
- What "age" is determined when each of the following rock types is dated by radioisotopes? Discuss your answers.
  - A. Igneous rocks
  - B. Metamorphic rocks
  - C. Sedimentary rocks
- Radioactive and other heavy elements formed by thermonuclear reactions in the centers of stars and nova before or during the formation of our solar system. The earth formed from some of this matter about 4.5 to 5 billion years ago. Given that the radioactive elements were all formed at approximately the same time, why are there rocks of different radiometric ages on the earth's crust today?
- How would you determine the accuracy of a radiometric date?
- How would you determine the precision of a radiometric date?
- How might you use tree-rings to determine the accuracy of the carbon-14 dating technique?
- Precision vs. accuracy
- Age of the Earth

  Historical approach

  Cooling rates

  Accumulation of salt in the oceans

  Sedimentation rates

  Modern approach

  Oldest known radiometric date on a rock from earth = 3.96 billion years

  Radiometric age of meteorites average about 4.5 b.y.

  Radiometric age of lunar rocks

  Oldest known lunar sample = 4.6 b.y.

  Lunar maria basalts = 3.1 to 3.8 b.y.

Historical Criteria for the Age of the Earth

Scientists	Basis	Age
Hemholtz and Kelvin	Cooling rates and contraction of the earth/tides	10–75 m.y.
Walcott	Rate of sediment accumulation	Approximately 100 m.y.
Joly and Others	Rate of salt accumulation in oceans	20 m.y. to 1.5 b.y.
Rutherford (1905)	Radiometric decay	Oldest known rock 4 b.y. (1989)

- Pass out in lecture a copy of the latest Geologic Time Scale published by the Geological Society of America.
- Metaphors for Geologic Time

  Consider all of Earth's history as the old measure of the English yard, the distance from the King's nose to the tip of his outstretched hand. Then, one stroke of a nail file on his middle finger would erase all of human history.

  A roll of Scott® toilet paper contains 1000 sheets. Compressing all of Earth's history into one roll results in each sheet representing 4,500,000 years.

- Why do rocks on Earth have different radiometric ages?

  Most radiometric ages represent the interval of time that has passed since a mineral crystallized. The "radiometric clock" gets reset whenever minerals are heated or melted, resulting in a loss or redistribution of accumulated daughter atoms. Radiometric dating works because parent and daughter atoms have significantly different physical and/or chemical properties.

Teaching Resources

Student Study Guide Highlights

In Part I: Chapters provide strategies for learning geology. Ideally, students would read these chapters early in the course.

> Chapter 1   Brief Preview of the *Study Guide for Understanding Earth* by Press, Siever, Grotzinger, and Jordan

> Chapter 2   Meet the Authors of *Understanding Earth, 4th Edition:* How to use your geology textbook

> Chapter 3   How to Be Successful in Geology (or just about any other challenging course)

Part II. Chapter 10: *The Rock Record and the Geologic Time Scale*

> Before Lecture:

>> Time Management Tip

>> Preview Questions & Brief Answers

>> Vital Information from Other Chapters

> During Lecture:

>> Note-Taking Tips

> After Lecture:

>> Check Your Notes

>> Intensive Study Session: Strategies for learning the Geologic Time Scale

> Exam Prep:

>> Chapter Summary

>> Practice Exercises: *Determining the Succession of Geologic Events*
>>   *Ordering Geological Events*
>>   *Marker Events for the Geologic Time Scale*
>>   *Geologic Time Scale Mnemonic*

Review Questions (Answers to all review questions are given at the end of the Study Guide.)

Folds, Faults, and Other Records of Rock Deformation

Chapter Summary

- All rocks may bend (behave ductilely) and break (behave brittlely) in response to the application of forces. Laboratory experiments have revealed that whether a rock exhibits ductile or brittle behavior depends on its composition, temperature, depth of burial (confining pressure), and rate with which tectonic processes apply force.

- In the field and on geologic maps, strike and dip of a formation shows its orientation at a particular place.

- Ductile behavior is more likely when a rock is exposed to higher temperatures, deeper burial, slower application of tectonic forces, and is a sedimentary rock. Brittle behavior is favored when rocks are cooler, closer to the Earth's surface, exposed to more rapid application of tectonic forces, and is an igneous or high-grade metamorphic rock.

- Folding is a result of ductile deformation. From the type of fold and its orientation, geologists can interpret the orientation of the tectonic forces and characteristics of the rock layers during deformation.

- Faulting and jointing are a result of brittle deformation. Jointing occurs when a rock fractures but there is little movement along the fracture planes. Faults are fractures along which there is appreciable movement (offset). The type and orientation of faults and joints provides valuable information about the tectonic forces and the characteristics of the rock layers at the time of deformation.

- The type of fold or fault provides a basis for geologists to interpret the type of tectonic force acting on the rock during deformation. Tectonic forces can be of three types: compressive, tensional, and shearing forces. These same kinds of forces are active at all three types of plate tectonic boundaries: compressive forces dominate at convergent boundaries, where plates collide or subduct; tensional forces dominate at divergent boundaries, where plates are pulled apart; and shearing forces dominate at transform faults, where plates slide horizontally past each other.

• Geologic structures such as folds, faults, and joints occur on all scales from microscopic to the size of a mountainside. Geologists deduce the geologic history of a region in part by unraveling the history of deformation, thereby reconstructing what the rock units looked like before deformation. Regional deformational fabrics can help geologists decipher the plate tectonic history for the region.

Learning Objectives

In this section we provide a *sampling* of possible objectives for this chapter. No class could or should try to accomplish all these. Choose based on your analysis of your class. Refer to Chapter 1: *Learning Objectives—How to Define Your Goals for the Class* in the Instructional Design section of this manual for thoughts and ideas about how to go about such an analysis.

Knowledge

• Know the factors that determine whether a rock breaks or bends.
• Understand what geologic structures result from compressional, tensional, shear stresses.
• Identify the major types of folds and faults.
• Know what styles of deformation are characteristic of each tectonic plate boundary.

Geology Skills/Applications/Attitudes

• Measure and record a strike and dip of a planar rock feature.
• Given information about geologic structures in an outcrop or series of outcrops, interpret the geologic circumstances responsible for the deformation.

General Education Skills

• Write an interesting piece for your local paper on a local example of deformation.

Freshman Survival Skills

• Encourage Students to preview Chapter 11 by awarding credit for restating in their own words acceptable answers to all Chapter Preview Questions and turning in their answers before the lecture. (Previewing/Textbook Reading)

Sample Lecture Outline

Digital copy is available from Instructor's CD and web site.
http://www.whfreeman.com/understandingearth
Sample lecture outlines highlight the important topics and concepts covered in the text. We suggest that you download a digital copy of this outline from the CD and web site, and customize it to your own lecture before handing it out to students. At the end of each chapter outline, consider adding a selection of review questions, representing a range of thinking levels.

Chapter 11: Folds, Faults, and Other Records of Rock Deformation

Measuring Strike and Dip
Constructing a Geo Map and Cross-Section
Forces—Types of Stress
    Compressive
    Tensional
    Shearing
Behavior (Plastic, Elastic, Brittle) of Rocks Depends on
    Composition
    Temperature
    Confining pressure
    Rate at which stress is applied (time)
    Small amounts of fluids
Deformation—Response to Force
Brittle Deformation
    Joints
    Faults
        Normal
        Reverse
        Thrust
        Strike-slip
        Rift Valley (horst and graben)
Folds—Symmetrical and Asymmetrical
    Monocline
    Syncline
    Anticline
    Overturned
    Plunging
    Domes
    Basins

CD and Web site Resources

Instructor's CD Highlights

• *Key Textbook Figures and Tables*

    Figure 11.4: Geologists use the strike and dip of a formation to define its orientation at a particular place.
    Figure 11.5: A geologic map and a cross section derived from it
    Figure Story 11.6: Rocks are deformed by folding and by faulting.
    Figure 11.11: Types of faults
    Figure 11.16: Types of folds
    Figure 11.22: Stages in the development of a fictitious geologic province.

• *Photo Gallery:* Includes slide set images from the previous three editions

Web site Highlights

http://www.whfreeman.com/understandingearth

• **Presentation Tools**

    Animations: Visit the web site for animations, including animations of figures from this chapter.
    PowerPoint Presentation

PowerPoint Presentation with Lecture Notes
Photo Gallery

- **Course Preparation**

    Instructor's Manual

    Sample Lecture Outline

    Sample Exercises

- **Student Study Resources—Assessable**

    Graded Online Quizzing

    Geology in Practice: Interpreting the Geologic History of Deformed (Bent and Broken) Rocks

    > This *Geology in Practice* contains exercises that can be used for in-class discussion, homework, or extra credit. Exercises ask students to identify and interpret patterns of deformation.

- **Student Study Resources—Non-Assessable**

    Online Review Exercises

    Tectonic Forces in Rock Deformation Review

    Identify the Type of Fold

    Rock Deformation Review

    San Andreas and Hayward Fault Field Trip

    Concept Self-Checker

    Flashcards

Teaching Tips

Cooperative Exercises and Assignments to Encourage Student Learning

Refer to Chapter 4: *Cooperative Learning Teaching Strategies* in the Instructional Design section of this manual for general ideas about conducting cooperative learning exercises in your classroom.

Practice Exercises 1 and 2 from Chapter 11 of the Student Study Guide work well as a Think/Pair/Share. Present the exercise on the board or as an overhead. Then, ask student teams to fill in the blanks.

Coop Exercise #1: Geologic Structures

For each of the following five illustrations of deformed rocks, name (a) the geologic structure, e.g., normal fault, syncline; (B) the type of force, e.g., compressional, tensional, shearing force, responsible for producing each geologic structure; and (c) the plate tectonic boundary, e.g., convergent, divergent, or shear, with which the geologic structure is commonly associated.

A. Geo structure _____

B. Type of force _____

C. Commonly associated plate tectonic boundary

_____

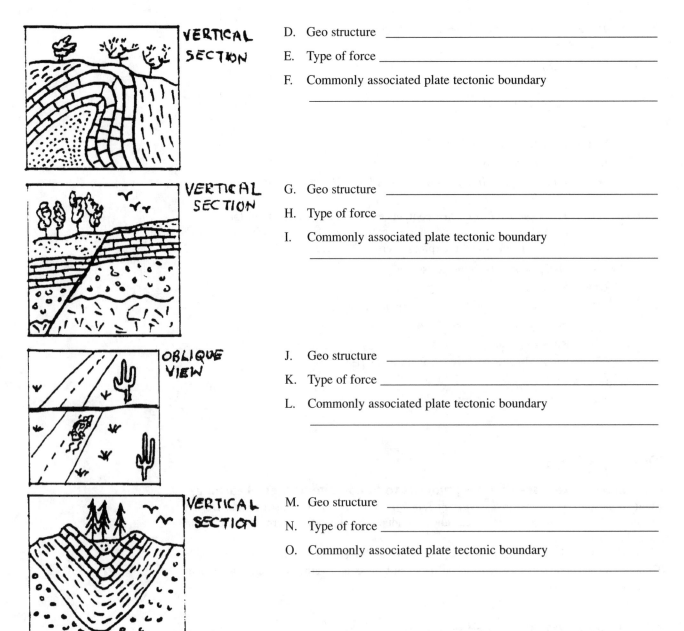

VERTICAL SECTION

D. Geo structure _____

E. Type of force _____

F. Commonly associated plate tectonic boundary

_____

VERTICAL SECTION

G. Geo structure _____

H. Type of force _____

I. Commonly associated plate tectonic boundary

_____

OBLIQUE VIEW

J. Geo structure _____

K. Type of force _____

L. Commonly associated plate tectonic boundary

_____

VERTICAL SECTION

M. Geo structure _____

N. Type of force _____

O. Commonly associated plate tectonic boundary

_____

Coop Exercise #2: Silly Putty®

Silly Putty® is a popular teaching aid (and toy) with geologists because it exhibits at room temperature all three kinds of deformation characteristic of solids. If you pull on the putty quickly, it will snap into two pieces. It is easy to bend and mold the putty into many shapes. Plus if you throw a ball of it on the floor, the ball will bounce. Compare the properties of silly putty with the behavior of rocks by completing the table below.

Behavior of Silly Putty®	Behavior of rock	Type of force	Geologic structure produced by this style of deformation
snaps into pieces		*tensional*	
bends	*ductile*		
bounces	*Elastic—Rocks do exhibit elastic behavior. More on this when we study earthquakes.*	*Compressional—The ball of putty is compressed by the impact with the floor.*	NOTE: *Earthquakes are attributed to the elastic properties of rocks.*

Freshman Survival Skills Assignment

If you encouraged your students to preview chapters before attending lecture, it is a good idea to reinforce this idea from time to time. One good approach is to preview Chapter 11 for extra credit. Tell the students they must write a brief paragraph in their own words for each of the **Chapter Preview Questions.** Credit should be given only for answers turned in before the lecture occurs. (Previewing/Textbook Reading)

Topics for Class Discussion

- Compare the behavior of rocks with that of Silly Putty®. Discuss. Refer to Coop Exercise #2 above.
- Rocks behave (deform) in principally three different ways in the Earth's crust. Characterize each type of behavior. What factors influence how a rock deforms? What is the field evidence for each style of deformation?
- What kind of deformation occurs when a tall building sways in the wind?
- **Deformation and metamorphism**
Rock deformation and metamorphism are closely linked. The following conceptual graph illustrates the relationship between rate of strain (deformation) and rate of (re-)crystallization (metamorphism). How a rock behaves under stress (brittlely or plastically) will depend in part on how quickly minerals within the rock can recrystallize, which depends on temperature, pressure, and the rock's composition. As temperature increases, ion mobility increases, and rates of recrystallization increase. Note the relationship between cataclastic and mylonitic metamorphic rocks.

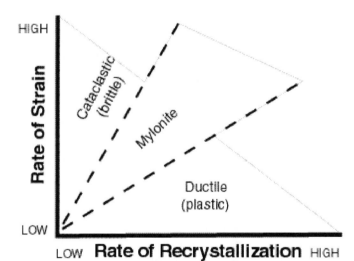

Brittle <= high rate of strain, low T & P
Ductile <= low rate of strain, high T & P

Strain Rate vs. Behavior of Solids
Low strain rate → elastic behavior
Slow strain rate → ductile behavior
Fast strain rate → brittle behavior

Teaching Resources

Student Study Guide Highlights

In Part I: Chapters provide strategies for learning geology. Ideally, students would read these chapters early in the course.

Chapter 1   Brief Preview of the *Study Guide for Understanding Earth* by Press, Siever, Grotzinger, and Jordan

Chapter 2   Meet the Authors of *Understanding Earth, 4th Edition:* How to use your geology textbook

Chapter 3   How to Be Successful in Geology (or just about any other challenging course)

Part II. Chapter 11: *Folds, Faults, and Other Records of Rock Deformation*

Before Lecture:

Study Tip

Preview Questions & Brief Answers

During Lecture:

Note-Taking Tip

After Lecture:

Check Your Notes

Intensive Study Session

Exam Prep:

Chapter Summary

Practice Exercises: *Silly Putty®*
Geologic Structures
Anticline vs. Syncline
Identifying Geologic Structures

Review Questions (Answers to all review questions are given at the end of the Study Guide.)

Mass Wasting

Chapter Summary

- Mass movements are slides, flows, or falls of large masses of rock material down slopes when the pull of gravity exceeds the strength of the slope materials. Such movements can be triggered by earthquakes, absorption of large quantities of water during torrential rain, undercutting by flooding rivers, human activities, or other geologic processes.

- The three most important factors enhancing the potential for mass movements are the steepness of the slope, the nature of the rock making up the slope, and the water content. Although steep slopes are prone to mass movements, slopes of only a few degrees of slope can also fail catastrophically.

- Slopes become unstable when they become steeper than the angle of repose, the maximum slope angle that unconsolidated material will assume. Slopes in consolidated material may also become unstable when they are oversteepened or denuded of vegetation. Erosion by rivers and glaciers and human activities can oversteepen slopes and, thereby, enhance the potential for mass movement.

- The composition, texture, and geologic structure of the slope material are other important factors influencing the potential for slope failure. For example, rocks with high clay content tend to be weak and may liquefy. Titled layers of sedimentary or volcanic rocks are more likely to fail along bedding planes when the bedding parallels the slope. Failure of foliated metamorphic rocks is more likely to occur parallel to the direction of foliation.

- Water absorbed by the slope material contributes to instability in two ways: (1) by lowering internal friction (and thus resistance to flow) and (2) by lubricating planes of weakness in the slope.

- The hazards and damage associated with mass movements can be minimized by careful geological assessment, engineering, and land use policies that restrict development on unstable slopes.

Learning Objectives

In this section we provide a *sampling* of possible objectives for this chapter. No class could or should try to accomplish all these. Choose based on your analysis of your class. Refer to Chapter 1: *Learning Objectives—How to Define Your Goals for the Class* in the Instructional Design section of this manual for thoughts and ideas about how to go about such an analysis.

Knowledge

- Understand mass wasting and how it results from the down-slope movement of rock material.
- Know the factors that enhance the potential for and trigger mass movements.
- Know how mass movements are classified.
- Know how damage from mass movements can be minimized.

Geology Skills/Applications/Attitudes

- Analyze a hillside plot for susceptibility to mass wasting.
- Understand the need for geological assessment to identify hazardous slopes and the role slope ordinances can play in reducing slope hazards.

General Education Skills

- Write a set of brief guidelines (less than one page) for use by your employer (a local developer) in regard to building homes in coastline areas of Southern California. (Writing/Critical Thinking)

Freshman Survival Skills

- Reinforce previewing the chapter by assigning Practice Exercise 1 before lecture. Explain that because the idea is to get them to preview the chapter you will give credit only for exercises turned in prior to the lecture on Mass Wasting.

Sample Lecture Outline

Digital copy is available from Instructor's CD and web site.
http://www.whfreeman.com/understandingearth
Sample lecture outlines highlight the important topics and concepts covered in the text. We suggest that you download a digital copy of this outline from the CD and web site, and customize it to your own lecture before handing it out to students. At the end of each chapter outline, consider adding a selection of review questions, representing a range of thinking levels.

Chapter 12: Mass Wasting

Factors that Influence Mass Movements
    Nature of slope materials—consolidated vs. unconsolidated
        Angle of repose
        Surface tension
        Cohesion
    Amount of water in the slope materials
        Liquefaction
    Steepness and instability of the slope
        Rock fabric and structure, e.g., jointing and other planes of weakness
Triggers
    Earthquakes
    Runoff and infiltration from storms
    Slope becomes steeper
        Undercutting
        Construction
        Cut/fill

Types of Mass Movement
    Rock mass movements
        Rockfall
        Rock slide
        Rock avalanche
    Unconsolidated mass movements
        Creep
        Solifluction
        Earthflow
        Debris flow
        Mudflow
        Debris avalanche
    Submarine mass movements
Natural Causes of Landslides
Human Activities that Promote or Trigger Slides

CD and Web site Resources

Instructor's CD Highlights

- *Key Textbook Figures and Tables*

    Figure Story 12.1: Slope material, slope steepness, and water content influence mass movement.

    Earth Policy box 12.1: Reducing Loss from Landslides and Preventing Landslides

    Figure Story 12.6: Mass movements are classified according to factors: nature of material (consolidated or unconsolidated), velocity, and the nature of the movement.

    Table 12.1: Factors that Influence Mass Movements

- *Photo Gallery:* Includes slide set images from the previous three editions

Web site Highlights

http://www.whfreeman.com/understandingearth

- **Presentation Tools**

    Animations: Visit the web site for animations, including animations of figures from this chapter.

    PowerPoint Presentation

    PowerPoint Presentation with Lecture Notes

    Photo Gallery

- **Course Preparation**

    Instructor's Manual

    Sample Lecture Outline

    Sample Exercises

- **Student Study Resources—Assessable**

    Graded Online Quizzing

    Geology in Practice: Assessing Potential Hazards from Mass Wasting

        This *Geology in Practice* contains exercises that can be used for class discussion, homework, or extra credit. The *Geology in Practice* exercises ask students to assess the potential for mass movement for various home site locations.

• **Student Study Resources—Non-Assessable**
  Online Review Exercises
      Identify the Rock Mass Movement
      Identify the Consolidated Rock Mass Movement
      Create a Mass Wasting Scenario
  Concept Self-Checker
  Flashcards

Teaching Tips

Cooperative Exercises and Assignments to Encourage Student Learning

Refer to Chapter 4: *Cooperative Learning Teaching Strategies* in the Instructional Design section of this manual for general ideas about conducting cooperative learning exercises in your classroom.

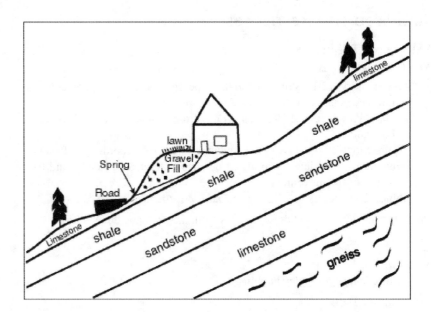

Coop Exercise #1: Evaluation of Slope Stability

Exhibit to the class the cross-section shown below (from Practice Exercise 3: Evaluation of Slope Stability in the Student Study Guide). Give teams of two to three students about 2 to 3 minutes to complete an assessment of potential problems with slope instability. Have them write down their answers on a sheet of paper with the names of all students in the team. Call on a variety of teams to share their assessments. Discuss their answers. Collect answers for attendance and credit, if you wish.

Coop Exercise #2 or Homework: Inventory of the Different Kinds of Mass Wasting

This is Practice Exercise 1 in the Student Study Guide.

As an aid to learning the circumstances that can trigger mass movement, use your textbook to fill in the blanks in the table below. Textbook figures, figure captions, and photographs will help you complete the table.

Tip: The students probably haven't seen many examples of mass wasting before, so in preparation for this exercise it may be helpful to show slides of mass wasting. During the exercises encourage them to use photos in the text by pinpointing figures relevant to the exercise. Explain to the students that:

If you are a visual learner this activity may be vital. Also, to get a kinesthetic feel for these movements imagine yourself trying to outrun each movement. Indicate in the space labeled "Speed" whether you could escape the mass movement by walking, running, or moving as fast as a speeding auto.

Collect the written answers for grading or to take attendance. Have them write down their answers even if you do not intend to collect them because it helps students to organize their thoughts. Plus if they are called on to share their answers, reading from their answer sheet provides a less intimidating way of presenting their analyses than asking them to do it from memory.

Kind of mass wasting	Composition of slope (consolidated vs. unconsolidated and wet vs. dry)	Characteristics
Rock avalanche		Speed: running or a speeding auto Slope angle: steep slopes Triggering event(s): earthquakes Notes: Occur in mountainous regions where rock is weakened by weathering, structural deformation, weak bedding, or cleavage planes
Creep		Speed: Slope angle: any angle Triggering event(s): none Notes:
Earthflows		Speed: Slope angle: any angle Triggering event(s): intense rainfall Notes: Fluid-like movement
Debris flow		Speed: Slope angle: any angle Triggering event(s): Notes:
	mostly finer rock materials with some coarser rock debris with large amounts of water	Speed: Slope angle: Triggering event(s): intense rainfall or catastrophic melting of ice and snow by a volcanic eruption. Notes: Contains large amounts of water
Debris avalanche	water-saturated soil and rock	Speed: Slope angle: Triggering event(s): Notes:
Slump		Speed: walking Slope angle: any slope Triggering event(s): rainfall Notes
	surface layers of soil	Speed: walking Slope angle: any angle Triggering event(s): Notes: Occurs only in cold regions when water in the surface layers of the soil alternately freezes and thaws. Water can not seep into the ground because deeper layers are frozen.

Freshman Survival Skills Assignment

In the beginning of your course it is prudent to include a few exercises to help the freshmen in your class learn how to learn and to reinforce mastery of the basics of good preparation for college level lectures. Learning skills are like critical thinking skills. They tend to be mastered slowly, over time with lots of practice: even upper division students and graduate students sometimes need coaching about how to learn. See Part I: *Instructional Design* for a discussion of why this is true and ideas about how to do it. Chapter 1 discusses freshman survival as a national educational priority. Chapters 5 and 6 discuss how to develop credit assignments to encourage students to learn how to learn.

As an alternative to doing the slope stability in class (see Teaching Tips) consider having the students complete the exercise before class. Doing it that way will reinforce the idea that you expect them to preview the chapter before lecture. Encourage them to use both text pictures and photos of mass wasting on the web site. Explain to your students that because the idea is to get them to preview the chapter you will give credit only for exercises turned in prior to the lecture on Mass Wasting.

Topics for Class Discussion

- You are about to purchase a hillside lot for use as a home site. What are three lines of evidence that would indicate the property was susceptible to mass movement?
- Water enhances mass movements by:
    - ✓ adding weight
    - ✓ buoyancy—weight of an object is decreased in water by the weight of the water
    - ✓ displaced by the object—Archimedes Principle
    - ✓ hydrostatic pressure
    - ✓ dissolution of cement, e.g., calcium carbonate cementing a sandstone
    - ✓ undercutting by streams
    - ✓ freeze/thaw
- Recognizing the signs for mass movement—what a prospective home buyer should look for:
    - ✓ evidence for old landslides
        - hummocky terrain
        - a scarp
        - lack of older vegetation
        - poorly sorted, angular blocks
        - lack of layering (bedding) in deposit
    - ✓ springs emerging from a slope
    - ✓ undercutting by a river, ocean waves, or construction
    - ✓ cut and fill foundation for building
    - ✓ fabric of the rock
        - bedding planes
        - foliation
        - jointing
    - ✓ damage to existing structures
        - cracks in the walls
        - cracks radiating from corners of window or door frames

Teaching Resources

Student Study Guide Highlights

In Part I: Chapters provide strategies for learning geology. Ideally, students would read these chapters early in the course.

Chapter 1   Brief Preview of the *Study Guide for Understanding Earth* by Press, Siever, Grotzinger, and Jordan

Chapter 2   Meet the Authors of *Understanding Earth, 4th Edition:* How to use your geology textbook

Chapter 3   How to Be Successful in Geology (or just about any other challenging course)

Part II. Chapter 12: *Mass Wasting*

Before Lecture:

Preview Questions & Brief Answers

During Lecture:

Note-Taking Tips

After Lecture:

Check Your Notes

Intensive Study Session

Exam Prep:

Chapter Summary

Practice Exercises: *Inventory of the Different Kinds of Mass Wasting*
Water's Role in Mass Wasting
Evaluation of Slope Stability

Test-Taking Tip

Review Questions (Answers to all review questions are given at the end of the Study Guide.)

CHAPTER 13

The Hydrologic Cycle and Groundwater

Chapter Summary

- The hydrologic cycle is a flow chart or model for the distribution and movement of water on and below the surface of the Earth. The major reservoirs for the hydrologic cycle are oceans, glaciers, groundwater, lakes and rivers, the atmosphere, and the biosphere in decreasing volumes. Water moves in and out of these reservoirs by various pathways and at varying rates. Over the short term a balance is maintained among the major reservoirs at and near the Earth's surface. However, climate change, longer-term tectonic processes such as mountain building, and human activity can alter the rate of water movement between reservoirs and impact the size of the reservoirs.

- Groundwater is estimated to be the third largest reservoir of water on Earth. The infiltration of water into the ground and groundwater flow are largely controlled by the porosity and permeability of the rock materials and topography. A groundwater aquifer is in dynamic balance between recharge (the amount of water that infiltrates into the aquifer) and discharge, which can occur from springs or wells.

- Darcy's Law describes the groundwater flow rate in relationship to the slope of the water table and the permeability of the aquifer.

- Human demand for groundwater has increased to a level where pumping discharges from many aquifers exceeds the natural rates of recharge. As a result, aquifers are being depleted and groundwater tables are lowering to a point where dependable, quality groundwater is becoming more and more of a challenge to supply.

- Water quality may be compromised by both natural and human sources of contamination. Various factors like recharge rate and aquifer size influence the amount of effort and effectiveness of attempts to clean up contamination.

- Caves, sinkholes, and associated karst topography is a result of the dissolution of carbonate rocks (limestone) by groundwater. Karst topography is well-developed in regions of high rainfall, abundant vegetation, an underlying extensively fractured limestone, and an appreciable hydrologic gradient to enhance groundwater flow rates. Environmental problems associated with karst regions include surface subsidence from collapse of underground space, and catastrophic cave-ins and sinkhole formation.

- All rocks below the groundwater table are saturated with water. With increasing depth, porosity and permeability typically decrease as confining pressure increases. Water temperature increases progressively with increasing depth and, as a result, the water dissolves more solids. Hot springs and geysers are surface expressions of the circulation of hydrothermal waters over a magma body or along a deep-seated fault.

Learning Objectives

In this section we provide a *sampling* of possible objectives for this chapter. No class could or should try to accomplish all these. Choose based on your analysis of your class. Refer to Chapter 1: *Learning Objectives—How to Define Your Goals for the Class* in the Instructional Design section of this manual for thoughts and ideas about how to go about such an analysis.

Knowledge

- Know the hydrologic cycle.
- Know how water moves below the ground surface.
- Know the characteristics of an aquifer.
- Know the factors that govern our use of groundwater resources.
- Know the geologic processes and features associated with groundwater.

Skills/Applications/Attitudes

- Given a cross-section illustrating the geologic circumstances for a well or spring, evaluate the potential yield and water quality from the water source.
- Have an appreciation for the value of water conservation.
- Understand the need for hydrological analyses to gain better information on water resources, water quality, and potential for pollution.

General Education Skills

- Participate in a class debate on the topic: Water is a Precious Resource: How Can We Conserve It? (Critical Thinking/Debate)

Freshman Survival Skills

- Encourage students to study strategically by delivering a brief lecture segment on the intensive study of this chapter. See details under Teaching Tips.

Sample Lecture Outline

Digital copy is available from Instructor's CD and web site.
http://www.whfreeman.com/understandingearth
Sample lecture outlines highlight the important topics and concepts covered in the text. We suggest that you download a digital copy of this outline from the web site and customize it to your own lecture before handing it out to students. At the end of each chapter outline, consider adding a selection of review questions, representing a range of thinking levels.

Chapter 13: The Hydrologic Cycle and Groundwater
Hydrologic Cycle
Flows/Fluxes
    Reservoirs

Hydrology and Climate
    Humidity, rainfall, runoff
    Drought
    Rain shadows
Ground Water
Movement of Groundwater
    Porosity
    Permeability
    Hydrostatic pressure
Water Table
    Unsaturated zone
    Saturated zone
    Perched water table
Aquifer vs. Aquiclude
Discharge vs. Recharge
    Springs
    Artesian springs
    Wells
    Geysers
    Ground subsidence due to excessive pumping
Rate of Groundwater Flow
    Hydraulic gradient
    Darcy's Law
Erosion by Groundwater—Dissolution
    Karst topography
        Caves
        Speleothems
            Stalagmite
            Stalactite
        Sinkholes
Water Quality
    Toxic waste
    Salt water encroachment
Water Deep in the Crust
    Hydrothermal waters

CD and Web site Resources

Instructor's CD Highlights

• *Key Textbook Figures and Tables*

    Figure 13.2: The hydrologic cycle
    Figure 13.7: Pores in rocks are normally filled partly or entirely with water.
    Figure 13.8: The groundwater table
    Figure 13.9: Dynamics of the groundwater table
    Figure 13.10: An artesian system
    Figure 13.11: A perched water table
    Figure 13.12: Cone of depression
    Figure 13.14: Salt water intrusion
    Figure 13.15: Darcy's law
    Figure 13.19: Some major features of karst topography

• *Photo Gallery:* Includes slide set images from the previous three editions

Web site Highlights
http://www.whfreeman.com/understandingearth

- **Presentation Tools**

  Animations: Visit the web site for animations, including animations of figures from this chapter.

  PowerPoint Presentation

  PowerPoint Presentation with Lecture Notes

  Photo Gallery

- **Course Preparation**

  Instructor's Manual

  Sample Lecture Outline

  Sample Exercises

- **Student Study Resources—Assessable**

  Graded Online Quizzing

  Geology in Practice: Tucson, Arizona, A Case Study in Groundwater Use and Policy

    This *Geology in Practice* exercise has students explore the implications of a declining water table and groundwater contamination in Tucson, Arizona, which is one of the largest cities in the world dependent on groundwater for its municipal water supply. Exercises can be used for in-class discussion, homework, or extra credit.

- **Student Study Resources—Non-Assessable**

  Online Review Exercises:

    Identify the Parts of the Hydrologic Cycle

    Create an Artesian Well

    Darcy's Law Review

  Concept Self-Checker

  Flashcards

Teaching Tips

Cooperative Exercises and Assignments to Encourage Student Learning
Refer to Chapter 4: *Collaborative Teaching Strategies* in the Instructional Design section of this manual.

Coop Exercise #1: The Characteristics of a Good Aquifer
The following Review Question from Chapter 13 of the Student Study Guide is a good basis for a short Think/Pair/Share exercise.

Which of the following would make the best aquifer?

	Porosity	Permeability
A. Rock A	5%	high
B. Rock B	10%	medium
C. Rock C	30%	low
D. Rock D	35%	medium

Coop Exercise #2: A Class Debate on Water Resources
Divide the class into four-person debate groups. Two people in each group are partners and are assigned a position to defend. The remaining two people in the group partner up to defend

the rival position. Then, randomly assign each four-person team paired topics listed below to debate. Tell them to develop arguments in favor of their position by referring to *Earth Issues* box 13.1 *Water is a Precious Resource: Who Should Get it?*

Team position	Rival team position
The western states should be given priority water rights.	The eastern states should be given priority water rights.
Industry should be given priority water rights.	Urban users should be given priority water rights.
Agriculture should be given priority water rights.	Urban users should be given priority water rights.
California should be given priority water rights to the water of the Colorado River.	Colorado should be given priority water rights to the water of the Colorado River.

This exercise has four phases:

Phase 1: Partners work together to develop arguments supporting their topic.

Phase 2: Each team has 3 minutes to present their arguments to the opposing team.

Phase 3: Partners write down as many of the opposing teams arguments as they can remember.

Phase 4: Arguments presented are scored for accuracy by the opposing team.

This exercise is designed to encourage development of Critical Thinking/Debate skills. The idea is to have students take a position, argue that position as persuasively as possible, then listen accurately to the arguments of the other team. It is important to explain to the students why listening accurately to your opponent's arguments is an invaluable debate skill.

Coop Exercise #3: Evaluating Rock Materials as Potential Aquifers
Practice Exercise 1 from the Student Study Guide makes a good Think/Pair/Share.

Form teams with two students and ask them to complete the table below, which you can provide as an overhead, a handout, or in a PowerPoint presentation.

You have recently purchased a rustic country cabin and need to drill a new well for a dependable water supply for the cabin. The geology around your cabin is complex due to ancient mountain building events. Because the rocks are folded and faulted, it is difficult to predict what rock might be encountered as the water well is drilled. Which of the following rock materials has the potential of yielding ground water to your well? Fill in the blank parts of the table below.

Hint: Keep in mind that, generally, permeability increases as porosity increases, but not always. Permeability also depends on the sizes of the pores, how well they are connected, and how tortuous a path the water must travel to pass through the material. Refer to Figure 13.7 and Table 13.2.

Rock material	Porosity (high, medium, low)	Potential as an aquifer (good, moderate, poor)
loose, well-sorted, coarse sand		
silt and clay	low	
granite and gneiss		poor
highly fractured granite		
sandstone	medium	
shale		
highly jointed limestone		moderate to good

Freshman Survival Skills Assignment

In the beginning of your course it is prudent to include a few exercises to help the freshmen in your class learn how to learn and to reinforce mastery of the basics of good preparation for college level lectures. In the Study Guide we laid out a strategic approach for student to use to master this chapter (quoted in full below). Consider delivering this material to your students in a brief lecture segment or converting it into an assignment.

Intensive Study Session

From the *Student Study Guide for Understanding Earth,* Chapter 13, section titled *After Lecture.*

Set priorities for studying this chapter. We recommend you give highest priority to activities that involve answering questions. Encourage your students to adopt the following strategy for learning the material in this chapter.

- **Add illustrations to your lecture notes.** First, preview the key figures in Chapter 13. They are Figures 13.2, 13.7, 13.9, 13.10, 13.11, 13.12, 13.14, 13.15, and 13.20. Insert simple sketches of these figures into your lecture notes.

- **Practice Exercises and Review Questions.** Next, complete Practice Exercises 1 and 2. You will get the greatest return on your study time by working on these exercises because they will help you remember important ideas in the chapter. Then work on answering each of the review questions to check your understanding of the lecture. Check your answers as you go, but do try to answer the question before you look at the answer. Pay attention to the test taking tips we provide. They will help you do better on quizzes and exams.

- **Text.** Sometime before the next exam complete all 11 exercises at the end of Chapter 13 in the text. These require short answers and won't take long if you know the material. Note that helpful animations are provided on the web site for Exercises 3, 5, and 6.

- **Web site Study Resources**
  http://www.whfreeman.com/understandingearth
  Complete the **Web Review Questions** and the **Concept Self-Checker** questions. Pay particular attention to the explanations for the answers. Be sure to check out the animations of an aquifer, a confined aquifer, and the dynamic balance between recharge and discharge. The **Geology in Practice** exercises involve you in an on-going case study involving ground contamination.

Topics for Class Discussion

- How does a river continue to flow during dry spells?
- A neighbor claims that you have contaminated his well by dumping waste in a nearby stream. Show in a cross-section how this might be possible.
- A farmer claims his shallow well has gone dry since a housing development put in several deep wells, and sues the developer. Show in a sketch how his claim might be correct.

Typical single family home indoor water use.

Water use	Without conservation (gallons per capita per day)	With conservation (gallons per capita per day)
Shower and bath	14.5, 19.6%	12.4, 23.9%
Toilet	19.3, 26.1%	9.3, 17.9%
Faucet	11.4, 15.4%	11.1, 21.5%
Dish and clothes washers	17.8, 24.1%	12.8, 24.7%
Other domestic use and leaks	10.0, 14.8%	6.3, 12.1%
Total water use	74 .0 gallons per capita per day	51.9 gallons per capita per day

This table can be displayed after a short cooperative exercise during which you ask student pairs to make an estimate of their approximate daily uses of water.

Teaching Resources

Student Study Guide Highlights

In Part I: Chapters provide strategies for learning geology. Ideally, students would read these chapters early in the course.

Chapter 1   Brief Preview of the *Study Guide for Understanding Earth* by Press, Siever, Grotzinger, and Jordan

Chapter 2   Meet the Authors of *Understanding Earth, 4th Edition:* How to use your geology textbook

Chapter 3   How to Be Successful in Geology (or just about any other challenging course)

Part II. Chapter 13: *The Hydrologic Cycle and Groundwater*

Before Lecture:

Preview Questions & Brief Answers

During Lecture:

Warm-up Activity

Note-Taking Tips

After Lecture:

Check Your Notes

Intensive Study Session

Exam Prep:

Chapter Summary

Practice Exercises: *Evaluating Rock Materials as Potential Aquifers*
Evaluating Groundwater Wells

Review Questions (Answers to all review questions are given at the end of the Study Guide.)

CHAPTER 14

Streams: Transport to the Oceans

Chapter Summary

- Streams erode, transport, and deposit sediments. The turbulence of streams allows water to transport sediment by suspension, saltation, rolling, and sliding. The tendency for particles to be carried in suspension is countered by gravity, pulling them to the bottom, and measured by the settling velocity. Deposition of sediments occurs when the velocity of the stream decreases.

- The physical features (drainage pattern, stream channel, floodplain, meander bends in the channel, alluvial fans, and deltas) of a stream system evolve over time.

- The longitudinal profile represents the stream gradient. It is a plot of the elevation of the stream channel bottom at different distances along the stream's course. The longitudinal profile is controlled by local (the river into which the stream flows or a lake) and regional (the ocean) base levels. Refer to Figures 14.7, 14.13, 14.14, and 14.15. Streams cannot cut below base level, because base level is the "bottom of the hill."

- Whether a stream is dominantly eroding or depositing, its sediment load is determined by the stream's velocity. Stream velocity in turn depends on the stream's gradient (slope), discharge (amount of water in the stream), load (sediment in transport), and channel characteristics. A stream's drainage patterns, the stream channel, and floodplain evolve in response to changes in stream velocity, gradient, sediment load, discharge, and the characteristics of the bedrock over which the stream flows. Alluvial fans form at mountain fronts, in response to an abrupt widening of the stream valley and a change in slope.

- Drainage networks exhibit different patterns depending on topography, rock type, and geologic structure in the drainage area. Refer to Figure 14.20. Streams can be antecedent and superimposed on geologic and topographic features as illustrated in Figures 14.21 and 14.22.

- Near its mouth, a river tends to branch downstream into distributary channels forming a delta. Deltas are major sites of sediment deposition. Where waves, tides, and shoreline currents are strong, deltas may be modified or even absent. Tectonics controls delta formation by uplift in the drainage basin and subsidence in the delta region.

Learning Objectives

In this section we provide a *sampling* of possible objectives for this chapter. No class could or should try to accomplish all these. Choose based on your analysis of your class. Refer to Chapter 1: *Learning Objectives—How to Define Your Goals for the Class* in the Instructional Design section of this manual for thoughts and ideas about how to go about such an analysis.

Knowledge

- How is flowing water in streams able to erode solid rock and to transport and deposit sediments?
- Understand the basic processes by which stream valleys and their channels and floodplains evolve.
- How is the stream's velocity (speed) linked to gradient (slope), discharge (amount of water), sediment load, and channel characteristics?
- Why do floods occur?
- How do drainage networks work as collection systems and deltas as distribution systems for water and sediment?

Skills/Applications/Attitudes

- Evaluate a flood-frequency plot for a location along a river. Refer to Figure 14.12.
- Predict the basic response of a river system to changes in the base level, discharge, gradient, availability of sediment load, and human interventions. Refer to Figures 14.14 and 14.15.
- Appreciate the need for flood hazard assessment and policies restricting land use within flood prone areas. Refer to *Earth Issues* box 14.1.

General Education Skills

- Write a position paper outlining flood potential and possible options for prevention/ containment. (Writing/Critical Thinking)
- Evaluate a flood-frequency plot for a location along a river. (Math/Critical Thinking/Writing)
- Write an essay on *The Development of Cities on Floodplains*. (Writing/Critical Thinking)
- Participate in a class debate on topics derived from *Earth Issues* box 14.1. (Public Speaking/Debate/Critical Thinking)

Freshman Survival Skills

- Distribute a chapter outline and a selection of mixed format study questions before the lecture on *Streams*. (Note-Taking)
- Encourage accurate note-taking by presenting a 15-minute segment of your *Streams* lecture. Then stop, have students pair-up and "check their notes." Then provide feedback on what you think should be in their notes with an overhead. (Note-Taking)

Sample Lecture Outline

Digital copy is available from Instructor's CD and web site.
http://www.whfreeman.com/understandingearth

Sample lecture outlines highlight the important topics and concepts covered in the text. We suggest that you download a digital copy of this outline from the web site and customize it to your own lecture before handing it out to students. At the end of each chapter outline, consider adding a selection of review questions, representing a range of thinking levels.

Chapter 14: Streams: Transport to the Oceans

Flow Characteristics
    Turbulent vs. laminar
    Viscosity
Sediment Load and Transport
    Suspended/bed/dissolved
    Particle size vs. flow velocity
    Capacity vs. competency
Erosion by Running Water
    Abrasion
    Undercutting
Stream Features and Characteristics
    Active channel—cross-section and roughness
    Floodplain
    Meanders and entrenched meanders
    Levees
    Channel patterns
    Discharge (amount of water)
    Gradient (slope)
        Longitudinal profile
        Concept of a graded stream
    Base level
        Local vs. regional
Floods
    Recurrence interval
    Flood-frequency
Response of a Stream System to a Change in Base Level and Gradient
    Lake
    Alluvial fans
    Terraces
    Dam and reservoir
Drainage Networks
    Drainage basin
    Tributaries
    Trunk stream
    Distributaries (delta, alluvial fan)
    Drainage patterns
        Dendritic
        Rectangular
        Trellis
        Radial
    Antcedent
    Superimposed
Deltas
    Distributaries channels
    Sedimentation
        Topset beds
        Foreset beds
        Bottomset beds
    Effects of waves, tides, and tectonics

CD and Web site Resources

Instructor's CD Highlights

- *Key Textbook Figures and Tables*

    Figure 14.3: The relationship between particle size and velocity

    Figure Story 14.9: Channel patterns

    Figure 14.10: The formation of levees by river floods

    Figure 14.12: The flood-frequency curve for annual floods on the Skykomish River at Gold Bar, Washington

    Figure 14.13: The longitudinal profile of the Platte and South Platte rivers

    Figure 14.14: The base level of a stream controls the lower end of its longitudinal profile

    Figure 14.15: A change in the base level of a river caused by human intervention

    Figure 14.17: Terraces

    Figure 14.20: Typical drainage networks

    Figure 14.21: Antecedent stream

    Figure 14.22: The development of a superimposed stream

    Figure 14.23: A typical large marine delta

    Figure 8.10: Sands and gravel in a typical alluvial cycle

- *Photo Gallery:* Includes slide set images from the previous three editions

Web Site Highlights

http://www.whfreeman.com/understandingearth

- **Presentation Tools**

    Animations: Visit the web site for animations, including animations of figures from this chapter.

    PowerPoint Presentation

    PowerPoint Presentation with Lecture Notes

    Photo Gallery

- **Course Preparation**

    Instructor's Manual

    Sample Lecture Outline

    Sample Exercises

- **Student Study Resources—Assessable**

    Graded Online Quizzing

    Geology in Practice: Why Do Rivers Meander?

    > Albert Einstein addressed this question in 1926. Einstein's son is well known for his work on hydrodynamics that describes how fluids behave. This *Geology in Practice* contains exercises that can be used for in-class discussion, homework, or extra credit. Students are asked to explore more about why rivers meander and how river systems operate.

- **Student Study Resources—Non-Assessable**

    Online Review Exercises:

    Identify the Parts of a Marine Delta

    Flooding

    Create a Flood

    Concept Self-Checker

    Flashcards

Teaching Tips

Collaborative Exercises and In-Class Activities

Refer to Chapter 4: *Collaborative Teaching Strategies* in the Instructional Design section of this manual.

You can use Review Questions from the *Student Study Guide for Understanding Earth* for in-class Think/Pair/Share exercises. Just pair-up the students and have them decide together what the correct answer should be. Below are sample selections of Review Questions from Chapter 14 in the *Study Guide.*

Suggestion: Some instructors find that doing such exercises in lecture and telling students that these exercise will be on the next exam encourages attendance and helps students to focus on the most important information.

Coop Exercise #1: Sample Review Questions from Study Guide for a Think/Pair/Share

- Entrenched meanders like those shown for the San Juan River in Figure 14.8 are evidence of a
    A. decrease in stream gradient.
    B. decrease in discharge.
    C. change, such that the river has renewed ability to erode.
    D. decrease in stream velocity.

- If a dam is placed across a stream that has been carrying a large volume of sediment, the stream would probably
    A. deposit downstream and erode upstream from the dam.
    B. erode downstream and not change upstream from the dam.
    C. erode downstream and gradually deposit upstream from the dam.
    D. not change downstream but would deposit upstream from the dam.
    Hint: Refer students to Figure 14.15.

- Active erosion in a meander bend takes place
    A. in the center of the stream.
    B. along the outer bank of a bend.
    C. along the inside bank of a bend.
    D. near a stream's headwaters.
    Hint: Refer students to Figure Story 14.9.

- The Kali Gandaki River cuts one of the deepest gorges on Earth right through the Himalayan Mountain Range. Briefly describe two ways that a river can cut through a mountain range.
    Hint: Refer students to Figures 14.21 and 14.22.
    A. _____
    B. _____

Coop Exercise #2: Five-Minute Write

The Five-Minute Write is done during the last five minutes of lecture. Ask students to put their name on a sheet of paper and then address the three questions on the overhead (see adjacent sample). Start the next lecture by discussing the answers to some of the questions students had about the previous lecture.

Freshman Survival Skills Assignment

In the beginning of your course, it is prudent to include a few exercises to help the freshmen in your class learn how to learn and to reinforce mastery of the basics of good preparation for college level lectures. Learning skills are like critical thinking skills. They tend to be mas-

Five-Minute Write

- What questions do you have about lecture?
- What did you find most interesting about lecture?
- How was lecture relevant to you?

tered slowly, over time with lots of practice: even upper division students and graduate students sometimes need coaching about how to learn. See *Part I: Instructional Design* for a discussion of why this is true and ideas about how to do it. Chapter 1 discusses freshman survival as a national educational priority. Chapters 5 and 6 discuss how to develop credit assignments to encourage students to learn how to learn.

Time Management Workshop. The semester is well along. About this time freshmen are starting to realize how much time college really requires. This is a perfect time to do something to help them develop time management skills. Consider motivational slides and quotations that encourage good time management. You can just put up the quote. You don't have to talk about it.

You can also encourage your students to take advantage of quality time management workshops that are offered on your campus. In business and industry busy executives sometimes pay hundreds or even thousands of dollars for help with time management. Often such help is available free on a college campus. Try calling your campus learning center or teaching center to see if they run time management seminars that your students can attend. Some instructors even bring in guest speakers to discuss time management with their students. Consider awarding students extra-credit for attending a time management workshop.

Topics for Class Discussion

- Practice Exercise 1: Stream Velocity in the Study Guide.
- Twenty years ago a family built a home adjacent to a small desert wash. In fact, they used the sandy bottom as a driveway and enjoyed the lush vegetation along its banks. Last year a large shopping center with many acres of paved parking lot was built upstream from this family's home. Exploring their wash, the kids walked up the wash about a half-mile and found themselves in the parking lot. What impact might storm runoff from the new parking lot have on their driveway, and potentially on their home? Explain. For example, how might discharge, sediment load, potential for erosion, and flooding be influenced?
- It is an observed fact that most rivers increase in velocity in a downstream direction ("lazy" Old Man River really may flow faster than the "rushing" mountain brooks at its head!). How can you account for this?
- A dam is built across a stream, impounding a lake. What effect would this have on the stream both above the lake and below the dam? Refer students to Figure 14.15.
- Why do streams continue to flow in some areas many months after precipitation has taken place in their watershed? Refer students to Figure 13.11.
- Overview of the 1993 Mississippi Flood
  (USGS Bulletins 1120 A, B, C, and D on the Mississippi River Flood of 1993)
  - Very stable weather conditions, resulting in about 200% more rainfall than average, caused the flood. Gauging records were broken all along the river.
  - The 1993 flood at 1,080,000 cfs is approximately a 100-year event based on a little more than 100 years of records and 60 years of good flow records.
  - Damage amounted to about $11 billion with more than 100,000 residences flooded.
  - The Mississippi River reached 9 feet above bank full.

Teaching Resources

Student Study Guide Highlights

In Part I: Chapters provide strategies for learning geology. Ideally, students would read these chapters early in the course.

> Chapter 1   Brief Preview of the *Study Guide for Understanding Earth* by Press, Siever, Grotzinger, and Jordan
>
> Chapter 2   Meet the Authors of *Understanding Earth, 4th Edition:* How to use your geology textbook
>
> Chapter 3   How to Be Successful in Geology (or just about any other challenging course)

Part II. Chapter 14: *Streams: Transport to the Oceans*

> Before Lecture:
>> Preview Questions & Brief Answers
>
> During Lecture:
>> Learning Warm-up Tip
>
> After Lecture:
>> Check Your Notes
>>
>> Web site Resources
>
> Exam Prep:
>> Chapter Summary
>>
>> Practice Exercises: *Stream Velocity*
>>> *Relationship Between Stream Flow and Groundwater*
>>> *How Do Rivers Cut Through Mountain Ranges?*

Review Questions (Answers to all review questions are given at the end of the Study Guide.)

CHAPTER 15

Winds and Deserts

Chapter Summary

- Deserts are regions where evaporation exceeds precipitation.
- Desert regions on Earth are the result of: global air circulation patterns that generate a relatively stationary zone of descending, warm, and dry air at about 15° to 30° north and south of the equator; distance from large bodies of water like the oceans; the rain shadow generated by high mountains which block the flow of moisture-rich air; cold ocean currents which reduce air temperatures and reduce the transport of moisture by the air; and polar climates where the air is so cold that it holds very little moisture at all.
- Wind is a major erosional and depositional agent, moving enormous quantities of sand, silt, and dust. Turbulent airflow erodes and transports particles by suspension, sliding, rolling, and saltation. As velocity decreases, sediment is pulled out of the air by gravity and deposited as a blanket or dunes of sand and dust.
- Only about 20% of the area of desert regions is covered by sand. The distinctive types of sand dunes are governed by the amount of sand available, the strength of the wind, and the variability in wind direction. Loess, wind blown dust, is another important eolian deposit.
- Geologic and topographic features associated with desert regions include: sand dunes, loess deposits, evaporite (salt) deposits in playas, desert pavement, ventifacts (sandblasted rocks), alluvial fans and alluvial sands and gravels, pediments, distinctive soils (pedocals, rich in calcium carbonate) and rusty orangish brown colors to weathered rock surfaces. Some of these features are preserved in the rock records and provide geologists clues to ancient desert regions that no longer exist.

Learning Objectives

In this section we provide a *sampling* of possible objectives for this chapter. No class could or should try to accomplish all these. Choose based on your analysis of your class. Refer to Chapter 1: *Learning Objectives—How to Define Your Goals for the Class* in the Instructional Design section of this manual for thoughts and ideas about how to go about such an analysis.

Knowledge

- Know how turbulent flow and forward motion combine to lift finer particles into the wind and carry them by suspension, sliding, rolling, and saltation.
- Know how winds deposit sand and dust.

- Know the relationship between the shape of sand dunes, the supply of sand, the strength and variability in wind direction.
- Know what factors contribute to the existence of desert regions on Earth.
- Know what features are characteristic of desert landscapes.

Skills/Applications/Attitudes

- Interpret wind direction and reconstruct paleowind directions using dune shape, ripples, and cross-bedding within the dune.
- Know how human activities may play a role in desertification.
- Know how ancient deserts can be recognized by geologists studying the rock record.

General Education Skills

- Write a two-page position paper for a United Nations committee, exploring the causes of desertification. Discuss at least one possible natural and one possible human cause for the expansion of desert conditions. Be sure to identify the time span (decades, centuries, millennium, or longer) over which each possible cause operates.

Freshman Survival Skills

- Encourage the students to develop time management skills by putting up a slide referring them to the time management tip in the Before Lecture section of Chapter 15 of the Student Study Guide. (Time Management/Previewing)

Sample Lecture Outline

Digital copy is available from Instructor's CD and web site.
http://www.whfreeman.com/understandingearth
Sample lecture outlines highlight the important topics and concepts covered in the text. We suggest that you download a digital copy of this outline from the web site and customize it to your own lecture before handing it out to students. At the end of each chapter outline, consider adding a selection of review questions, representing a range of thinking levels.

Chapter 15: Winds and Deserts
Deserts are where evaporation exceeds precipitation
Wind
    Turbulence
    Wind belts
    Coriolis effect
Wind Transport
    Suspension
    Saltation
    Rolling
    Sliding
Wind-Transported Materials
    Loess/dust
    Sand
Wind Erosion
    Ventifacts
    Deflation
    Desert pavement

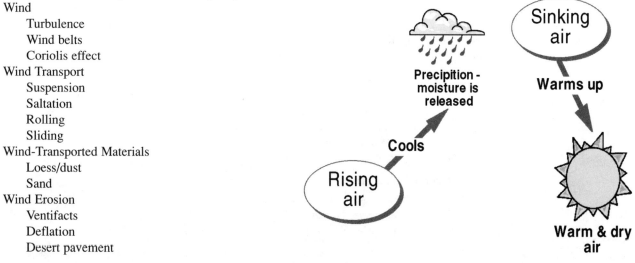

Wind Deposits
    Sand dunes
        Barchan
        Transverse
        Blowout
        Linear
    Loess/dust
Factors Contributing to Desert Conditions
    Global air circulation
    Distance from oceans
    Topography
    Ocean currents
Desert Weathering
    Rusty color
    Desert varnish
Sediments
    Alluvial
    Eolian
    Evaporites
Desert Landscape Features
    Dry washes/wadis
    Alluvial fans
    Pediments
    Playas–dry lake beds

A Hadley Cell —
atmospheric circulation pattern
generated by the differential
heating of the Earth's surface

Decending air

Cold, dry high altitude winds

Warm dry surface winds

30°N
Clear Skies
Hot & Dry
Southwestern
U. S. A.

Air picks up more & more moisture

Rising air

Equator
Cloudy & Rainy

CD and Web Site Resources

Instructor's CD Highlights

- *Key Textbook Figures and Tables*

    Figure 15.1: The circulation of Earth's atmosphere
    Figure 15.7: Desert pavement in the Kofa Mountains of Arizona, in the Sonoran Desert
    Figure Story 15.11: A ripple or dune advances by the movement of individual grains
    Figure 15.12: Dune types in relation to prevailing winds
    Figure 15.15: Major desert areas of the world (exclusive of polar deserts)
    Figure 15.20: Stages in the evolution of a typical pediment

- *Photo Gallery:* Includes slide set images from the previous three editions

Web site Highlights

http://www.whfreeman.com/understandingearth

- **Presentation Tools**

    Animations: Visit the web site for animations, including animations of figures from this chapter.
    PowerPoint Presentation
    PowerPoint Presentation with Lecture Notes
    Photo Gallery

- **Course Preparation**

    Instructor's Manual
    Sample Lecture Outline
    Sample Exercises

• **Student Study Resources—Assessable**
  Graded Online Quizzing
  Geology in Practice: Dust Storms, Rainforests, and Coral Reefs
      Geology in Practice exercises explore the link between dust
      storms and the nutrient cycle in rainforests and coral reefs.
      Exercises can be used for in-class discussion, homework, or extra
      credit.

• **Student Study Resources—Non-Assessable**
  Online Review Exercises:
      Identifying the World's Major Deserts
      Understanding Global Air Circulation Patterns
  Concept Self-Checker
  Flashcards

Teaching Tips

Collaborative Exercises and Assignments to Encourage Student Learning

Refer to Chapter 4: *Collaborative Teaching Strategies* in the Instructional Design section of
this manual.

Coop Exercise #1: Quick Think/Pair/Share Exercises

The following question from the Student Study Guide could be used in Think/Pair/Share
exercise.

• While hiking through a dune-filled coastal plain on a windless morning, you
  become surrounded by a dense fog and realize you are lost. You know you are
  near a shoreline and that the beach will lead you back to camp, but you don't
  know which direction to go. You recognize the crescent-shaped dunes that
  wrap moderate depressions as blow-out dunes! According to your compass,
  the tapered arms of the dunes point south. Then, remembering that in this
  region strong, gusty winds come onto the coastal plain off the ocean, you
  immediately remember which direction to head to the beach:
    A. North
    B. South
    C. East
    D. West
  Hint: Refer to Figure 15.12.

• You are lost in the Goblin Desert. The nearest town is due south. Winds
  blow from the south to the north but there is no wind blowing today.
  Furthermore, the sun is totally obscured by clouds. Without a compass,
  which direction are you going to hike, given the orientation of the barchan
  dune shown below?
    A. Direction A
    B. Direction B
    C. Direction C
    D. Direction D
  Hint: Refer to Figure 15.12.

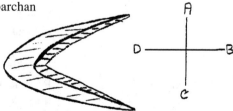

Sample Exercise from the Student Study Guide

Digital copy is available from Instructor's CD and web site.
http://www.whfreeman.com/understandingearth

Exercise 1: Sand Dune Types
Complete the table below by filling out the blank spaces. Figure 15.12 and the section in your text on *Dune Types* will be helpful. Also refer to pictures of dunes in the Photo Gallery on the web site.

Dune type	Characteristics	Sand supply	Wind direction/strength
Barchan			
Transverse			
Blowout		*limited to moderate*	*unidirectional/gusty*
Linear			
See Figure 15.8			

Freshman Survival Skills Assignment

Refer students to the following study tip in the Student Study Guide or put it up as a slide before your lecture while students are arriving in the classroom.

Time Management Tip: Preview Just Before Lecture

The best time to preview is right before lecture. Why? Because the preview questions will be fresh in your mind as the lecture begins. If you can arrive 30 minutes before lecture that is ideal. But even five minutes of previewing done just before the lecture begins will improve your ability to understand the material. Here's a program for using whatever time you have efficiently.

How much time do you have before lecture begins?	How to use it:
30 minutes or more	With this much time you can dig deep into the chapter. Do as many of the following as your time allows. ✓ Read the **Chapter Preview** questions and brief answers. ✓ Read the suggestions for **During Lecture.** ✓ Study the key figure(s) for this chapter (usually shown at the beginning of the Study Guide chapter). ✓ Study and annotate any additional figures, hints, or suggestions alluded to in the **Chapter Preview** ✓ If time allows do the **Practice Exercises.**
15–20 minutes	Do a brief but intense preview: ✓ Read the **Chapter Preview** questions and brief answers. ✓ Read the suggestions for **During Lecture.** ✓ Study the key figure for this chapter (always shown at the beginning of the Study Guide chapter).
5–10 minutes	Read the **Chapter Preview** questions and brief answers. Focus on getting the questions clearly in mind. Then listen for answers during lecture. Even five minutes of previewing helps!

Topics for Class Discussion

• Geoscientists are studying fossil sand dunes to estimate paleowind directions (wind directions hundreds of millions of years ago). Explain how the dune shapes and cross-bedding within the fossil dunes can be used in this way.

- There are several types of dunes. How are the dune types influenced by wind direction and velocity, quantity of sand available, and amount and type of vegetation or other obstacles to sand movement?
- Consider an in-class exercise, homework, or extra credit exercise that asks students to discuss what evidence might be found in the rock record for ancient deserts. Possible answers include:

    Geologic Record of Deserts
    Sediments
        Loess
        Evaporites
        Sandstone
    Sedimentary structures
        Large-scale, planar cross-bedding
        Ripples
        Raindrop imprints
        Salt casts
    Physical weathering dominates over chemical weathering
        Preservation of less stable minerals, e.g., feldspars
        Poorly developed paleosols
    Rusty color to sediments
    Paleosols rich in carbonate and deficient in organic (plant) matter
    Lack of fossils

Teaching Resources

Student Study Guide Highlights

In Part I: Chapters provide strategies for learning geology. Ideally, students would read these chapters early in the course.

    Chapter 1   Brief Preview of the *Study Guide for Understanding Earth* by Press, Siever, Grotzinger, and Jordan

    Chapter 2   Meet the Authors of *Understanding Earth, 4th Edition:* How to use your geology textbook

    Chapter 3   How to Be Successful in Geology (or just about any other challenging course)

Part II. Chapter 15: *Winds and Deserts*

    Before Lecture:
        Preview Questions and Brief Answers
        Time Management Tip box
        Vital Information from Other Chapters
    During Lecture:
        Note-Taking Tip
    After Lecture:
        Check Your Notes
        Intensive Study Session
    Exam Prep:
        Chapter Summary
        Practice Exercise: *Sand Dune Types*

Review Questions (Answers to all review questions are given at the end of the Study Guide.)

Additional Web Sites

The two web sites below are an excellent source for additional information and images. They may also be useful as a reference for student assignments.

http://pubs.usgs.gov/gip/dcscrts/

http://www.desertusa.com/glossary.html

CHAPTER 16

The Work of Ice

Chapter Summary

- Glaciers form in cold and snowy climates where snow accumulation exceeds the ablation of ice due to melting, sublimation, wind erosion, and iceberg calving. Glacial ice moves by plastic flow and slip along the base, which may be lubricated by melt water. The rate of ice flow varies typically from meters per year to meters per week.

- Glaciers are described as advancing or retreating depending on the balance between snow accumulation and ablation. Refer to Figure 16.10. When ablation exceeds accumulation, the shrinking glacier "retreats" as the toe or terminus migrates upslope. When accumulation exceeds ablation, the expanding glacier "advances" as its toe or terminus migrates downslope.

- Glaciers are powerful agents of erosion and deposition. Glaciers erode by scraping, plucking, and grinding rock.

- Landscapes sculptured by ice have distinctive features that have provided geologists with evidence for reconstructing the position of ice sheets during the ice ages and deciphering the existence of ice ages throughout Earth's history. U-shaped and hanging valleys, moraines, aretes, cirques, drumlins, kames, eskers, erratics, and striated rock characterize a glacial landscape.

- Ice-laid deposits of rock material are called till, consisting of a heterogeneous mixture of rock, sand, and clay. Accumulations of till are called moraines; each type of moraine is named for its position relative to the glacier that formed it. Ancient tills, called tillites, provide evidence for ancient glaciations numerous times during Earth's history.

- Water-laid deposits from glaciers are called outwash, consisting of sand, gravel, and fine rock flour.

- The ice sheets of the last major advance were gone by about 10,000 years ago, the beginning of the Holocene Epoch. Studies of the geologic ages of glacial deposits on land and sediments of the seafloor show that the Pleistocene glacial epoch consisted of multiple advances (glacial intervals) and retreats (interglacial intervals) of the continental ice sheets. Each advance corresponded to a global lowering of sea level that exposed large areas of continental shelf; during the interglacial intervals, sea level rose and submerged the shelves.

- Although the causes of the ice ages remains uncertain, the general cooling of the Earth leading to glaciation appears to have been the result of plate tectonics that gradually moved continents to positions where they obstructed the general transport of heat from the equator to polar regions.

- A favored explanation for the alternation of glacial and interglacial intervals is the effect of astronomical cycles, by which very small periodic changes in Earth's orbit and axis of rotation alter the amount of sunlight received at the Earth's surface. There is also evidence that decreased levels of carbon dioxide in the atmosphere diminished the greenhouse effect and triggered glaciation.

Learning Objectives

In this section we provide a *sampling* of possible objectives for this chapter. No class could or should try to accomplish all these. Choose based on your analysis of your class. Refer to Chapter 1: *Learning Objectives—How to Define Your Goals for the Class* in the Instructional Design section of this manual for thoughts and ideas about how to go about such an analysis.

Knowledge

- Understand how glaciers form and how they move.
- Understand how geoscientists study climate change.
- Understand why geologists think that ice ages have occurred in the ancient geologic past.
- Understand how glaciers erode bedrock, transport and deposit sediments, and shape the landscape.
- Be able to define what is meant by "the ice ages" and understand the factors that caused them.

Skills/Applications/Attitudes

- Sees clearly how human activities are linked to climate change (attitude) and can articulate examples of the human activity/climate change connection in a short answer question.
- Can recognize, in the field or from photos, the characteristic landforms of a glacially sculptured region.
- Can recognize, in the field or from photos, the major kinds of rock deposits associated with glacial ice and periods of glaciation.

General Education Skills

- Write a letter to the editor of a local newspaper criticizing an article with the following headline: Antarctic Ice Shelves Melting: Sea Levels Expected to Rise in the Future. (Writing/Critical Thinking)
- Write a brief review of an article that deals with global climate change.

Freshman Survival Skills

- Freshman retention research has documented the importance of out-of-class contact with faculty as a positive influence on student retention. To encourage contact, consider developing assignments that will make it necessary for students to come by during your office hours to discuss their work. Example: assign students a two-page paper entitled: What Caused the Ice Ages?

  Require them to stop at your office with a half-page outline of their paper. Review their outline

  with them and discuss any questions they may have on the topic.

Sample Lecture Outline

Digital copy is available from Instructor's CD and web site.
http://www.whfreeman.com/understandingearth
Sample lecture outlines highlight the important topics and concepts covered in the text. We suggest that you download a digital copy of this outline from the web site and customize it to your own lecture before handing it out to students. At the end of each chapter outline, consider adding a selection of review questions, representing a range of thinking levels.

Chapter 16: The Work of Ice

Glacial Ice (metamorphic rock)
- Snow
- Firn
- Ice

Types of Glaciers
- Continental ice sheets
- Mountain/valley glaciers

How Do Glaciers Form?
- Climate
- Altitude
- Latitude
- Glacial Budget: Growth = Accumulation Minus Ablation
  - Zone of accumulation
  - Zone of ablation
    - Melting
    - Calving
    - Sublimation
    - Wind erosion

Movement of Ice
- Plastic flow
- Basal slip
- Surges
- Ice streams

Isostasy, Ice Shelves, and Sea Level Change
- Isostasy: Dynamic balance between buoyancy and gravity
- When an iceberg melts, sea level does not change

Erosional and Abrasional Features
- Striations/glacial polish
- U-shaped valley
- Hanging valley
- Fjords
- Cirque
- Horn
- Arete
- Roche moutonée

Ice and Melt Water Deposited Sediments/Drift
- Glacial till
- Rock flour
- Erratic boulders
- Outwash
- Loess

Depositional Features
- Moraines (end, terminal, lateral, medial)
- Eskers
- Drumlins

Kettles
Kames
Varves
Permafrost
Ice Ages: the Pleistocene Glaciations
Multiple advances and retreat of ice
Causes of climate change
Climate since the last glacial period
Record of Ancient Glaciation

CD and Web site Resources

Instructor's CD Highlights

• *Key Textbook Figures and Tables:*

Figure 16.8: Stages in the transformation of snow crystals
Figure 16.10: Glacial Budget
Figure 16.12: Glaciers move by plastic flow and basal slip
Figure 16.16: Melting ice shelves and icebergs will not change the sea level
Figure 16.18: A *rouche moutonée*
Figure 16.19: Before and after glaciation
Figure 16.29: Glacial drift
Figure 16.21: Glacial deposits
Figure 16.22: North Pole
Figure 16.26: Sea-surface temperatures, ice extent, and ice elevation 18,000 years ago
Figure 16.27: Three components of variations in Earth's orbit around the Sun
Figure 16.28: Thermohaline circulation of the North Atlantic Ocean
Figure 16.29: Ancient glacial epochs
Table 16.1: Glacial Moraines

• *Photo Gallery:* Includes slide set images from the previous three editions

Web site Highlights

http://www.whfreeman.com/understandingearth

• **Presentation Tools**

Animations: Visit the web site for animations, including animations of figures from this chapter.
PowerPoint Presentation
PowerPoint Presentation with Lecture Notes
Photo Gallery

• **Course Preparation**

Instructor's Manual
Sample Lecture Outline
Sample Exercises

• **Student Study Resources—Assessable**

Graded Online Quizzing
Geology in Practice: Layers of Ice, Layers of Sediment, Packrat Mittens, Pollen, Oxygen Isotopes and Tree Rings

Geology in Practice exercises will involve students with various proxies for climate change and can be used for in-class discussion, homework, or extra credit.

• **Student Study Resources—Non-Assessable**

Online Review Exercises:
　　　Identify the Glacial Landscape Feature
　　　Understanding Glacial Mass Balance
Concept Self-Checker
Flashcards

Teaching Tips

Cooperative Exercises and Assignments to Encourage Student Learning

Refer to Chapter 4: *Cooperative Learning Teaching Strategies* in the Instructional Design section of this manual for general ideas about conducting cooperative learning exercises in your classroom.

Coop Exercise #1: Glacial Advances and Retreats

From the *Student Study Guide for Understanding Earth,* Chapter 16, Practice Exercise. Students commonly misunderstand and get confused about advancing and retreating glaciers. Some students actually think the glacial ice flows uphill when a glacial retreats. This exercise is good for an in-class Think/Pair/Share activity. Divide students into pairs and tell them to write an answer to the following question.

　　A glacier advances, halts, and retreats. Will the glacier continue to deposit material at its snout while it is halted, and even while it is retreating? Discuss.

　　You can use the following summary as a slide to provide students feedback to their responses to Coop Exercise #1.

　　Rarely does a glacier remain stationary—especially in the summer. Driven by the force of gravity, glacial ice and the rock material that it carries move downhill. The words advancing, retreated, and halted are used to describe the movement, or location, of the toe or terminus of the glacier and do not actually refer to the movement of glacial ice within the glacier. The terminus of the glacier will remain stationary (halted), retreat up the valley, or advance down the valley depending on the glacial budget. (Show students Figure 16.10.) For example, if the snow accumulating in the upper reaches of the glacier equals the loss (ablation) of glacial ice from the lower and warmer reaches of the glacier, the size of the glacier will remain constant and the glacial terminus will remain stationary. Nevertheless, the glacial ice is still flowing down slope with rock material and may pile up a sizeable end moraine. (Show students Table 15.1 and Figure 16.20.)

Coop Exercise #2: Climate Change and the Ice Ages

From the *Student Study Guide for Understanding Earth,* Chapter 16, Review Questions. The following review question might generate considerable discussion between student pairs and within the class because all three factors contribute to climate change but do so over different time frames. Debate may center on the relative role each factor may have played in causing the last ice age.

Which of the following may have influenced climate fluctuations during the ice ages?

    A. Variations in Earth orbital characteristics
    B. Changes in the composition of the atmosphere
    C. Plate tectonic movements of the continents
    D. All of the above

General Education Skills Assignment

Climate Change—Possible long-term causes (Writing/Critical Thinking)

Students write a short review of one of three *Scientific American* articles that discuss possible long-term causes for global climate change. You might choose a different selection of articles.

Prerequisite: Each article establishes possible links between geologic processes and climate change. The Greenhouse Effect is an integral part of the models proposed by these articles. So, be sure that students are familiar with the Greenhouse Effect before assigning this as homework.

Assignment: Read one of the three articles, listed below. Write a short review of the article. Briefly review the principle theme(s) of the article. Your review should be about one to three pages long.

"Plateau Uplift and Climate Change" by W. F. Ruddiman and J. E. Kutzbach, *Scientific American* (March 1991).

"Large Igneous Provinces" by M. F. Coffin and O. Eldholm, *Scientific American* (October 1993).

"The Supercontinent Cycle" by R. D. Nance, T. R. Worsley, and J. B. Moody, *Scientific American* (July 1988).

Helpful Hints for Students:

- Start by outlining the important ideas and evidence cited by authors that support their ideas.

- Write the review as though you were an author of the article. Think of your review as the executive summary. There is no need to mention the authors throughout the review. Be sure the title and author(s) of the article are included in the title of your report.

- Each article in some way links one or more geologic processes to global climate change. Be sure to discuss how climate change may be linked (caused by) geologic processes on earth. Include in your discussion evidence cited by the authors to support their model for the cause(s) of climate change.

- Consider illustrating your discussion with diagrams.

Topics for Class Discussion

- How is the advance and retreat of glaciers linked to changes in sea level?

- What is the evidence for the rock debris, which covers northern United States and southern Canada, being deposited by glaciers?

- Why do geologists think that there was more than one glacial advance during the Pleistocene Epoch?

- How can the centers from which the ice sheets advanced be located?

- Compare and contrast the North and South Pole of the Earth.

- What would be the effect on sea level of melting the ice at the North Pole? The South Pole?

- What distinguishes a glacial till from other types of rock materials like alluvium, lake sediments, and soil?

• Oxygen isotope ratios as a paleo-ice recorder. The match in the change of the oxygen isotopic ratios with the change in sunlight reaching Earth due to orbital variations provides convincing evidence for the role orbital variations played in driving climate change during the Ice Ages. Consider reviewing this topic in some detail with your students, using the following illustrations:

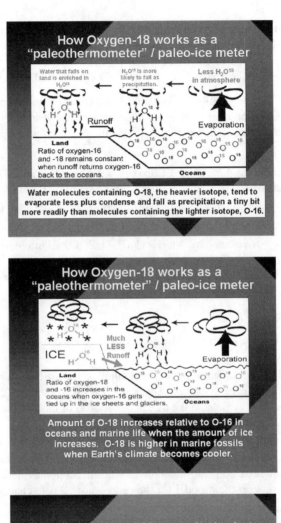

• What were the diverse effects of an ice age?
    Refer to box on the right.

Teaching Resources

Student Study Guide Highlights

In Part I: Chapters provide strategies for learning geology. Ideally, students would read these chapters early in the course.

Chapter 1   Brief Preview of the *Study Guide for Understanding Earth* by Press, Siever, Grotzinger, and Jordan

Chapter 2   Meet the Authors of *Understanding Earth, 4th Edition:* How to use your geology textbook

Chapter 3   How to Be Successful in Geology (or just about any other challenging course)

Part II. Chapter 16: *The Work of Ice*

Before Lecture:

Preview Questions & Brief Answers

Vital Information from Other Chapters

During Lecture:

List of landscape features discussed in this chapter

After Lecture:

Check Your Notes

Study Tip

Intensive Study Session

Exam Prep:

Chapter Summary

Practice Exercises: *The Glacial Sculptured Landscape*
                    Your Personal Budget as a Metaphor for a Glacial Budget
                    Glacial Advances and Retreats

Review Questions (Answers to all review questions are given at the end of the Study Guide.)

Diverse Impacts of the Ice Ages

• Modification of river drainages - -
    Ice blocks or deflects drainage.
    Rivers carry greater discharges.
• Formation of the Great Lakes
• Pluvial period in S.W. U.S.A.
    Lake Bonneville, Lahontan
    Lake Searles and Manly
• Ice dams and floods due to:
    catastrophic failure of dams, e.g.,
    Channel Scablands, E. Washington
• Sea level changes
    Bering Straits land bridge
• Isostatic adjustment of crust
    Rebound of crust after glaciation
• Changes in plant and animal communities

CHAPTER 17

Earth Beneath the Oceans

Chapter Summary

- The deep seafloor is constructed by volcanism at the mid-oceanic ridges and at oceanic hot spots. Sedimentation also plays a secondary role in constructing the deep seafloor.

- Ocean ridges (spreading centers), trenches, abyssal plains and hills, seamounts (guyots), hot-spot island chains, and plateaus are the main features of the deep ocean floor.

- Continental margins are flooded portions of the continent. The continental slope and rise mark the edge of the continent and a transition to deeper water and the ocean floor.

- Passive continental margins form where rifting and seafloor spreading carry continental margins away from plate boundaries. Active continental margins form where oceanic lithosphere is subducted beneath a continent or a transform fault coincides with the continental margin. Continental shelves are broad and relatively flat at passive continental margins and are narrow and uneven at active margins.

- Turbidity currents transport fine sediments off the continental shelf and onto the adjacent abyssal ocean floor. Turbidity currents can both erode and transport sediments. Submarine canyons and fans are formed by turbidity currents.

- In the deep sea fine-grained pelagic terrigenous and biochemically precipitated sediments settle to the seafloor. Foraminiferal oozes, composed of tiny foraminiferal shells, are the most abundant biochemical component of pelagic sediments. Foraminiferal and other carbonate oozes are abundant at depths less than about 4 km. Below a certain depth, called the carbonate compensation depth, carbonate sediments dissolve in deep seawater. Deep ocean water is colder, contains more carbon dioxide, and is under higher pressure. All these factors increase the solubility of carbonate sediments. Silica ooze is produced by sedimentation of the silica shells of diatoms and radiolaria.

- Waves and tides shape the shoreline. Waves are created by the wind blowing over the surface of the water. Ocean tides on Earth are a result of centrifugal force and gravitational forces acting between the Earth, the Moon, and the Sun.

- The beach is a result of the dynamic balance between waves and longshore currents that erode and transport rock material along the coast within the surf zone and the supply of sand from rivers that deliver sand to the surf zone. Longshore currents result from the zigzag movement of water on and off the beach. Waves typically splash onto shore at an angle in part due to wave refraction. The backwash—off the beach—runs down the beach slope at a small but opposite angle to the swash. The net results of this swash and backwash of water on and off the beach slope is a longshore current that transports sand parallel to the beach within the surf zone.

- The topography along the shoreline is a product of tectonic forces elevating or depressing the Earth's crust and changes in sea level.
- Global sea level has risen by 10 to 25 cm over the last century.

Chapter 8: *Sediments and Sedimentary Rocks* contains important information about sedimentation in marine environments and sedimentary basins. Consider reviewing the following highlights in Chapter 8:

- Coral reefs and atolls are constructed by coral and other marine organisms. The reef construct plays an important role in modulating wave energy and creating a favorable environment for shallow marine life.
- Conditions that favor the deposition of marine evaporites are:
  —Restricted sea
  —Arid climate where evaporation rates are high
  —Limited supply of freshwater from rivers

- Tectonic mechanism for the formation of sedimentary basins include:
  —Rifting
  —Thermal sag
  —Flexure of the lithosphere

Learning Objectives

In this section we provide a *sampling* of possible objectives for this chapter. No class could or should try to accomplish all these. Choose based on your analysis of your class. Refer to Chapter 1: *Learning Objectives—How to Define Your Goals for the Class* in the Instructional Design section of this manual for thoughts and ideas about how to go about such an analysis.

Knowledge

- Know the major components of the continental margins and adjacent ocean floor?
- Understand how the deep seafloor is formed.
- Understand turbidity currents and how they transport fine sediments off the continental shelf and onto the adjacent abyssal ocean floor.
- Know the carbonate compensation depth and how it figures into the carbon cycle on Earth.
- Know which types of sediments are deposited on the deep ocean floor.
- Understand how waves and tides shape the shoreline.
- Know how beaches form and can change due to natural factors and human activities.
- Know what causes ocean tides.
- Understand how changes in sea level affect a coastline.

Skills/Applications/Attitudes

- Can explain how waves advance even though the water molecules do not.
- Can explain how a sand beach is in dynamic balance determined by sediment input, output, and longshore currents. For example, describe the impact of the construction of a groin.

General Education Skills

- a team project, which requires the team to evaluate a proposal to construct a groin up the coast from a local county beach. (Team Work/Critical Thinking/Writing)

Freshman Survival Skills

- The amount of material in Chapter 17 means that previewing will be even more important than usual. Encourage your students to answer all the preview questions before they come to lecture.

Sample Lecture Outline

Digital copy is available from Instructor's CD and web site.
http://www.whfreeman.com/understandingearth
Sample lecture outlines highlight the important topics and concepts covered in the text. We suggest that you download a digital copy of this outline from the web site and customize it to your own lecture before handing it out to students. At the end of each chapter outline consider adding a selection of review questions, representing a range of thinking levels.

Chapter 17: The Oceans

Oceans vs. Continents
Origin of the Ocean Crust
How Geologists Study the Ocean Floor
Major Features of the Ocean Basins
    Continental slope and margins
    Submarine canyons and fans
    Abyssal sea floor
    Plateaus
    Oceanic ridge system, rift valley, and associated transform faults
    Ocean trenches and associated island arcs, i.e., Japan and Aleutian Islands
    Seamounts/guyots
    Hot-spot island chains; i.e., Hawaiian Islands–Midway–Emperor Seamounts
Continental Margins
    Active vs. passive
    Continental shelf, slope, rise
    Submarine canyons
    Turbidity currents
Sedimentation
    Continental margins
        Clastic
        Biochemical
    Deep sea
        Pelagic
        Carbonate and silica oozes
        Carbonate compensation depth
Waves and Wave Refraction
Surf Zone
    Longshore drift
    Headward erosion
Tides
Shoreline Features
    Beaches/sand budget

Spits
Barrier islands
Sea stacks
Wave-cut terraces
Changes in sea level
Reefs and atolls
Rising Sea Level

CD and Web site Resources

Instructor's CD Highlights

• *Key Textbook Figures and Tables*

Figure 17.1: Earth topography showing the major features of the ocean floor
Figure 17.2: High-technology methods for exploring the deep seafloor
Figure 17.4: A topographic profile across the Atlantic Ocean
Figure 17.6: Topographic profile of the floor of the Pacific Ocean
Figure 17.8: Schematic profiles of three types of continental margins
Figure 17.9: How turbidity currents form in the ocean
Figure 17.11: The carbonate-compensation depth
Figure Story 17.13: The refraction and breaking of waves
Figure 17.14: Origin of the ocean tides
Figure 17.17: Profile of a beach
Figure 17.18: The sand budget

• *Photo Gallery:* Includes slide set images from the previous three editions.

Web site Highlights

http://www.whfreeman.com/understandingearth

• **Presentation Tools**

Animations: Visit the web site for animations, including animations of figures from this chapter.
PowerPoint Presentation
PowerPoint Presentation with Lecture Notes
Photo Gallery

• **Course Preparation**

Instructor's Manual
Sample Lecture Outline
Sample Exercises

• **Student Study Resources—Assessable**

Graded Online Quizzing
Geology in Practice: Why Are the Oceans Salty?
   Geology in Practice exercises can be used for in-class discussion, homework, or extra credit.

• **Student Study Resources—Non-Assessable**

Online Review Exercises:
Identify the Parts of the Beach
   Identify the Main Features of the Ocean Floor
   Find the Sea Floor Hot Spot
   Understanding Waves and Currents
Concept Self-Checker
Flashcards

Teaching Tips

Cooperative Exercises and Assignments to Encourage Student Learning

Refer to Chapter 4: *Cooperative Learning Teaching Strategies* in the Instructional Design section of this manual for general ideas about conducting cooperative learning exercises in your classroom.

Coop Exercise: Passive vs. Active Continental Margins

From the *Student Study Guide for Understanding Earth,* Chapter 17, Practice Exercises.

The following exercise from the Study Guide makes a good in-class think/pair/share exercise. After you have lectured on the plate tectonic aspects of the oceans, take a break and ask the students to do some thinking by pairing up and completing the following exercise. Present the following questions on a slide. Allow a minute or two for each question. If you are short of time just omit some of the questions by covering them. After the teams have completed their work, you can either collect and grade their answers, or ask teams to report and discuss their answers, or show the answers on a slide and ask for question.

Characterize each locality described below as either a *passive (Andean Type)* or *active (Marianas Type)* continental margin. Figures 17.4, 17.6, 17.8 are useful references.

    A. Far from a crustal plate boundary _____

    B. East coast of North America _____

    C. West coast of South America _____

    D. Very broad, featureless continental shelf _____

    E. California coast along the San Andreas Fault _____

    F. Continental margin with no volcanic activity for millions of years _____

Sample Exercise from the Student Study Guide

Digital copy is available from Instructor's CD and web site.
http://www.whfreeman.com/understandingearth

Exercise 1: Profile from the Atlantic shoreline to the Ocean Floor.

From the *Student Study Guide for Understanding Earth,* Chapter 17, **Practice Exercises and Review Questions.** Fill in the blanks to correctly label this profile. **Hint:** Refer to Figure 17.8a.

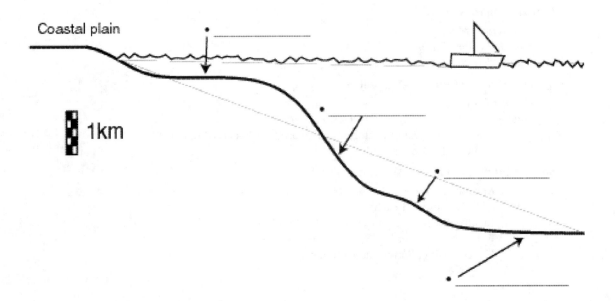

General Education Skills Assignment

Long-Term Team Project

You will find a full outline of this assignment at the end of Chapter 17 in *Understanding Earth*. The project requires the instructor to set up teams at the beginning of the semester. Each team visits a local beach after every storm, measures the width of the beach, and makes other observations. Using sources of information specified, the team then investigates the approach that has been taken to protect the beach. Based on material in Chapter 17, each team writes a critique of the protection implemented by the Corps of Engineers or local officials. This exercise will foster team work, critical thinking, and writing skills, as well as a greater sensitivity to the issues of beach protection.

Topics for Class Discussion

- Is wave action most intense in a bay or at a headland? Explain.
- Discuss how wave-cut terraces can be used to interpret tectonic movements of the land. Refer students to Figure 17.19.
- A beach has been characterized as a "river of sand." Explain.
- Apply the concept of Dynamic Equilibrium, used to model the behavior of streams, to beaches. For example, what factor or factors might cause a beach to be eroded or deposited? Refer students to Figure Story 17.13 and Figure 17.18.
- No matter what the initial shape and outline of the shoreline, waves hitting the coastline will eventually produce a straight shoreline with no major irregularities, such as headlands and bays, especially if sea level changes or tectonic disturbances do not interrupt the process. Evaluate this statement.

Teaching Resources

Student Study Guide Highlights

In Part I: Chapters provide strategies for learning geology. Ideally, students would read these chapters early in the course. But it's never too late to recommend or assign these chapters.

Chapter 1   Brief Preview of the Study Guide for *Understanding Earth* by Press, Siever, Grotzinger, and Jordan

Chapter 2   Meet the Authors of *Understanding Earth, 4th Edition:* How to use your geology textbook

Chapter 3   How to Be Successful in Geology (or just about any other challenging course)

Part II. Chapter 17: *Earth Beneath the Oceans*

Before Lecture:

Preview Questions & Brief Answers

Vital Information from Other Chapters

During Lecture:

Note-Taking Tip

After Lecture:

Check Your Notes

Intensive Study Session

Study Tip

Exam Prep:

Chapter Summary

Practice Exercises: *Profile from the Atlantic Shoreline to the Ocean Floor*
Passive vs. Active Continental Margins

Review Questions (Answers to all review questions are given at the end of the Study Guide.)

CHAPTER 18

Landscapes: Tectonic and Climate Interaction

Chapter Summary

- Landscapes are described in terms of their topography: elevation, the altitude of the surface of the Earth above sea level; relief, the difference between the highest and the lowest spots in a region; and the varied landforms produced by erosion and sedimentation by rivers, glaciers, mass wasting, and wind. Elevation is a balance between tectonic activity and erosion rate.

- Tectonics (uplift and subsidence), erosion, climate, and the type of bedrock control the evolution of landscapes. Water, wind, and ice act to erode and transport rock material from the high spots and deposit it in the low spots. Over time, relief is subdued by both erosion and sedimentation.

- Landscapes go through different phases depending on tectonic activity and climate. For example, a landscape with high relief will form if tectonic activity is high, which in turn stimulates erosion. Erosion will at first enhance relief but over time, water, wind, and ice will wear down the high spots and fill in the low spots with sediment.

- Current views of landscape evolution emphasize the competition between erosion and tectonic uplift. If uplift is faster, the mountains will rise; if erosion is faster, the mountains will be lowered. When tectonics dominates, mountains are high and steep, and they remain so as long as the balance is in favor of tectonics. When erosion exceeds uplift, slopes become lower and more rounded.

- Mountain building processes dominate convergent plate boundaries. Various feedback mechanisms may influence evolution of a mountain system at a convergent boundary. As the mountains become higher, glaciers can form. Ice is a very effective agent of erosion. Therefore, a negative feedback develops where, as mountains get higher, glaciers become bigger and more numerous, and the ice can erode faster. Over the long term (tens to hundreds of millions of years) this feedback mechanism probably speeds up the wearing down of high mountains. However, over the short term (thousands to millions of years) erosion may promote uplift and actually result in the highest peaks rising even higher, due to isostatic adjustments associated with erosional unloading.

Learning Objectives

In this section we provide a *sampling* of possible objectives for this chapter. No class could or should try to accomplish all these. Choose based on your analysis of your class. Refer to

Chapter 1: *Learning Objectives—How to Define Your Goals for the Class* in the Instructional Design section of this manual for thoughts and ideas about how to go about such an analysis.

Knowledge

- Know how landscapes are described in terms of their topography: elevation, the altitude of the surface of the Earth above sea level, and relief (the difference between the highest and the lowest spots in a region).
- Understand how the great variety of landscapes results from sculpturing geologic processes such as erosion and sedimentation by rivers, glaciers, mass wasting, and wind.
- Understand how landscapes go through different phases depending on tectonic activity and climate.
- Know the major landform provinces for North America.
- Know characteristic landforms associated with active tectonic plate boundaries.
- Understand how Earth systems and plate tectonics control landscapes.
- Understand the relationship between tectonics and erosion.

Skills/Applications/Attitudes

- Given facts about a region's elevation, relief, and climate, can make predictions about the landforms one would expect to find there.
- Given a particular topography (mesa, cuesta, hogback, valley and ridge topography), can sketch and describe its features.

General Education Skills

- Write a review of an article out of *Scientific American* or a professional journal. (Writing/Critical Thinking)

Freshman Survival Skills

- This might be a good time to give your students a brief workshop on simple sketching techniques that will facilitate their note-taking during class and field trips. (Note Taking)

Sample Lecture Outline

Digital copy is available from Instructor's CD and web site.
http://www.whfreeman.com/understandingearth
Sample lecture outlines highlight the important topics and concepts covered in the text. We suggest that you download a digital copy of this outline from the web site and customize it to your own lecture before handing it out to students. At the end of each chapter outline, consider adding a selection of review questions, representing a range of thinking levels.

Chapter 18: Landscapes: Tectonic and Climate Interaction

Topography, Elevation, and Relief
    Contour lines
    Topographic maps
Landforms
    Types
        Plateaus
        Mountains and hills
        Badlands
        Mesas

CD and Web site Resources

Instructor's CD Highlights

- *Key Textbook Figures and Tables*

  Figure 18.3: Relief is the difference between the highest and lowest elevations

  Figure 18.5: A digital shaded-relief map of landforms in the contiguous United States

  Figure Story 18.12: Erosion is controlled by a balance between stream power and sediment load.

  Figure 18.17: Uplift stimulates erosion/Isostatic mantle rebound raises mountain elevation

  Figure 18.19: Classic models of landscape evolution

- *Photo Gallery*: Includes slide set images from the previous three editions

Web site Highlights

http://www.whfreeman.com/understandingearth

- **Presentation Tools**

  Animations: Visit the web site for animations, including animations of figures from this chapter.

  PowerPoint Presentation

  PowerPoint Presentation with Lecture Notes

  Photo Gallery

- **Course Preparation**

  Instructor's Manual

  Sample Lecture Outline

  Sample Exercises

- **Student Study Resources—Assessable**

  Graded Online Quizzing

  Geology in Practice: Can Erosion Make Mountains Higher?

   Geology in Practice exercises can be used for in-class discussion, homework, or extra credit.

- **Student Study Resources—Non-Assessable**

  Online Review Exercises:

   Identify the Plate Boundary

Identify North America's Landforms
Understanding Landform Evolution
Concept Self-Checker
Flashcards

Teaching Tips

Cooperative Exercises and Assignments to Encourage Student Learning

Refer to Chapter 4: *Cooperative Learning Teaching Strategies* in the Instructional Design section of this manual for general ideas about conducting cooperative learning exercises in your classroom.

Coop Exercise #1: Landscapes: Tectonic and Climate Interaction Flowchart

The following exercise from the Study Guide makes a good in-class exercise. Display the flowchart below as a slide or overhead. Then have students pair up with a neighbor to fill in the blanks.

Instructions: Place the following words in the correct positions on the flowchart:

tectonic activity
high relief
low relief
erosion
physical weathering
chemical weathering

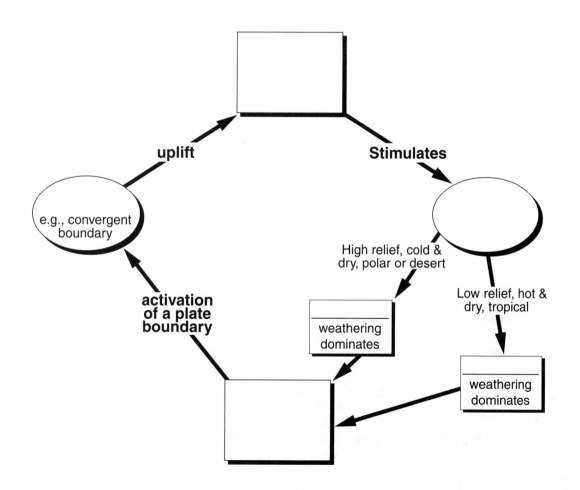

Coop Exercise #2: Comparison of Some of the Landforms

Chapter 18 provided a virtual fieldtrip experience. To master the landforms discussed in this chapter it will be helpful to develop a comparison chart identifying the important features that distinguish each landform you learned about. Fill in the missing information under "Important Features." **Hint:** Use the text figures, captions, and accompanying text to help you. Then, make a very simple sketch of each landform. Sketching is both a thinking tool and a great kinesthetic learning tool. When you draw you tap the part of the brain that learns by moving.

General Education Skills

The *Geology in Practice* exercises offer an opportunity for students to think about feedback relationships between uplift, erosion, and isostatic adjustments. The article entitled "A Review of How Erosion Builds Mountains" by Nicholas Pinter and Mark T. Brandon, *Scientific American* (April 1997): 74–79 provides a basis for this investigation. Below is a brief summary of this article.

Major Themes Discussed in "How Erosion Builds Mountains"

- Mountains are a product of plate tectonics, erosion, and climate.
- Plate tectonics determines the location of mountains on Earth, and plate tectonic processes produce the thick crustal root that helps to support many mountain ranges.
- Erosion and climate are closely linked and act together to determine how fast rock is removed off the mountain.
- Erosion coupled with isostatic compensation can result in a positive feedback, whereas rock is removed from a mountain range by erosion; the buoyant response of the crustal root results in additional uplift.

Additional Themes

- Orographic effects can help to determine the ultimate shape of mountains.
- The history of a mountain range can be characterized in three basic stages:
  1. Tectonics acts to thicken crust and induce uplift at rates greater than erosion.
  2. Rate of uplift and erosion are about equal, so the highest areas within the mountain range can get even higher.
  3. Erosion surpasses uplift and the mountain range wears down.

- There is continued debate about the relationship between mountain building and global climate.

Topics for Class Discussion

Introduce the concept of isostatic adjustment due to loading, e.g., accumulation of ice, and unloading, e.g., the retreat of the ice sheets, erosion of high mountains.

Teaching Resources

Student Study Guide Highlights

In Part I: Chapters provide strategies for learning geology. Ideally, students would read these chapters early in the course. But it's never too late to recommend or assign these chapters.

Chapter 1   Brief Preview of the Study Guide for *Understanding Earth* by Press, Siever, Grotzinger, and Jordan

Chapter 2   Meet the Authors of *Understanding Earth, 4th Edition:* How to use your geology textbook

Chapter 3   How to Be Successful in Geology (or just about any other challenging course)

Earthquakes

Chapter Summary

- An earthquake is a shaking of the ground caused by seismic waves, emanating from the focus along a fault that moves suddenly. When the fault moves, the strain built up over years of slow deformation by tectonic forces is released in a few moments as seismic waves.

- Elastic rebound theory explains why earthquakes occur. Over a period of time the application of stress causes rock to slowly deform (bend) elastically until its breaks, and the rock snaps back as the fault moves. This is analogous to stretching a rubber band until it breaks and snaps back to sting your hand.

- There are three major types of seismic waves. Two types of waves travel through the Earth's interior: P (primary/compressional) waves, which move through all forms of matter and move the fastest, and S (secondary/shear) waves, which move through solids only and move at about half the speed of P waves. Surface waves need a free surface like the Earth's surface to ripple. They move more slowly than the interior waves but cause most of the destruction associated with earthquakes.

- Earthquake magnitude is a measure of the size of the earthquake. The Richter magnitude is determined from the amplitude of the ground motion. The movement magnitude is closely related to the amount of energy radiated by the earthquake. The moment magnitude scale depends on the product of the slip of the fault when it broke, the area of the fault break, and the rigidity or stiffness of the rock. The Modified Mercalli Intensity Scale provides a way of estimating the intensity of an earthquake shaking, directly from an event's destructive effects.

- Most earthquakes occur along crust plate boundaries but not all. Earthquakes at divergent plate boundaries are usually shallow, lower magnitude, and a consequence of tensional stress. Convergent plate boundaries produce shallow and deep earthquakes of low to high magnitudes and are commonly due to compressive stress. Transform faults produce shallow to moderately deep earthquakes of low to high magnitude and are usually in response to shear stress.

- The destructiveness of an earthquake does not depend on the magnitude alone. In addition to ground motion, the duration of the earthquake, avalanches, fires, liquefaction, tsunamis, proximity to population centers, and the construction design of buildings all help to determine the destructiveness of an earthquake.

- The damage caused by earthquakes can be mitigated by: regulating the construction design of buildings in earthquake zones; bolting houses to their foundation; in your home, securing appliances connected to gas lines and tall furniture to walls; keeping heavy items at low levels; and having a community plan for dealing with emergencies generated by earthquakes. Geologists generate seismic-risk maps to aid public authorities with their evaluations.

- Scientists can characterize the degree of risk in a region, but they cannot consistently predict earthquakes. Recurrence intervals—the average time between large earthquakes—is used for *long-term forecasting* of earthquakes.

Learning Objectives

In this section we provide a *sampling* of possible objectives for this chapter. No class could or should try to accomplish all these. Choose based on your analysis of your class. Refer to Chapter 1: *Learning Objectives—How to Define Your Goals for the Class* in the Instructional Design section of this manual for thoughts and ideas about how to go about such an analysis.

Knowledge

- Know the factors that define an earthquake (ground shaking caused by seismic waves that emanate from a fault that moves suddenly).
- Know the three types of seismic waves and their basic characteristics.
- Understand what is meant by earthquake magnitude and intensity, and the scales use to measure them.
- Know that most earthquakes are associated with active tectonic plate boundaries.
- Know that earthquake activity at each type of tectonic plate boundary has distinctive characteristics.
- Know what governs the type of faulting that occurs in an earthquake.

Skills/Applications/Attitudes

- Evaluate the geologic circumstances that contribute to the destructiveness of earthquakes
- Appreciate the importance of mitigating damage by earthquakes, and understand the steps that should be taken by threatened communities.

General Education Skills

- Given the arrival time of S and P waves at an observation point and the graph in Figure 19.6, compute distance from the observation point to the epicenter of an earthquake.

Freshman Survival Skills

- Encourage students to study strategically by making the intensive study recommendations for this chapter a credit assignment. (Study Skills)
- Distribute a chapter outline and a selection of mixed format study questions before your lecture on earthquakes. (Note-Taking)

Sample Lecture Outline

Digital copy is available from Instructor's CD and web site
http://www.whfreeman.com/understandingearth

Sample lecture outlines highlight the important topics and concepts covered in the text. We suggest that you download a digital copy of this outline from the web site and customize it to your own lecture before handing it out to students. At the end of each chapter outline, consider adding a selection of review questions, representing a range of thinking levels.

Chapter 19: Earthquakes

What is an Earthquake?
Causes
    Elastic rebound theory—
        Release of strain energy built up in the Earth's crust beyond the elastic limit
    Volcanism
    Explosions
    Landslides
Detecting and Measuring Earthquakes
    Seismometer
    Seismograph
Seismic Waves
    Body waves
        P-waves—compressional
        S-waves—shear
    Surface waves
Location
    Focus
    Epicenter
Measuring the Size of an Earthquake
    Magnitude
        Richter Scale (ground motion)
        Moment magnitude (energy released)
    Intensity
        Mercalli Scale (damage)
Earthquakes and Patterns of Faulting
    Three main types of fault movements
    First motions
Global Pattern of Earthquake Activity
    Divergent boundaries
    Transform-fault
    Convergent boundaries
    Intraplate
Destructiveness of Earthquakes
    Ground motion
    Tsunamis
    Landslides
    Earth cracks and fissures
    Fires
    Building materials and methods
    Protection programs
Earthquake Risk Assessment and Prediction
What Should You Do Before and During an Earthquake?

CD and Web site Resources

Instructor's CD Highlights

    • *Key Textbook Figures and Tables:*
        Figure Story 19.1: The elastic rebound theory

• *Photo Gallery:* Includes slide set images from the previous three editions

Web site Highlights

http://www.whfreeman.com/understandingearth

- **Presentation Tools**

  Animations: Visit the web site for animations, including animations of figures from this chapter.

  PowerPoint Presentation

  PowerPoint Presentation with Lecture Notes

  Photo Gallery

- **Course Preparation**

  Instructor's Manual

  Sample Lecture Outline

  Sample Exercises

- **Student Study Resources—Assessable**

  Graded Online Quizzing

  Geology in Practice: Can We Predict Earthquakes?

  > *Geology in Practice* exercises can be used for in-class discussion, homework, or extra credit. In this exercise, students will explore recent literature about new ideas for predicting earthquakes.

- **Student Study Resources—Non-Assessable**

  Online Review Exercises: Identify the Plate Boundary

  Concept Self-Checker

  Flashcards

Teaching Tips

Cooperative Exercises and Assignments to Encourage Student Learning

Refer to Chapter 4: *Cooperative Learning Teaching Strategies* in the Instructional Design section of this manual for general ideas about conducting cooperative learning exercises in your classroom.

Coop Exercise # 1: Seismic Risk Assessment

This question is a Review Question from Chapter 19 of the Student Study Guide.

The following question works well as an in-class Think/Pair/Share exercise. It taps critical thinking by requiring students to identify the first key step in solving a risk management problem. As teams defend their reasoning, there is potential for lively discussion.

Ask students to team up with a partner, develop an answer to the following question, then report back their answer and the reasoning that led them to it. Allow teams a few minutes to discuss their answer and to make a few notes documenting the reason(s) for their choice.

- You have just started a job as a county planner in Colorado when the Board of Supervisors mandates earthquake risk assessment. Your first task is to assess the potential for a major seismic event in an area that has experienced only a few minor earthquakes. So, you decide to

    A. install a state-of-the-art seismic recording station to monitor earthquake activity.

    B. develop a seismic risk map showing the likelihood of an earthquake based on the number that have occurred in the past.

    C. develop an earthquake protection plan with local and state officials.

    D. investigate the records for tsunamis.

Coop Exercise #2: Five-Minute Write

The Five-Minute Write is done during the last five minutes of lecture. Ask students to put their name on a sheet of paper and then address the three questions on the overhead (see adjacent sample). Start the next lecture by discussing the answers to some of the questions students had about the previous lecture.

Sample Exercise from the Student Study Guide

Digital copy is available from Instructor's CD and web site.
http://www.whfreeman.com/understandingearth

Exercise 1: Earthquake Focus vs. Epicenter

Label the diagram below by filling in the blanks using the following terms: fault scarp, focus, fault zone, and epicenter. Use arrows to show the relative motion along the fault zone. The star marks the location from which fault movement propagated.

What type of fault is this? _____

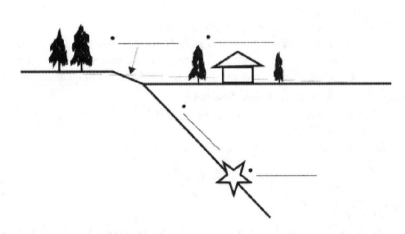

General Education Skills Assignment

Chapter 19 offers some good possibilities for assignments that require students to do some very simple mathematics. For example, below is Review Question 12 from the Student Study Guide.

We recommend that you review Figure 19.6 with students before assigning this task.

Mathematics: Graph Interpretation

- Your seismograph has just recorded an earthquake. You are curious whether the earthquake occurred in North America or somewhere else in the world.

Given the arrival time of 5 minutes for the first P waves and 10 minutes for the first S waves, you determine that the approximate distance between you and the earthquake is

    A. 100 kilometers

    B. 1000 kilometers

    C. 3000 kilometers

    D. 7000 kilometers

Hint: Use the graph in Figure 19.6 to determine the distance between you and the earthquake.

Topics for Class Discussion

- Describe how the elastic rebound theory accounts for the earthquakes.

- Use Silly Putty to illustrate the three ways solids respond to stress by breaking, bending, or elastically. The elastic behavior (rebound) of Silly Putty is very easy to demonstrate in lecture. A ball of Silly Putty bounces due to its elastic behavior. Silly Putty breaks when pulled apart quickly and will even shatter when hit very abruptly with a hammer. Plus Silly Putty will bend (deform plastically) when pulled apart slowly.

- If a seismic wave travels faster in olivine than it does in quartz, what does it tell you about the density and rigidity of olivine relative to quartz?

- Can sections of the Earth's surface move relative to one another even though an earthquake does not occur? Discuss aseismic movements such as isostatic rebound, associated with glacial erosional unloading.

- Seismic Risk Assessment:
  Identify seismic sources, e.g., fault zones, neotectonic features
      Geologic mapping of
          Fault scarps and lineaments
          Offset landforms
          Spurs and facets to mountain slopes
          Uplifted stream and beach terraces
      Problems
          Erosion obscures feature
          Blind thrusts/buried faults
  Estimate the probability of a large earthquake at a known source
      Recurrence intervals
      Identify seismic gaps
  Monitor potential earthquake sites for
      Change in small quakes activity
      Uplift or tilt of ground surface
      Radon in wells
      Change in electrical resistivity
      Change in seismic wave velocity
      Animal behavior
      Change in geyser activity
  Estimate intensity pattern that might be associated with seismic events at a specific site.
      This involves the assessment of the local geologic characteristics such as
          Bedrock/ground stability.
      Soils/liquefaction, e.g., San Francisco Bay; Anchorage, Alaska
      Potential for amplification, e.g., Mexico City
      Quake magnitude and distance are not necessarily the most important factor affecting intensity (damage).
  Building design
      Most damage occurs with strong horizontal ground motion and when natural vibrations of the building coincide with ground motion.

Teaching Resources

Student Study Guide Highlights

In Part I: Chapters provide strategies for learning geology. Ideally, students would read these chapters early in the course. But it's never too late to recommend or assign these chapters.

Chapter 1   Brief Preview of the *Study Guide for Understanding Earth* by Press, Siever, Grotzinger, and Jordan

Chapter 2   Meet the Authors of *Understanding Earth, 4th Edition:* How to use your geology textbook

Chapter 3   How to Be Successful in Geology (or just about any other challenging course)

Part II. Chapter 19: *Earthquakes*

Before Lecture:

Preview Questions & Brief Answers

Vital Information from Other Chapters

Web Site Preview

During Lecture:

Note-Taking Tip: Marking Possible Test Items

After Lecture:

Check Your Notes

Intensive Study Session

Exam Prep:

Chapter Summary

Practice Exercises: *Elastic Rebound*
Characteristics of Seismic Waves
Factors that Amplify the Damage Caused by an Earthquake

Review Questions (Answers to all review questions are given at the end of the Study Guide.)

Seismic Eruption Program

http://www.eas.purdue.edu/~braile/edumod/svintro/svintro.htm

This is a very useful software program available for computer instruction or lecture, if you can project a computer screen. Instructional ideas, examples, and the software download are available from the web site above.

The Seismic Eruption Program is excellent for use in lecture to illustrate:

• Global distribution of earthquakes

• The plunging zone of earthquake foci (the Benioff Zone) associated with sub-duction zones

• The comparison of earthquake activity (depth and magnitude) at divergent vs. convergent plate boundaries.

To show the global distribution of earthquakes:

• Open program to "World" menu (display of a world map with seismic regions marked with labels).

• Select "World" and run plot on "Fast."
Discuss with class how this distribution of earthquakes defines active plate boundaries. It is a great example of pattern/process in nature. And there is more that can be learned from this pattern (distribution of earthquakes) if we can plot earthquake activity in three dimensions or, at least, in cross-section. Be sure to carefully point out how earthquake magnitude and depth are represented. Also, be sure to mention the interval of time represented by this display of global seismicity.

To show the Benioff Zone (plunging plane of earthquake foci with depth to one side of an oceanic trench):

- Begin back at the "World" menu.
- Select the "Kuriles" and "Kamchatka" region by clicking on the label.

  Various other subduction zones, like the west coast of South America, Aleutians, work well also.
- Run plot of seismic activity for magnitude 5.0 and greater, on "Fast."
- Ask students if they see a systematic pattern in the distribution of earthquakes along this plate boundary. Occasionally, a student will recognize that earthquakes get progressively deeper to one side of the trench.
- Now go to the "Control" menu in the menu bar on the top of the display and select "Set up cross-section."
- Click on map to see a box.

  Within this box will be plotted earthquake foci for a region of the plate boundary. The size of the box is set by the instructions given below. The box is positioned by dragging it into position.
- Set azimuth at about 30 degrees.
- Set length at about 800 km.
- Set width at about 400 km.
- Depth is probably already set at about 500 km but you can check this setting, too.
- Click on "OK."
- Go to "Control" menu.
- Then, go to "Map/3D/Cross section" and select "Cross section."
- The plunging plane (Benioff Zone) of earthquake foci will be mapped within the area of the box.

  The cross-sectional plot will not work if you do not run the plot of seismic activity to start.

  The Kuriles/Kamchatka boundary provides one of the clearest plots of earthquake foci to a depth of about 500 km. The plot shows a pattern of foci where the shallow earthquakes are relatively broadly distributed across the plate boundary but the deeper foci are restricted to a plunging zone to one side of the trench. The relatively cold, rigid, and brittle subducting ocean lithosphere breaks to generate earthquakes to a depth of about 500 km along this boundary. The deepest earthquake foci go down to about 700 km. Ask students why the deeper earthquakes are only associated with subduction zones.

Now that you are more familiar with the **Seismic Eruption Program,** you can navigate the controls to show cross-sectional plots that compare earthquake foci along the Chile-Peruvian convergent boundary with that along the Mid-Atlantic Ridge.

Sample Exercise

Web-Based Exercise on Earthquakes

National Earthquake Information Center (NCEI): http://neic.usgs.gov/

The National Earthquake Information Center (NCEI) is located in Boulder, Colorado, and is operated by the United States Geological Survey as part of its Geologic Hazards information and research services. NCEI operates a World Wide Web site that provides excellent background information on earthquakes and posts information about recent earthquakes, including maps.

In this exercise, you will "surf" through the NCEI web site to gain some background knowledge on earthquakes and then investigate recent earthquake activity.

Part I: Frequently Asked Questions

• First, log on to the NCEI web site home page at http://neic.usgs.gov/

• From the list of subtopics along the left column, choose "General earthquake information."

• Scroll down to the "Education" subheading.

• Choose "Earthquake frequently asked questions."

Answer the following questions using the information provided. Scroll down to find these questions.

1. Can we cause earthquakes?

2. Do earthquakes cause volcanoes?

3. What states have the smallest number of earthquakes?

4. What is liquefaction of soil?

5. How many earthquakes worldwide occur each day?

6. Draw a graph showing the number of earthquakes per year of a given magnitude within the magnitude range 8+ down to 5.0. Use the plot provided to the left. A bar graph is a good way to display the data because the number of earthquakes are given in "bins" or a range of magnitudes, e.g., 8 and greater, 7.0 to 7.9. The number of earthquakes in the 6.0–6.9 range has been plotted for you to illustrate how to complete this graph.

Part II: Earthquake Activity in the United States

• Return to the "General earthquake information" page and choose "World seismicity 1975–1995."

• Choose "United States."

• Answer the following questions based on the map.

7. Which area has the most earthquakes? The western, central, or eastern U.S.?

8. Are there any obvious concentrations of earthquakes along "bands" or "lines" on the map? Where are these bands?

9. Are there seismically active regions that you did not expect to see (earthquakes in areas that you thought did not have earthquakes)? Explain why you were surprised by the location of this earthquake activity.

Part III: World's Largest Earthquakes

• Return to the "General earthquake information" page.

• Choose "Largest earthquakes in the world."

• Choose "World."

• Observe the resulting map of the ten largest earthquakes of this century and answer the following questions.

10. Where and when were the two largest earthquakes in the 21st century?

11. Which state of the United States has experienced three of the ten largest earthquakes in the 21st century?

Part IV: Current Earthquake Activity

• Return to the NCEI home page.

• Select "Current earthquake information."

• Scroll down to the section labeled "Current earthquake map."

• Select "World."

• Answer the following questions using the map of the global seismicity over the last week.

   12. Where was the most recent event?

   13. If there are any earthquakes shown within the United States, where [in what state(s)] were they located?

Part V: Magnitude and Intensity

• Return to the "General earthquake information" page.

• Scroll down to and click the label "Magnitude and intensity."

• Select "U.S. earthquakes causing damage."

• Using the map of Mercalli Intensity for earthquakes since 1750, answer the following questions.

   14. Where were the most damaging earthquakes (shown by red squares) located within the contiguous 48 states? **Hint:** There are about five general areas where especially damaging earthquakes have occurred within the contiguous 48 states.

   15. Are you surprised at the location(s) of some of these most damaging earthquakes? Justify your surprise by giving one reason why you thought a large earthquake was unlikely in the region.

CHAPTER 20

Evolution of the Continents

Chapter Summary

- Large-scale geologic features of North America, like the other continents, are organized into a pattern that reflects the continent's long-term geologic evolution. Major continental features include the stable interior, shield, mountain belts, coastal plain, and continental shelves.

- The North American continent today contains a large central stable shield and platform that have been relatively undistributed by orogenic events since the Precambrian. Surrounding the stable interior are younger orogenic belts—the mountainous Cordillera and Appalachians, which were deformed during plate convergence at various times in the Paleozoic, Mesozoic, and Cenozoic eras.

- Plate convergence initiates orogeny and the associated crustal deformation and other processes that build mountains. If plate convergence initiates along a pre-existing passive continental margin, sediments that have collected over time along that margin will be involved in the deformation and metamorphism. Folding, thrusting, emplacement of plutons, extrusion of volcanic rock, and collisions with microplates or full-sized continents all act to thicken the crust in active orogenic zones. Thicker continental crust leads to uplift and mountains.

- Continents can grow by a succession of orogenies over geologic time in several ways:

  1. Accretion of sediments on continental shelves and fragments of pre-existing crust. Mechanisms for accretion include:

     A. Transfer of a crustal fragment from a subducting plate to the overriding plate.

     B. Closure of a marginal sea that separates an island arc from a continent, resulting in the accretion of the island arc.

     C. Transport of crustal fragments along continental margins by strike-slip faulting.

     D. Collision of two continents that sutures them together.

  2. Addition of batholiths and volcanic rocks derived from melting and magmatic differentiation in subduction zones.

- Orogenic zones that are actively modifying continents today include the Alpine-Himalayan and Cordilleran orogenies.

- The supercontinent, Pangaea, was assembled by a series of orogenies during the Paleozoic. Refer to Figure 20.17. An idealized sequence of events in the opening and closing of ocean basins is named the Wilson cycle, after J. Tuzo Wilson. Refer to Figure 20.18.

- Epeirogenic (gradual vertical) movements of the continents are thought to be caused by isostatic adjustments associated with loading and unloading or heating of the crust. Refer to Figure 20.20.

- A hotter and more actively convecting mantle probably contributed to the formation of cratonic nuclei during the Archean era. Lithosphere beneath the cratons extends into the deeper mantle, like a keel of a boat into water. The cratonic keels appear to have formed at about the same time as the cratons. The cold, strong, and somewhat buoyant keels help to explain why some Archean cratons have managed to survive through many continental collisions without much internal deformation.

Learning Objectives

In this section we provide a *sampling* of possible objectives for this chapter. No class could or should try to accomplish all these. Choose your learning objectives based on your analysis of your class. Refer to Chapter 1: *Learning Objectives—How to Define Your Goals for the Class* in the Instructional Design section of this manual for thoughts and ideas about how to go about such an analysis.

Knowledge

- Know the major tectonic features of North America.
- Know the geologic events that typify an orogeny (mountain building episode) caused by plate convergence.
- Know the distinction between epeirogeny and orogeny.
- Describe the general sequence of geologic events that formed the Appalachian, Himalayan, and North America Cordillera and how these orogenic systems related to plate tectonic processes.
- Describe mechanisms for vertical movements of the Earth's crust.

Skills/Applications/Attitudes

- Interpret the general plate tectonic setting for an orogenic system, given some basic geologic knowledge about the mountain range.

General Education Skills

- Draw upon the material in Chapter 20 and additional instructor-provided resources to write a brief newspaper article about the long-term history of the tectonic area in which students live. (Writing/Critical Thinking)

Freshman Survival Skills

- As the end of the semester approaches, students will appreciate helpful ideas for preparing for and taking exams.

Sample Lecture Outline

Digital copy is available from Instructor's CD and web site.
http://www.whfreeman.com/understandingearth
Sample lecture outlines highlight the important topics and concepts covered in the text. We suggest that you download a digital copy of this outline from the web site and customize it to your own lecture before handing it out to students. At the end of each chapter outline, consider adding a selection of review questions, representing a range of thinking levels.

Chapter 20: Evolution of the Continents

Major Components of the Continents
 Shield—Canadian/Baltic
 Stable platform—Great Plains
 Sedimentary basins—Michigan basin
 Mountain belts—Appalachians/Cordilleran
 Coastal plain—Gulf and east coast of North America
 Continental shelf
Case Histories
 Appalachian fold belt
 North American Cordillera
Tectonic Ages—Refer to Figure 20.8
How Continents Grow
 Magmatic differentiation—buoyant, silica-rich crust is generated in subduction zones
 Accretion
  Crustal fragments accreted by subduction
  Island arc crust accreted when a marginal sea closes
  Transport of crustal fragments along a strike-slip fault, like the San Andreas
  Continental collision sutures two continents
Modification of Continents by Orogeny
 Alpine-Himalayan orogeny
 Paleozoic orogenies assemble Pangaea
 Wilson cycle
Epeirogeny—Regional Vertical Movements of the Crust
 Isostatic adjustments
  Loading and unloading, e.g., accumulation and melting of glacial ice
  Heating and cooling, e.g., mantle plumes, hot spots
Archean Cratonic Nuclei
 Oldest known continental crust formed about 4.0 billion years ago
 Granite-greenstone terrains
 High-grade metamorphic terrains
 Cratonic keels
  Extend to depths of more than 200 km into the mantle beneath the cratons
  Cold, strong, and relatively buoyant
  May protect cratons from subsequent deformation

CD and Web site Resources

Instructor's CD Highlights

 • *Key Textbook Figures and Tables:*
  Figure 20.1: Major tectonic features of North America
  Figure 20.3: Map of sedimentary thickness on the interior platform of North America

- *Photo Gallery:* Includes slide set images from the previous three editions

Web site Highlights

http://www.whfreeman.com/understandingearth

- **Presentation Tools**

    Animations: Visit the web site for animations, including animations of figures from this chapter.
    PowerPoint Presentation
    PowerPoint Presentation with Lecture Notes
    Photo Gallery

- **Course Preparation**

    Instructor's Manual
    Sample Lecture Outline
    Sample Exercises

- **Student Study Resources—Assessable**

    Graded Online Quizzing
    Geology in Practice: Floating Continents
        This *Geology in Practice* exercise poses the question: Do continents float on the mantle? Students make estimates for and compare the density of continental and ocean crust, and the upper mantle. These exercises can be used for class discussion, homework, or extra credit.

- **Student Study Resources—Non-Assessable**

    Concept Self-Checker
    Flashcards

Teaching Tips

Cooperative Exercises and Assignments to Encourage Student Learning

Refer to Chapter 4: *Cooperative Learning Teaching Strategies* in the Instructional Design section of this manual for general ideas about conducting cooperative learning exercises in your classroom.

Coop Exercise #1: Evolution of the Continents

Present the conceptual flowchart below to the class. Give pairs of students about 2–3 minutes to complete it. Then discuss questions students have on the flowchart and the Wilson cycle.

This may be used as a preview or review to your presentation on the Wilson cycle. This is Exercise 1 in Chapter 20 of the Student Study Guide.

Complete the sentences in the flowchart below by filling-in-the-blank using words from the list below. Refer to Figures 20.12, 20.15, and 20.18.

accretion & collision	intrusion of magmas	subducts
continental plate	magmatism	thick
erosion	ocean basin	thrust faulting
folding	passive margin	
hot	stable craton	

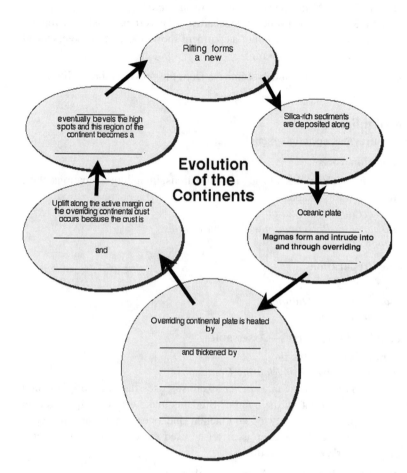

Ask students where orogeny fits into the flowchart above.

Coop Exercise #2: Orogeny Review

The following sequence of questions can be used as a Think/Pair/Share exercise.
(From the *Student Study Guide for Understanding Earth,* Chapter 20, Review Questions)

Which of the following statements about orogenic systems is not valid?

   A. Orogeny is initiated by rifting as extension begins to open up a new ocean basin.

   B. Orogeny is initiated by subduction and the evolution of an active convergent margin.

   C. Large volumes of granite are intruded during orogenies.

   D. Folding and thrusting of preexisting rocks contributes to crustal thickening in the orogeny.

The Cordilleran orogeny was initiated by formation of

   A. a continental rift in western North America.

   B. a new subduction zone and convergent plate boundary along the western edge of North America.

C. an impact of a comet-size object in the Pacific Ocean adjacent to the western edge of North America.

D. a line of mantle or hot spots that caused doming and rifting through out western North America.

The western Cordillera of North America is topographically higher than the Appalachians mainly because

A. orogeny occurred more recently in the Cordillera.

B. granite batholiths were intruded in the Cordilleran belt.

C. the Appalachians eroded faster because they consist mostly of soft sedimentary rocks.

D. the Appalachians never reach the elevation of the Cordillera because collisions do not generate high mountains.

Note: If you are short of time you can eliminate the last question and answer it yourself during discussion. To avoid confusion between orogeny and the broader idea of continental evolution you may need to underscore the point that rifting *is* part of the Wilson cycle of continental evolution and orogeny (mountain building) is initiated with subduction.

Sample Exercise from the Student Study Guide

Digital copy is available from Instructor's CD and web site.
http://www.whfreeman.com/understandingearth

Coop Exercise #3: The Ocean Crust vs. Continental Crust

Using information in Chapters 2, 5, 17, 18, and 20, complete the table below by filling in the blank boxes.

Characteristics	Ocean crust	Continental crust
Composition Rock type(s)		Very heterogeneous—can contain any rock but dominantly granitic and gneissic with a cover of sediments.
Density	3.0 g/cm^3	2.7 g/cm^3
Thickness	10 km	
Age		The ages of continental crust spans 4 billion years.
Topographic features	Abyssal floor Ridge with axial rift Trenches Seamounts Hot spot island chains Plateaus	
Structure/ Architecture	A model for the structure of the ocean crust is the ophiolite suite: deep-sea sediments, basaltic pillow lavas and dikes, and gabbro. (Note: peridotites are part of the mantle lithosphere, not the ocean crust.)	The architecture of the continents is complex. It consists of preexisting cratons, accreted microplates, island arcs, volcanic arcs, suture zones, ophiolite suites, and belts representing ancient orogenic zones. Sediments cover basement rock in the interior platform of the continent.
Origin		Orogenic processes and accretion of preexisting crustal blocks along convergent plate boundaries.

General Education Skills Assignment

Chapter 20 affords some great opportunities for students to apply the geology they have learned this semester to their home area. Writing a brief but accurate newspaper article allows some room for creativity in the form of cute headlines and metaphors that may occur to the students as they think about geological history. Here is a sample assignment you can use or modify.

Your Home-Town Tectonic History

Assignment: Draw on the material in Chapter 20 and additional materials from the web and library to write a brief newspaper article about the geologic history of the tectonic area in which you live. (Writing/Critical Thinking) Begin by determining from Figure 20.1 the tectonic province you live in. Think about local topographic features you are familiar with and ask yourself whether or how these features may be associated with the tectonic evolution of the region. For example, the valleys and ridges in central and western Pennsylvania, refer to Figure 20.4, are a topographic expression of the Appalachian fold belt.

The material in Chapter 20 in the section entitled: *The Tectonic History of North America* provides an excellent base of information for this exercise. You may want to add a list of web site resources or other information you have on file for students to incorporate in their articles.

Freshman Survival Skills Resources

As the end of the semester approaches, students will appreciate helpful ideas for how to effectively prepare for and take final exams. This is the perfect time to put up slides on test preparation during lecture. You may also want to recommend helpful test preparation workshops that may be offered by your campus learning or teaching center. Finally, if you have a class web site, consider posting some materials or links that will help students prepare for exams.

Sample Material (From the Student Study Guide, Chapter 20)

Top Ten Tips for Taking a Multiple-Choice Exam

Number 10: Answer the questions you know first. Mark items where you get stuck. Come back to harder questions later. Often you will find the answer you are looking for embedded in another, easier question.

Number 9: First, try to answer the item without looking at the options.

Number 8: Eliminate the distracters. Treat each alternative as a true-false item. If "False," eliminate it.

Number 7: Use common sense. Reasoning is more reliable than memory.

Number 6: Underline key words in the stem. This is good to try when you are stuck. It may help you focus on what question is really being asked.

Number 5: If two alternatives look similar, it is likely that one of them is correct.

Number 4: Answer all the questions. Unless points are being subtracted for wrong answers (rare) it pays to guess when you're not sure. Research indicates that items with the most words in the middle of the list are often the correct items. But be cautious. Your professor may have read the research too!

Number 3: Do not change answers. Particularly when you are guessing, your first guess is often correct. Change answers only when you have a clear reason for doing so.

Number 2: If the first item is correct, check the last. If it says "all (or none) of the above" you obviously need to read the other alternatives carefully. Missing an "all of the above" item is one of the most common errors on a multiple-choice exam. It is easy to read carelessly when you are anxious.

Number 1: Read the directions before you begin!

Topics for Class Discussion

- Young mountain ranges are commonly located at the margins of continents. Why?
- How do mountains form within the interior of continental crust?
- How is an iceberg floating in the ocean analogous to a continent on the Earth?
- What is isostasy, and explain how isostatic adjustment helps to explain vertical movements of the Earth's crust.
- Do continents get subducted? Discuss.
- In the context of plate tectonics, explain the observation that belts of different aged rocks in continents tend to get younger toward the margins of the continent—but not always. Refer to Figure 20.8.

Teaching Resources

Student Study Guide Highlights

In Part I: Chapters provide strategies for learning geology. Ideally, students would read these chapters early in the course. But it's never to late to recommend or assign these chapters.

Chapter 1   Brief Preview of the *Study Guide for Understanding Earth* by Press, Siever, Grotzinger, and Jordan

Chapter 2   Meet the Authors of *Understanding Earth, 4th Edition:* How to use your geology textbook

Chapter 3   How to Be Successful in Geology (or just about any other challenging course)

Part II. Chapter 20: *Evolution of the Continents*

Before Lecture:

Preview Questions & Brief Answers

Study Tip

Vital Information from Other Chapters

During Lecture:

Keeping the "Big Picture" in Mind

After Lecture:

Check Your Notes

Intensive Study Session

Exam Prep:

Chapter Summary

Practice Exercises: *Evolution of the Continents*
The Ocean Crust vs. Continental Crust

Review Questions (Answers to all review questions are given at the end of the Study Guide.)

Web site on Critical Thinking

The *Foundation for Critical Thinking* (www.criticalthinking.org) publishes useful guides on using critical thinking in problem solving. Two examples of their miniature guides are:

"Critical Thinking Concepts & Tools" by Dr. Richard Paul and Dr. Linda Elder, and "How to Study & Learn a Discipline" by Dr. Richard Paul and Dr. Linda Elder.

CHAPTER 21

Exploring Earth's Interior

Chapter Summary

- Seismic waves reveal that the Earth has a concentrically zoned internal structure. The silicate-rich crust lies on a denser mantle consisting of iron-rich silicates. The Moho or Mohorovicic discontinuity in seismic wave velocities marks the boundary between the crust and the mantle. Earth's tectonic plates are large fragments of the lithosphere, which includes the crust and uppermost, rigid mantle. Below the lithosphere, in the upper mantle is a hot, weak zone called the asthenosphere. Abrupt increases in seismic wave velocities coupled with high pressure laboratory studies of materials suggest that there are zones at progressively greater depths within the mantle where the crystal structure of minerals collapses under the intense pressure to form more compact atomic structures and therefore, different minerals.

- P wave and S wave shadow zones reveal a liquid outer core and a solid inner core. P wave velocities in the core, the natural abundance of iron in nature, the existence of iron-nickel meteorites, the Earth's strong magnetic field, and the need for a very dense core to account for the overall mass of the Earth all support an iron-nickel composition for the Earth's core.

- The principle of isostasy proposes that continents float on the denser mantle, supported by a buoyant root that projects into the mantle. Seismic waves reveal the existence of these roots. The principle of isostasy implies that, over longer periods, the mantle has little strength and behaves like a viscous fluid when it is forced to support the weight of continents and mountains.

- Earth heated up in the process of becoming a planet, and its temperature was increased further by the heat released by the decay of radioactive elements. Heat transfer within the Earth is thought to be largely a result of convection. Convection occurs when a heated fluid expands and rises because it becomes less dense than the surrounding material. Convection can occur in solids that "flow" over longer periods, similar to the way a ball of Silly Putty will spread out into a pancake shape under its own weight over a relatively short period. Convection is driven by the force of gravity and density differences between hotter and cooler materials.

- The average increase in temperature with depth measured for the upper crust is about 20° to 30°C per kilometer. The rate of increase of Earth's internal temperature must decrease rapidly within the mantle, otherwise the entire Earth would be hot enough to melt. Seismic waves tell us that most of the Earth is solid.

- Seismic tomography provides a three-dimensional view of structure within the mantle. Tomographic sections through the Earth have revealed a mantle plume rising from the core, and remnants of the subducted Farallon Plate under the North American Plate.

- The main component of the Earth's magnetic field is thought to be generated by electrical fields within a moving liquid iron-rich outer core. The Earth's magnetic field flips back and forth over geologic time. Preserved in some rocks is a clear record of past changes in the orientation of Earth's magnetic field. The chronology of magnetic field reversals has been worked out so that the direction of remnant magnetization of a rock formation is often an indicator of its stratigraphic age.

Learning Objectives

In this section we provide a *sampling* of possible objectives for this chapter. No class could or should try to accomplish all these. Choose based on your analysis of your class. Refer to Chapter 1: *Learning Objectives—How to Define Your Goals for the Class* in the Instructional Design section of this manual for thoughts and ideas about how to go about such an analysis.

Knowledge

- Understand what seismic waves reveal about the Earth's internal structure, composition, and physical state.
- Know the principle of isostasy and what evidence supports it.
- Know the sources for Earth's internal heat and how heat is transferred through the Earth.
- Know how geoscientists use tomography and gravity to study Earth's internal structure.
- Know how geoscientists think the Earth's magnetic field is generated.
- Know that the Earth's magnetic field flips back and forth over geologic time and that preserved in some rocks is a record of past changes in the orientation of Earth's magnetic field.

Skills/Applications/Attitudes

- Be able to distinguish between observation (S-wave shadow zone) and inferences made from observations (molten inner core).
- Describe how the behavior of seismic waves is linked to the physical properties of the Earth's interior.

General Education Skills

- Can interpret simple seismic wave data plots such as those in Figures 21.2, 21.4, 21.5, and 21.7.
- Can interpret temperature curves such as those shown in Figure 21.9. (Mathematical Skills)

Freshman Survival Skills

As the end of the semester approaches, students will appreciate helpful ideas for preparing for and taking exams. Hint: You will find lots of test-taking and exam preparation tips in the Student Study Guide and in the teaching tips section of many chapters in this manual.

- Show slides with exam preparation tips as background during your lecture.
- Provide students a thorough exam review session close to the time of the final.
- Show slides with test-taking tips during your exam review section.

Sample Lecture Outline

Digital copy is available from Instructor's CD and web site.
http://www.whfreeman.com/understandingearth
Sample lecture outlines highlight the important topics and concepts covered in the text. We suggest that you download a digital copy of this outline from the web site and customize it to your own lecture before handing it out to students. At the end of each chapter outline, consider adding a selection of review questions, representing a range of thinking levels.

Chapter 21: Exploring Earth's Interior

Probing the Earth's Interior with Seismic Waves
Paths of Seismic Waves in the Earth
    Travel times
    Refraction
    Reflection
    Shadow zones
    Major discontinuities
Constraints on Composition
    Seismic wave velocities
    Earth's average density = 5.52 g/cc
    Rock samples from depth brought to the surface by volcanism
    Meteorites
    Natural abundance of the elements
Model for the Earth's Interior
    Crust (silica-rich silicates)
        Continental
        Oceanic
    Mohorovicic discontinuity ("Moho")
    Mantle (iron-rich silicates)
        Lithospheric mantle
        Asthenosphere & low-velocity zone
        Phase transitions at 400 and 600 km depth
        Lower mantle
    Core (mostly iron/nickel)
        Outer core (molten)
        Inner core (solid)
Earth's Internal Heat
    Geothermal gradient (20°C/km) in normal continental crust
    Sources of internal heat
        Radioactive decay
        Residual heat
        Accretion of planet
        Core formation
    Heat flow
        Convection
        Effects of convection
Three-Dimensional Structure of the Mantle
    Seismic tomography
    Gravity field variations
    The Geoid: Shape of the Earth
Earth's Magnetic Field
    Magnetic reversals
    Paleomagnetism
    Magnetic stratigraphy

CD and Web site Resources

Instructor's CD Highlights

- *Key Textbook Figures and Tables*

    Figure 21.2: P- and S-wave shadow zones

    Figure 21.5: Earth's layering revealed by seismology

    Figure 21.7: The structure of the mantle

    Figure 21.9: One estimate of the geotherm

    Figure 21.10: Cross-section showing the variations in S-wave velocity derived from seismic tomography

    Figure 21.11: Earth's magnetic field is much like the field that would be produced if a giant bar magnet were placed at the Earth's center.

    Figure 21.14: Newly formed sedimentary deposits can become magnetized in the same direction as the contemporaneous magnetic field of the Earth.

    Figure 21.15: The paleomagnetic time scale from 160 million years ago to the present

- *Photo Gallery:* Includes slide set images from the previous three editions.

Web site Highlights

http://www.whfreeman.com/understandingearth

- **Presentation Tools**

    Animations: Visit the web site for animations, including animations of figures from this chapter.
    PowerPoint Presentation
    PowerPoint Presentation with Lecture Notes
    Photo Gallery

- **Course Preparation**

    Instructor's Manual
    Sample Lecture Outline
    Sample Exercises

- **Student Study Resources—Assessable**

    Graded Online Quizzing
    Geology in Practice: Cleopatra's Emeralds (Peridot)(Journey from the Upper Mantle or A Window into the Upper Mantle
    > This *Geology in Practice* exercise can be used for in-class discussion, homework, or extra credit. Students are asked to hypothesize how peridote nodules in a lava flow formed and at what depth. Ultramafic nodules are one way geoscientists learn more about Earth's upper mantle.

- **Student Study Resources—Non-Assessable**

    Online Review Exercises:
    > Review the Terminology of the Earth's Interior
    > Review the Geography of the Earth's Interior

    Concept Self-Checker
    Flashcards

Teaching Tips

Cooperative Exercises and Assignments to Encourage Student Learning

Refer to Chapter 4: *Cooperative Learning Teaching Strategies* in the Instructional Design section of this manual for general ideas about conducting cooperative learning exercises in your classroom.

Coop Exercise #1: The Wave

by Randall Richardson, Department of Geosciences, University of Arizona, Tucson, Arizona

This is one of the most effective activities I've ever used. Before using it, students had a difficult time understanding the difference between longitudinal (P) and transverse (S) waves, which made it difficult to communicate that P and S waves give us different information about the Earth. Not only do students really learn the difference, they discover the relationship between wavelength, frequency, and speed, applicable to all waves.

The Wave

I have the class leave their seats and form a circle around the edge of the classroom (if necessary, they could make a double loop). I then ask them to do The Wave, as seen at football games, starting with a volunteer student. Then I ask them how long it took. To get data, they do it again, and measure the time (let's say 10 seconds). I ask them how many cycles they completed in the 10 seconds (one). "So, it's one cycle per ten seconds." What was the frequency of your wave? They work together and come up with 0.1 Hz. I ask them the distance around the circle (i.e., the wavelength; let's say it's 30 meters). "So, how fast did the wave go?" Again, in groups, they figure it went 30 m in 10 s, or 3 m/s. I ask them to do The Wave again in 5 seconds. They do, almost invariably laughing at the effort to speed it up. I ask them what frequency the wave had this time, and they figure out it is 0.2 Hz. "How fast did the wave go?" They realize it's 6 m/s, or twice as fast when the frequency is doubled. I ask them to work out a relationship between frequency (Hz, or 1/s), velocity (m/s), and wavelength that works out unit-wise and is consistent with their observations of the velocity doubling when the frequency is doubled (velocity = wavelength × frequency). I let them design further Wave experiments to verify the relationship.

An important concept for students to learn is the difference between longitudinal (or compressional) waves and transverse (or shear) waves. I ask them to do The Wave again, and ask them to notice how their hands move as the wave passes. They realize that The Wave moves horizontally from person to person, but their hands only move up and down, at right angles to the motion of The Wave. This is a transverse (at right angles) wave. Then I ask them to generate a longitudinal wave. They usually come up with something along the lines of stepping left or bumping shoulders, or (gently!) pulling on each other. They do this kind of a wave, and realize that their motion is horizontal, or aligned with the direction the wave moves. Then I tell them that sound waves are longitudinal waves and that water waves have a transverse component (an oversimplification). Longitudinal and transverse (P and S) waves in the Earth travel at different speeds, and hence give us different information about Earth structure.

Another concept I want them to learn is that energy is transported in waves without the medium actually moving the distance the wave travels. In their longitudinal wave I ask them if any student went all the way around the circle. "Of course not!" But it's clear that the energy did!

Finally, I play with waves reflecting off boundaries by having one student "bounce" the wave back when it gets to him/her, so that they can see it "reflect" off a boundary and travel in the other direction. I also let part of the wave be transmitted through the boundary and part reflected, and they have a lot of fun trying to have the wave go both ways.

There are probably endless variations on this, but I've never seen students come away with a better understanding of the differences between transverse and longitudinal waves, or the relationship between velocity, wavelength, and frequency, than when I've used this activity.

Sample Exercise from the Student Study Guide

Digital copy is available from Instructor's CD and web site.
http://www.whfreeman.com/understandingearth

Evidence for the Asthenosphere and Its Significance

This is a homework or extra credit exercise that requires students to articulate the evidence for the asthenosphere and its significance to plate tectonic theory.

Assignment

1. Briefly discuss one line of evidence supporting the presence of an asthenosphere in the upper mantle.

2. What is the significance of the asthenosphere to Plate Tectonic Theory?

Hint: Information in both Chapters 2 and 21 will help you complete this assignment.

Answers

1. Lines of evidence for the asthenosphere include:

    • Low Velocity Zone—Seismic waves travel slower through the asthenosphere than they do in shallower layers suggesting that this zone may be closer to the melting temperature of the rock and therefore softer. Refer to Figure 21.7.

    • Post-glacial isostatic rebound—Isostatic adjustments of the crust requires plastic flow in some part of the mantle in order to account for the displacement of the crust by the mantle as the crust is pushed down by the weight of the ice. Refer to *Earth Issues* boxes 21.1 and 21.2.

    Other evidence not discussed in the textbook includes:

    • Reduction in the frequency and magnitude of earthquakes between a depth of 175 and 350 km would be explained by a more ductile zone that is less likely to break and, if it does break, it does so with less build up of elastic strain energy.

    • When the projected geothermal gradient is plotted with the melting point curve for the rock thought to be in the mantle, the two curves converge and almost touch at a depth of between 100 to 150 km. This suggests that the rocks at this depth due to the combined effects of temperature and pressure are at or very close to melting.

    Note: For full credit, answers must clearly describe how the evidence supports the presence of an asthenosphere.

2. Essentially, the asthenosphere allows the lithosphere to be decoupled from the mantle. Plates apparently move due to the force of gravity, but without a ductile zone across which the plates can "slide," plate tectonics would probably not operate. Students may also discuss the possible role of convection currents within the upper mantle as a driving mechanism for plate tectonics.

General Education Skills Assignments

Chapter 21 develops ideas concerning seismology and paleomagnetism. Both of these content areas offer rich opportunities for assignments focused on mathematical skills. Consider adding special assignments that tap the following skills:

• Provide students simple graphs such as those in Figures 21.2, 21.5, and 21.7 and ask the students to summarize their interpretation of each graph.

• Ask them to interpret temperature curve such as the one shown in Figure 21.9.

   Suggestion: If you have not experimented with math-based assignments in the past you may be surprised at the difficulties some students have with graph interpretation. To anticipate some of these difficulties ahead of time, it will be helpful to talk to other faculty who have had success in structuring math assignments. Possible sources of help include: faculty in your home department and your campus learning and/or teaching centers. Also your math or math education department may be helpful. For example, at the University of Arizona we tapped a group of post-doctoral students in math-education who developed math assignments and trained special "math preceptors" to monitor and support the students as they worked on math assignments. Refer to Chapter 6 in the Instructional Design section and Appendices A–C in this manual for details about preceptors and contact information.

Freshman Survival Skills Resources

As the end of the semester approaches, students will appreciate helpful ideas for preparing for and taking exams. This is the perfect time to put up slides on test preparation during lecture. You may also want to recommend helpful test preparation workshops that may be offered by your campus learning or teaching center. Finally, if you have a class web site, consider posting some materials or links that will help students prepare for exams. **Hint:** There are some useful exam prep and test-taking tips in Chapter 21 of the Student Study Guide. See **Student Study Guide Highlights** below.

Topics for Class Discussion

- Where do you think scientists should start to drill if they want to reach the Moho in the shortest distance?
- If the Earth's outer core is molten, why doesn't the molten material rise to the surface and erupt from volcanoes?
- What would happen to the size of the P- and S-wave shadow zones if the size of the outer core was larger; was smaller?
- How deep have we drilled into the Earth and what have we learned from the hole?

  The deepest oil/gas wells in the United States are in Wyoming and Anadarko Basin. They range from about 7–8 kilometers (20,000 to 25,000 feet) deep. The deepest well is in the Russian Kola Peninsula near Finland where continental crust is about 35 kilometers thick. This well is down to about 10 kilometers (32,810 feet). In comparison, the Earth's center is 6400 km from the surface. The Kola well starts out about the size of an elevator shaft and is probably now between 0.5 to 1.0 meter in diameter. One surprising discovery from the Kola well is that rock at 10 km contained water-filled fractures. Conventional thinking was that at that depth pressures would be too great to maintain open fractures, even if they were fluid-filled. It was also thought that fluids would be very chemically reactive and combine with the silicate minerals. It's possible that the fractures and fluids are in some way a consequence of the drilling but apparently there is good evidence that they actually exist down at 10 km.

Teaching Resources

Student Study Guide Highlights

In Part I: Chapters provide strategies for learning geology. Ideally, students would read these chapters early in the course. But it's never to late to recommend or assign these chapters.

Chapter 1   Brief Preview of the *Study Guide for Understanding Earth* by Press, Siever, Grotzinger, and Jordan

Chapter 2   Meet the Authors of *Understanding Earth, 4th Edition:* How to use your geology textbook

Chapter 3   How to Be Successful in Geology (or just about any other challenging course)

Energy and Material Resources from the Earth

Chapter Summary

- Discovered resources consist of reserves—known deposits that can be mined economically today—and deposits that are known but that are currently subeconomic to mine.

- Oil and natural gas form from organic matter deposited in marine sediments. The organic materials are buried as the sedimentary layers grow in thickness. Heat, pressure, and bacterial action transform the organic matter into fluid hydrocarbons. The fluid hydrocarbons tend to migrate out of the source rock and accumulate in geologic traps that confine the fluids within impermeable barriers. Petroleum resources will be significantly depleted within about a century.

- Coal is formed by the compaction and mild metamorphism of buried wetland vegetation. The process by which coal beds form begins with the deposition of vegetation. Protected from complete decay and oxidation in a wetland environment, the deposit is buried and compressed into peat. Subjected to further burial, peat undergoes mild metamorphism, which transforms it successively into lignite, subbituminous and bituminous (soft) coal, and anthracite (hard) coal, as the deposit becomes more deeply buried, temperature rises, and structural deformation may occur. Coal currently accounts for about 23 percent of the energy consumed in the United States.

- Environmental concerns associated with the use of fossil fuels include mine reclamation, pollution, acid rain, and carbon dioxide emissions.

- Alternative energy resources include nuclear, geothermal, hydroelectric, wind, biomass, and solar. Like fossil fuels, there are significant economic, technological, environmental, and political concerns associated with alternative energy resources.

- Mineral deposits become ore deposits when they are rich and valuable enough to mine economically. Hydrothermal, metamorphic, chemical and mechanical weathering and sedimentary processes can enrich metal-bearing minerals to form economical deposits. Important non-metallic mineral deposits include limestone for cement, quartz sand for glass and fiber optics, gravel for concrete, clays for ceramics, evaporites like gypsum for plaster and wallboard, plus salts and fertilizers.

• Many metal ore deposits are formed by magmatic and hydrothermal processes, which are closely linked to both modern and ancient plate boundaries. Knowledge on how mineral deposits form and their association with plate boundaries has greatly facilitated the discovery of new deposits.

Learning Objectives

In this section we provide a *sampling* of possible objectives for this chapter. No class could or should try to accomplish all these. Choose based on your analysis of your class. Refer to Chapter 1: *Learning Objectives—How to Define Your Goals for the Class* in the Instructional Design section of this manual for thoughts and ideas about how to go about such an analysis.

Knowledge

- Know the difference between resources and reserves.
- Know how fossil fuels form.
- Know some of the ways the use of fossil fuels impacts our environment.
- Understand alternative sources of energy and the tradeoffs associated with their use.
- Know what an economical mineral deposit is.
- Know how ore deposits of metal-bearing minerals form.
- Understand and describe in a short essay how the formation of many natural resources is related to plate tectonics.

Skills/Applications/Attitudes

- Can think critically about energy issues.
- Appreciates that many of the natural resources we use today are non-renewable.
- Appreciates the long-range importance of energy and materials resources.

General Education Skills

This is a unique chapter. For your students, Chapter 22 represents a marvelous opportunity to do some clear thinking about some of the greatest challenges humans must face during the next hundred years.

Following are some learning objectives that lend themselves to writing, thinking, and debate.

- Can engage in an articulate debate concerning the tradeoffs involved with the use of energy and mineral resources, enumerating and discussing competing arguments.
- Can write a personal position paper defending one of the alternative positions (sustainable development, simpler lifestyle) described in *Earth Issues* box 22.3.
- Can defend one position by recognizing and addressing the best arguments of the opposition. (This could apply to either of the above activities. It is primarily a grading rubric suggestion.)
- Can differentiate between proven fact and opinion in a writing activity or debate. (Also a grading rubric suggestion.)
- Can lay out an argument in logical and convincing order. (Also a grading rubric suggestion.)
- Develops solutions that consider all relevant givens of the stated problem. (Also a grading rubric suggestion.)

Freshman Survival Skills

This is the next to last chapter and students will be very preoccupied with end-of-semester activities and getting ready for finals. It is a logical time to provide aids with exam preparation, test taking, or time management skills.

Sample Lecture Outline

Digital copy is available on the Instructor's CD and web site.
http://www.whfreeman.com/understandingearth
Sample lecture outlines highlight the important topics and concepts covered in the text. We suggest that you download a digital copy of this outline from the web site and customize it to your own lecture before handing it out to students. At the end of each chapter outline, consider adding a selection of review questions, representing a range of thinking levels.

Chapter 22: Energy and Material Resources from the Earth

Resources vs. Reserves
Energy Resources
    Fossil fuels
        World supply and demand
        Cost
    Petroleum/Natural gas
        Marine or delta environment
        Abundant organic debris
        Preservation/burial
        Prolonged bacterial activity
        Diagenesis (heat, pressure, time)
        Accumulation
        Migration of fluid hydrocarbons
        Geologic traps—structures, salt domes
        Source rock/reservoir rock/cap rock
    Coal
        Swamp environment
        Abundant *terrestrial plant* matter
        Relatively rapid burial—transgression
        Compaction
        Types
            Bituminous (soft coal)
            Anthracite (hard coal)
        Major periods of coal formation in the U.S.
            Mississippian/Pennsylvanian
            Cretaceous
    Alternative energy sources
        Nuclear
        Solar
        Geothermal
        Wind
        Hydroelectric
        Biomass
    Energy conservation and environmental policy
Mineral Resources
    Ore minerals
        Concentration factors
        Supply and demands

Geology of mineral deposits
    Hydrothermal
        Vein
        Disseminated
    Igneous
        Pegmatites
        Kimberlites
    Sedimentary
        Evaporites
            Gypsum
            Halite
            Phosphates
        Banded iron
        Placer
        Salt domes/oil
    Ore deposits and plate tectonics
The Need to Find New Mineral Deposits

CD and Web site Resources

Instructor's CD Highlights

- *Key Textbook Figures and Tables:*
  - Figure 22.3: Percentages of various types of energy used in the United States
  - Figure 22.5: Oil traps
  - Figure 22.8: The process by which coal beds form
  - Figure 22.13: World energy demand
  - Figure 22.16: Many ore deposits are found in hydrothermal veins
  - Figure 22.22: Enormous quantities of sulfide ores are found at mid-ocean spreading centers.
  - Figure 22.23: The role of plate tectonics in the accumulation of mineral deposits
  - Table 22.1: Economical Concentration Factors of Some Commercially Important Elements

- *Photo Gallery:* Includes slide set images from the previous three editions

Web site Highlights

http://www.whfreeman.com/understandingearth

- **Presentation Tools**

  Animations: Visit the web site for animations, including animations of figures from this chapter.
  PowerPoint Presentation
  PowerPoint Presentation with Lecture Notes
  Photo Gallery

- **Course Preparation**

  Instructor's Manual
  Sample Lecture Outline
  Sample Exercises

- **Student Study Resources—Assessable**

  Graded Online Quizzing
  Geology in Practice: "The Tempest in the Teapot"

This *Geology in Practice* exercise can be used for in-class discussion, homework, or extra credit.

For this exercise students are provided a reflection seismic section and background information on Teapot Dome in Wyoming and are asked to evaluate the best places to drill for oil based on their interpretation of the subsurface geologic structures.

- **Student Study Resources—Non-Assessable**

  Online Review Exercises:

  Identify the parts of the fossil fuel cycle
  Where do mineral deposits occur?
  Understanding our mineral resources
  Understanding mineral consumption and sustainability
  Drilling for oil (Part I)
  Drilling for oil (Part II)

  Concept Self-Checker
  Flashcards

Teaching Tips

Cooperative Exercises and Assignments to Encourage Student Learning

Refer to Chapter 4: *Cooperative Learning Teaching Strategies* in the Instructional Design section of this manual for general ideas about conducting cooperative learning exercises in your classroom.

Coop Exercise #1: Predict Which Well Will Pump Oil

The following review question would make a good in-class, Think/Pair/Share question.

(From the Student Study Guide, Chapter 22, Review Questions.)

Predict which well would give the best potential for oil and gas production.

A. Well A

B. Well B

C. Well C

D. Well D

Hint: Refer to Figure 22.5.

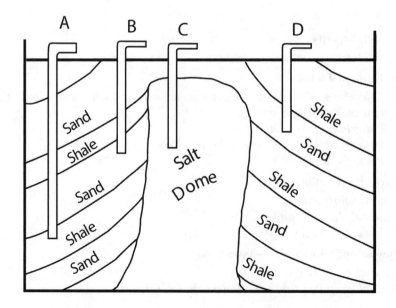

General Education Skills

Suppose your state's future governor happens to take your class this semester. Would that individual leave, better able to think and formulate rational energy policy? If any chapter in this book deserves a writing or thinking type of assignment, this is it. The following *Earth Policy* features in Chapter 22 lend themselves to writing, thinking, and class debate.

Earth Policy box 22.1: Subsurface Toxic and Nuclear Waste Contamination

Earth Policy box 22.2: Use of Federal Lands in the United States

Typically, the end of the semester is not a time when students do their best critical thinking. Consider the option of making this chapter a focal point for your course by assigning it early in the semester at a time when you think student energy can be galvanized to seriously consider the topics. Getting students to think about controversial topics is a key focus for some social science courses. Consider also a team effort with a colleague who teaches in a complimentary discipline in the social sciences and is accustomed to handling classroom debate.

Sample Critical Thinking Exercise
Oil Exploration Debate
by Randall Richardson, Department of Geosciences, University of Arizona, Tucson, Arizona

The effectiveness of this exercise is outstanding. Students, even years later, remembered not only the activity, but the content. The role-playing is extremely effective at helping students see other points of view and the complexity of such problems.

The Activity

Divide class into groups of four as they enter class. I have each person take a card upon entering, which gives a Group #, Role #, and Seat #. I do not tell them what the roles mean at this point. I ask them to take their assigned seat, take out a piece of paper and write their name and the information from the card on it (I don't want them later changing roles to something they are more comfortable with). An example of a card follows:

Group #7

Role #2

Seat #48

Sometimes in a 1.5-hour lecture, I first lecture on fossil fuels for 20–30 minutes. Other times I have handed out the lecture notes a day in advance and had them read them before class. Then I start with the exercise at the beginning of class.

The student roles are defined as follows:

#1: Ardent Supporter of Oil Exploration

#2: Ardent Opponent of Oil Exploration

#3: Mediator

#4: Reporter/Summarizer/Communicator

First, I have all the Role #1 students (ardent supporter of oil exploration) take two uninterrupted minutes to present their case for why we should continue an aggressive exploration program, in as flamboyant and convincing a case as possible, to the other students. If it doesn't sound like pandemonium, I tell them I can't hear them!

I tell the mediators (Role #3) to make sure that Role #1 is not interrupted, and that he/she sticks to the issues (no name calling, etc.).

Then I have Role #2 students (ardent opponent) take two minutes to present their case for why we should cease and desist with oil exploration immediately. I have the mediators (Role #3) play the same role as before.

I have the reporters take notes during both presentations. I tell them that they will have to provide a one paragraph "story" at the end summarizing the entire debate, and that some of them will be called upon to give a 90 second sound bite at the end, as if they were giving a news conference.

Then, I divide the class into the four corners of the room, with all the Role #1's in one corner, etc. I have each group talk among themselves. I tell Roles #1 and #2 to see if they come up with any more arguments as a group for their position than they were able to as individuals. I spend quite a bit of time with the mediators (Role #3), who often aren't sure what they are supposed to be doing. We talk about their feelings about being in the middle of a conflict. Do they feel "safe"? Are they uncomfortable in that situation? Do they feel they have to "solve" the conflict? I tell them that conflict is natural, that conflict resolution is an important skill, and that their role is to see that the other presenters play fair, not necessarily try to get them to agree with each other. We talk about what qualities a mediator should have (fair; trustworthy to both sides; keeps own opinion to themselves). I ask the reporters (Role #4) what it feels like trying to be an accurate reporter. What do they do with their own opinions? This whole part of the exercise takes about 10 minutes.

Then I have them return to their original groups of four and continue the debate. Only this time, they don't have to be rigid or flamboyant. They see if they can reach any consensus (not a requirement).

Then I ask one or two of the reporters to "report" to the class the results of the exercise for their group. I give them only 90 seconds each.

Then I have each one do some writing. I ask Roles #1 and #2 to put down the arguments they came up with by themselves first, followed in a second paragraph by any more that came up in the larger groups. For the mediators (Role #3), I ask them to list some skills a mediator should possess. I ask the reporters to write, in less than one page, a summary of the debate. I then ask all of them to finish by writing about whether or not their appreciation for the problem (its complexity in terms of societal and personal changes required to significantly reduce our dependence on oil) changed as a result of this exercise, and whether their own position had changed.

I have them turn in their reports, and either grade them as a quiz (separating all the roles so they can be compared to each other), or simply make comments on them before returning them.

Some of the points raised by those with various roles follow:
Role #1 (ardent supporter):

> Society needs oil for transportation, life style, etc.
>
> Enough oil for decades, at least. Why disrupt society now?
>
> Large parts of economy are dependent on oil exploration, production.
>
> No other option is currently available for cars on societal scale.
>
> When oil becomes scarce, prices will go up until it is economically feasible to pursue other energy sources.

Role #2 (ardent opponent):

> Major source of pollution and a continual risk to habitats.
>
> Cleaning up pollution is very expensive.
>
> We need to slow down using our limited natural resources.
>
> Global warming related to CO_2 from burning fossil fuels; we must curtail our usage or face possible global consequences.
>
> If we don't develop other sources now, then when oil becomes scarce, it will be very disruptive to society. Better to prepare now.

Role #3 (mediator):

> Skills of mediator include: flexibility, diplomacy, open mind (don't impose your own opinions), the ability to see both sides of an issue clearly and without bias, and the ability to allow both sides to communicate freely.

The entire exercise can be done in 1.5 hours, although sometimes it seems rushed. It's important to tell the students that they do not have to actually believe the position/role I've asked them to take. After all, they don't have a choice about the roles! I tell them that it is role playing, and an opportunity to explore an important issue that may well be pivotal in their lives.

Student response has been very positive. The exercise is often mentioned in course evaluations as one of the most positive experiences in the course. Even a year after this exercise, I sometimes see students who not only remember the exercise, but the issues. Thus, this seems a very effective way to improve retention.

The exercise can be generalized to a wide range of topics. Ones that come to mind immediately are global warming, use of any natural resource (water, for example), urban development, use of pesticides/fertilizers, etc.

Freshman Survival Skills Resources

As the end of the semester approaches, students will appreciate helpful ideas for preparing for and taking exams. This is the perfect time to put up slides on test preparation during lecture. You may also want to recommend helpful test preparation workshops that may be offered by your campus learning or teaching center. Finally, if you have a class web site, consider posting some materials or links that will help students prepare for exams.

Sample Tip

From the *Student Study Guide for Understanding Earth,* Chapter 22, Exam Prep

Tips for Surviving Finals Week

☐ Be organized and systematic. Use the **Final Exam Prep Worksheet (Appendix B)** to help you get organized for finals. Use the **Eight-Day Study Plan (Appendix A)** for every course where the final exam will be an important factor in determining your grade.

☐ Stick to priorities. Say no to distractions.

☐ Build in moments of relaxation: Take regular short breaks, exercise, and be sure to get enough sleep.

☐ Be confident. By now you have built up a good set of study habits. You are a competent learner.

Topics for Class Discussion

- Compare and contrast the conditions that led to the formation and accumulation of oil, gas, and coal.
- What makes a mineral deposit an ore deposit?
- Describe igneous processes and weathering processes that can form an ore deposit.
- T. S. Lovering said, "Deposits must be mined where they occur. Each deposit has its limits." Discuss what this statement mean.
- What is an evaporite? What is meant by the statement: "Man can live without gold but not without salt"?
- Formation of Ore Deposits

    Mobilize Earth's materials to form ore deposits with—
    Solvent = water + salt
    Increase heat and/or pressure
    Increase fluid flow through fractured rock.

- Generalized Stages of Copper Enrichment

    Average natural abundance of copper $\approx 0.005\%$ Cu
    Igneous and volcanic processes $\rightarrow 0.5\%$ Cu
    Weathering processes $\rightarrow 1.0\%$ Cu
    Mining, smelting, and refining $\rightarrow 99.999\%$ Cu

• Copper Concentrations in the Natural Environment

100 ppm (part per million) = 0.01%
Copper in people ≈ 1.7 ppm
Copper in plants ≈ 10 ppm
Copper in soils ≈ 20 ppm
Copper in drinking water ≈ 0.03 ppm
Copper in ocean water = 0.003 ppm
Copper in continental crust ≈ 15 ppm
Copper in ocean crust = 100 ppm

Teaching Resources

Student Study Guide Highlights

In Part I: Chapters provide strategies for learning geology. Ideally, students would read these chapters early in the course. But it's never too late to recommend or assign these chapters.

Chapter 1   Brief Preview of the *Study Guide for Understanding Earth* by Press, Siever, Grotzinger, and Jordan

Chapter 2   Meet the Authors of *Understanding Earth, 4th Edition:* How to use your geology textbook

Chapter 3   How to Be Successful in Geology (or just about any other challenging course)

Part II. Chapter 22: *Energy and Material Resources from the Earth*

Before Lecture:

Preview Questions & Brief Answers

Vital Information from Other Chapters

During Lecture:

Note-Taking Tip

After Lecture:

Check Your Notes

Intensive Study Session

Exam Prep:

Tips for Surviving Finals Week

Chapter Summary

Review Questions (Answers to all review questions are given at the end of the Study Guide.)

Web site on Critical Thinking

The Foundation for Critical Thinking (www.criticalthinking.org) publishes useful guides on using critical thinking in problem solving. Two examples of their miniature guides are:

Critical Thinking Concepts & Tools by Dr. Richard Paul and Dr. Linda Elder, and *How to Study & Learn a Discipline* by Dr. Richard Paul and Dr. Linda Elder.

You may find this literature helpful in constructing critical thinking exercises and fostering debate in the classroom.

U.S. Geological Survey Web Site: Are We Running Out of Oil?

by L. B. Magoon

http://geopubs.wr.usgs.gov/open-file/of00-320/

This publication is a poster approximately 33 inches wide by 17 inches high. For your convenience, we have provided the poster as a PDF document and as a PostScript file. This report is only available on the web.

This publication is an excellent source of current information and graphics for lectures on fossil fuels.

Science, Sustainability, and the Human Prospect

by Peter H. Raven

American Academy for the Advancement of Science, Presidential Address, February, 2002.

Science, August 9, 2002, vol 297, pages 954–958. (www.sciencemag.org)

This article is a superb basis for a one- to two-page review and analysis by students. (Writing/Critical Thinking)

CHAPTER 23

Earth's Environment, Global Change, and Human Impacts

Chapter Summary

- Humans are geologic agents with global impacts of a magnitude equal or greater than natural processes.

- Quantitative models manipulated with large computers help geoscientists better understand complex geosystems, like climate and Earth's interior.

- Components of the climate system are the atmosphere, hydrosphere, lithosphere, and biosphere.

- Albedo of the Earth's surface, plus the greenhouse effect, are significant factors in Earth's energy balance. Human activities significantly impact both these factors.

- Much of the radiant energy from the Sun passes through the atmosphere and is absorbed by Earth's surface. The warmed surface radiates heat back to the atmosphere as infrared radiation. Carbon dioxide and other trace atmospheric gases are transparent to sunlight but absorb heat (infrared radiation). In this way, the atmosphere acts like the glass in a greenhouse, allowing solar radiant energy to pass through but trapping heat.

- Positive and negative feedback mechanisms can stabilize or destabilize the climate system. Positive feedbacks tend to amplify changes in the system, whereas negative feedbacks tend to stabilize the system against change. Examples of some feedbacks within the climate system are water vapor, albedo, radiation, and plant growth.

  Various factors contribute to long and short-term climate change. The Pleistocene cycles of glacial and interglacial climatic conditions may have been triggered by changes in Earth's orbital parameters (Milankovitch cycles). Changes in ocean circulation (North Atlantic) and sea-surface temperatures (El Niño in the equatorial Pacific) are linked to shorter-term fluctuations in climate.

- Twentieth-century warming of global climate is linked to a human-induced enhanced greenhouse effect from the burning of fossil fuels.

- Geochemical cycles trace the flux of Earth's elements like carbon from one reservoir to another. Understanding the carbon cycle is important because of its strong link to life processes, climate change, and plate tectonic processes.

  • Acid rain, ozone depletion, and global warming due to the release of carbon dioxide from the burning of fossil fuels are major environmental concerns.

Learning Objectives

In this section we provide a *sampling* of possible objectives for this chapter. No class could or should try to accomplish all these. Choose based on your analysis of your class. Refer to Chapter 1: *Learning Objectives—How to Define Your Goals for the Class* in the Instructional Design section of this manual for thoughts and ideas about how to go about such an analysis.

Knowledge

  • Know that the primary source of water and gases on the Earth's surface is volcanic gas, which is released from the planet's interior over geologic time.

  • Know that oxygen gas was and continues to be added to Earth's atmosphere and oceans by photosynthetic organisms.

  • Know when life appeared on Earth and how life evolved over geologic time.

  • Understand how carbon dioxide and other trace atmospheric gases are transparent to sunlight but absorb heat (IR radiation), which warms Earth's surface environments, as in a greenhouse.

  • Know how cycles trace the flux of Earth's elements like carbon from one reservoir to another.

  • Understand how human activities (pollution/CFCs/acid rain) and natural events (bolide impact) can significantly alter geochemical cycles and therefore impact Earth's environmental conditions.

Skills/Applications/Attitudes

  • Appreciate and describe how life processes are an integral part of many of Earth's geochemical cycles.

  • Understand and appreciate the significance of linkages between the carbon cycle, life processes, and climate change.

General Education Skills

  • Articulate in a short position paper important global change issues, such as the Greenhouse Effect and population growth, and their potential impact on individuals and societies. (Writing/ Critical Thinking)

  • Given an unlabeled version of the graph shown in Figure 23.7, student can identify the 100,000 year glacial and interglacial periods. The graphs in this chapter offer another opportunity for students to practice graphic interpretation.

  • Given an unlabeled version of the graph in Figure 23.8, student can identify and interpret the industrial revolution or other interesting features specified.

Freshman Survival Skills

As the end of the semester approaches, students will appreciate helpful ideas for preparing for and taking exams. **Hint:** You will find lots of test-taking and exam preparation tips in the Student Study Guide and in the teaching tips section of many chapters in this manual.

  • Show slides with exam preparation tips as background during your lecture.

  • Provide students a thorough exam review session close to the time of the final.

- Show slides with test-taking tips during your exam review section.
- Encourage students to use the **Eight-Day Study Plan** and the **Final Exam Prep Worksheet** to ensure organized review for their end-of-semester exams. These materials are **Appendices A** and **B** of the *Student Study Guide for Understanding Earth*.

Sample Lecture Outline

Digital copy is available on the Instructor's CD and web site.
http://www.whfreeman.com/understandingearth
Sample lecture outlines highlight the important topics and concepts covered in the text. We suggest that you download a digital copy of this outline from the web site and customize it to your own lecture before handing it out to students. At the end of each chapter outline, consider adding a selection of review questions, representing a range of thinking levels.

Chapter 23: Earth's Environment, Global Change, and Human Impacts
Studying Geosystems with Quantitative Models
The Climate System
    Components
        Atmosphere
        Hydrosphere
        Lithosphere
        Biosphere
    Albedo
    Greenhouse Effect
        Maintains earth's surface temperature at about 33°C warmer
        Greenhouse gases: water, carbon dioxide, methane, others
    Feedback Mechanisms
        Positive—amplifies changes
        Negative—stabilizes changes
        Some feedbacks within climate system
            Water vapor
            Albedo
            Radiation
            Plant growth
Limitations of Climate Models
Natural Climate Variability
    Long-term variations
        Milankovitch cycles—glacial/interglacial
        Concentration of greenhouse gases in Earth's atmosphere
    Short-term variations
        Ocean circulation
        Volcanic eruptions
        El Niño—Southern Oscillation
Twentieth-Century Warming
    Mean surface temperature rose by about 0.6°C
    Enhanced greenhouse effect due to the release of carbon dioxide from the burning of fossil fuels
Geochemical Cycles
    Residence time
    Chemical reactions

Transport across interfaces
Calcium cycle
Carbon Cycle
Air-sea exchange
Photosynthesis and respiration in the terrestrial biosphere
Dissolved organic carbon
Carbonate weathering and precipitation
Human perturbations
Human Activity and Global Change
Acid rain
Stratospheric ozone depletion
Global warming

CD and Web site Resources

Instructor's CD Highlights

- *Key Textbook Figures and Tables*

    Figure 23.3: Components and interactions of Earth's climate system
    Figure 23.6: Earth's radiation budget
    Figure 23.7: Climate data from the Vostok ice core
    Figure 23.6: Twentieth-century warming
    Figure 23.10: The calcium cycle
    Figure 23.11: The geochemical carbon cycle
    Figure 23.12: Fluxes of carbon
    Table 23.1: Potential Climate-Change Effects on Various Systems

- *Photo Gallery:* Includes slide set images from the previous three editions.

Web site Highlights

http://www.whfreeman.com/understandingearth

- **Presentation Tools**

    Animations: Visit the web site for animations, including animations of figures from this chapter.
    PowerPoint Presentation
    PowerPoint Presentation with Lecture Notes
    Photo Gallery

- **Course Preparation**

    Instructor's Manual
    Sample Lecture Outline
    Sample Exercises

- **Student Study Resources—Assessable**

    Graded Online Quizzing

        Geology in Practice: How many pounds of coal does it take to copy MP3's (electronic music files) from the Internet? This exercise explores the inefficiencies of electric power generation and transmission. Students will discover that it takes about two pounds of coal and that four pounds of carbon dioxide are released into the atmosphere for each megabyte. *Geology in Practice* exercises can be used for in-class discussion, homework, or extra credit.

• **Student Study Resources—Non-Assessable**

Online Review Exercises:

> Identify the Parts of the Carbon Cycle
> Understanding the Types of Waste Produced by Humans
> Landfill Field Trip

Concept Self-Checker

Flashcards

Teaching Tips

Cooperative Exercises and Assignments to Encourage Student Learning

Refer to Chapter 4: *Cooperative Learning Teaching Strategies* in the Instructional Design section of this manual for general ideas about conducting cooperative learning exercises in your classroom.

Coop Exercises

The following questions are thought provoking and make good, brief in-class Think/Pair/Share exercises. (From the *Student Study Guide for Understanding Earth,* Chapter 23, Review Questions.)

It has been suggested that the uplift of the Himalayan Mountains and the Tibetan Plateau could have contributed to or even caused a global cooling. The link between the Himalayan Mountains and climatic cooling is likely related to

> A. the collision of India with Asia, triggering volcanism and increasing the CO_2 concentration in the atmosphere.
> B. the uplift intensifying the monsoon and associated physical and chemical weathering, which resulted in a drawdown of carbon dioxide from the atmosphere.
> C. the fact that high mountains generate more clouds, and their albedo (reflectivity) cools the Earth's surface.
> D. El Niño and the North Atlantic deep water current.

Answer: B. Refer to Pages 556–557: *Carbonate Weathering and Precipitation*

Ozone is a very reactive gas, so, as a pollutant in the lower atmosphere, ozone presents a significant health hazard. Why does ozone exist in the stratosphere?

> A. It is constantly leaking from the troposphere, where it is produced, up to the stratosphere.
> B. It is formed from the release of gasses out of the micrometeoric dusts that bombard the upper atmosphere.
> C. It is formed continuously in the stratosphere by solar radiation and cannot mix or react with other gasses because of the thin atmosphere at that altitude.
> D. It is produced constantly from the oceans and rises through the troposphere to the stratosphere.

Answer: C. Refer to page 560: *Stratospheric Ozone Depletion.*

As the oceans become warmer, _____ CO_2 is released from the oceans into the atmosphere resulting in a _____ feedback.

> A. more/positive
> C. more/negative
> B. less/negative
> D. less/positive

Hint: Is CO_2 more or less soluble in warmer water? Refer to Chapter 17.

Answer: A.

Sample Exercise from the Student Study Guide for Understanding Earth
Digital copy is available on the Instructor's CD and web site.
http://www.whfreeman.com/understandingearth

Exercise 3: Flow of Carbon Through Earth's Systems and Reservoirs
Carbon dioxide is an important greenhouse gas, which can greatly impact Earth's surface temperatures. Because the Earth is a closed system, the carbon cycle and distribution of carbon in the various reservoirs is a very important component to any model for how climate changes.

Fill out the table below to summarize the flow of carbon through Earth's systems and reservoirs. Flux is the amount of energy or matter flowing through a given area or reservoir in a given time. Refer both to Figures 23.6, 23.11, 23.12, and the accompanying text in Chapter 23.

Carbon fluxes	Brief description of flux	Direction of flux	Climatic impact/ implications
Life processes	Carbon is fixed in living organisms, which ultimately contribute to organic matter in sediments, coal, and oil.	Carbon flows from the atmosphere and oceans into rock—the lithosphere.	
Sedimentation	Calcium and carbonate ions combine to produce calcium carbonate, which can precipitate and collect to form limestone or help cement other rock particles.		**Climate cools.** Carbon dioxide is drawn out of the oceans and atmosphere. The loss of CO_2 from the oceans will result in a reduction of CO_2 in the atmosphere.
Volcanism			
Chemical weathering	CO_2 in rainwater combines with minerals in rock to form calcium carbonate.	Carbon flows from the atmosphere and oceans into the crust.	**Climate cools.** Carbon is being drawn out of surface environments and stored in the crust. Uplift of high plateaus and mountains may enhance this flux.
Metamorphism	Heating, recrystallization, and decomposition of rocks during metamorphism can release large amounts of CO_2.	Carbon flows from the rocks (the crust) into the atmosphere and oceans.	**Climate warms.** Increased CO_2 in the atmosphere enhances the Greenhouse Effect, which acts to trap heat energy and slow down the loss of heat to space.
Human activities combustion of fossil fuels	The burning of fossil fuels releases large amounts of CO_2 into the atmosphere.	Carbon flows from the lithosphere (coal, oil, and gas) into the oceans and atmosphere.	

General Education Skills Assignment
If you had your students try some graphic interpretation in relation to earlier chapters, then Chapter 23 offers an opportunity to reinforce those skills with a follow-up exercise. This could take the form of an extra credit assignment, an in-class exercise, or even an item on your exam.

Example
Provide an unlabeled version of the graph shown in Figure 23.7 and have students identify the 100,000 year glacial and interglacial periods. There are many possible variations on this assignment. For example, you could give the students unlabeled graphs showing 10,000-year climate cycles or 1000-year climate cycles or other interesting climate temperature features you have discussed during your lecture.

Freshman Survival Skills Resources

As the end of the semester approaches, students will appreciate helpful ideas for preparing for and taking exams. This is the perfect time to put up slides on test preparation during lecture. You may also want to recommend helpful test preparation workshops that may be offered by your campus learning or teaching center. Finally, if you have a class web site, consider posting some materials or links that will help students prepare for exams.

Topics for Class Discussion

- How can a major volcanic eruption cause climate change?
- Outline the carbon cycle and briefly describe the relationship between silicate rock weathering, the concentration of CO_2 in the atmosphere, and the temperature of the atmosphere.
- Discuss three things you can do to mitigate the Greenhouse Effect.
- What are the long-term ecological, economic, and geological consequences of acid rain?

pH of Common Substances

Substance	pH
Lime juice	2
Tomato juice	4
Black coffee	5
Milk	6
Pure water & blood	7
Seawater	8
Household ammonia	12

Teaching Resources

Student Study Guide Highlights

In Part I: Chapters provide strategies for learning geology. Ideally, students would read these chapters early in the course. But it's never too late to recommend or assign these chapters.

Chapter 1   Brief Preview of the *Study Guide for Understanding Earth* by Press, Siever, Grotzinger, and Jordan

Chapter 2   Meet the Authors of *Understanding Earth, 4th Edition:* How to use your geology textbook

Chapter 3   How to Be Successful in Geology (or just about any other challenging course)

Part II. Chapter 23: *Earth's Environment, Global Change, and Human Impacts*

Before Lecture:

Preview Questions & Brief Answers

Vital Information from Other Chapters

During Lecture:

After Lecture:

Check Your Notes

Intensive Study Session

Exam Prep:

Chapter Summary

Practice Exercises: *Conceptual Map/Flowchart of a Climate Factor*
Release of Carbon Dioxide from Burning of Fossil Fuels
Flow of Carbon Through Earth's Systems and Reservoirs

Review Questions (Answers to all review questions are given at the end of the Study Guide.)

Test-Taking Tip

Web sites on Climate Change, Global Warming, and the Kyoto Protocol

Exploring Climate Events and Human Development
http://www.ngdc.noaa.gov/paleo/ctl/cliihis.html

A Paleo Perspective on Global Warming
http://www.ngdc.noaa.gov/paleo/globalwarming/home.html

The National Academy of Sciences Report: *A Closer Look at Global Warming*
http://www4.nationalacademies.org/onpi/webextra.nsf/web/climate?OpenDocument

U.S. Global Change Program
http://www.usgcrp.gov/

The Intergovernmental Panel on Climate Change (IPCC) was established by WMO and UNEP to assess scientific, technical, and socio-economic information relevant for the understanding of climate change, its potential impacts, and options for adaptation and mitigation.
http://www.ipcc.ch/

Kyoto Protocol to the United Nations Framework Convention on Climate Change
http://www.unfccc.de/resource/docs/convkp/kpeng.html

English Conference of the Parties, Third Session Kyoto, 1–10 December, 1997
http://www.cnn.com/SPECIALS/1997/global.warming/stories/treaty/

"The farther backward you can look,
the farther forward you are likely to see."

—WINSTON CHURCHILL

Geosciences Preceptorship/ Teaching Workshop

Congratulations and welcome!! I am very glad that you, a distinguished student at the U of A, have chosen to participate in this Undergraduate Teaching Workshop. Teaching and sharing your excitement for something with others is personally very rewarding. I predict that you will look back at your experiences as an Undergraduate Teaching Assistant (UTA) as one of the most meaningful opportunities of your college career. What is a UTA? You are a leader, an enthusiast, a nurturer, a coach, a facilitator, a cheerleader, and much more!

Our principal goal is to enhance our effectiveness as teachers by improving our ability to communicate, motivate, organize, and work as an enthusiastic team to facilitate students' learning experiences. I expect nothing less than consistent and responsible dedication and professionalism toward our departmental efforts to provide the best possible environment for learning.

PERFECTION
Aspire to it;
Desire it;
Admire it;
But don't
require it.

—ANNIE KOMOMY

Opportunities/Moral Obligations/Burden of Proof!
Primary Responsibilities

1. Work as a team with the Graduate Teaching Assistant in teaching one lab section per week. Plus, serve as the principal instructor for one lab exercise, as preplanned with your graduate partner and faculty sponsor.

NOTE: This handout is given to new preceptors—undergraduate teaching assistants. Preceptors are an important part of our teaching team. They are excellent undergraduate students who have completed the course for which they will be serving as a teaching assistant. Preceptors participate in a workshop on teaching and communication skills concurrently with their service as a teaching assistant in a lab, workshop, or lecture.

2. Participate in weekly workshop meetings to discuss communication, motivational, and teaching skills.
3. Serve as a tutor in the Geosciences Learning Center for one hour per week.
4. Serve as an assistant for at least one lecture field trip.
5. Prepare a journal that characterizes your experiences (both accomplishments and challenges) teaching this semester. Journal is submitted to the faculty sponsor by the last day of classes.
6. Prepare a career portfolio with a resume and career statement.

Secondary Responsibilities

1. Help grade lab work.
2. Help with lectures.
3. Proctor lecture exams.
4. Provide feedback.

Special Opportunities

1. Plan and lead a new field trip.
2. Develop and grade a new extra credit exercise for lab or lecture.
3. Find, preview, and prepare videos for lab or lecture.
4. Design, build, and perform demonstrations for lab or lecture.
5. Give guest lectures at local schools on request.

Your Journal and Career Portfolio (due on the last day of classes)

The main purpose of your Journal is to provide both of us with candid and thoughtful feedback on your experiences both in class and in the workshop while serving as a preceptor. You may choose to address anything in your Journal that is relevant to being a UTA. For example, you might share how a positive (or negative) comment by one of your students affected you. Or, you might run across an article or quote in the newspaper, a magazine, or a book that inspires and motivates you with respect to your teaching. Record this cerebral and/or emotional encounter and share your thoughts on it.

Be creative and perceptive in your thoughts and observations. I would imagine that each Journal will be unique to its creator. Nevertheless, here is a general format to follow:

A. A statement on your philosophy of teaching
B. All materials you developed and/or used for teaching your lab exercise
C. A statement summarizing each preceptor workshop, what you contributed, and what you found particularly useful about the workshops
D. Your career portfolio
   Resume
   Career goals statement

Feedback/Evaluation/Basis for a Grade

We are all in this as a team! The graduate teaching assistants and I expect you to freely express constructive feedback to us throughout the semester and you can expect us to reciprocate. Our goal is to improve your teaching skills and enhance the general environment for learning. Please do not take things personally. I expect people to be responsive and to react! If we ever come on too strong, it's an expression of how much we care about your efforts and growth.

Your final evaluation (grade) will be based on the following:

1. A written evaluation by Graduate Teaching Assistant
2. Student, graduate teaching assistant, and faculty evaluations
3. Your career portfolio
4. Your Journal

Think as wise men do, but speak as the common people do.

—Aristotle

Sample Course Schedule for the Geoscience Preceptorship/ Teaching Workshop

Workshop Date	Topic
August 27	Organizational meeting
September 3	Creating a positive learning environment
September 10	Your best teacher exercise / career portfolio info
September 17	Communications
September 24	Round table discussion
October 1	Evaluating performance / grading (Dr. Beth Harrison)
October 8	Constructive feedback
	Career Portfolios due for preliminary review / feedback
October 15	Personality types
October 22	Learning styles
October 29	Learning and the structure of the brain
November 5	Career planning
November 12	Special topics: Teaching and public speaking
November 19	Reports on career exploration interview with a professional
November 26	No class (Thanksgiving)
December 3	Showcase display / Course evaluations/ *Portfolios due*

Basic Premises of the Preceptorship

- Almost anyone can teach if they want to and work at it.
- Teaching is not just regurgitation—it is not just the spilling out of information!
- Teaching involves:
  - Motivating people to learn
  - Making topics relevant
  - Being creative
  - Being enthusiastic

Geoscience Preceptor's Journal/Career Portfolio

Goals and Purpose of Your Journal/Career Portfolio

- Summary of your skills, experience, personal and professional development
- Presentation at a job or graduate school interview

Portfolio Contents

- Personal Information
    - Resume
    - Career statement
- Awards/Honors
- Evaluations
    - Student, preceptor, and supervisor evaluations
    - Letters of recommendation
- Preceptor workshops
    - Examples of what you did in the workshops
    - Summary of your activities
    - Assignments
    - Analysis of workshops and their application as applied by you in the classroom
    - Samples of instructional materials you developed and contributed to
- Samples of your work
    - Materials you developed for a presentation in lab, lecture, or on a field trip

Sample Guidelines for Team Roles and Responsibilities

Below are guidelines for effective and efficient teamwork. You may find these guidelines useful, especially for organizing teamwork for the Plate Tectonics and Water Resources Projects. Print your name in the box indicating which role you will serve as a team member. Whether team members rotate roles each week or hold the same role for the entire project is up to the each team to decide.

DATES
Leader
Recorder and
Spokesperson
Monitor

Description of Roles

Leader

- Makes sure everyone understands the assignment and logistics.
- Ensures that all members participate and work productively.
- Facilitates resolution of any conflicts among team members.
- Organizes team work sessions outside of the weekly workshop session.
- In case of an emergency, appoints or serves as a substitute for any absent team member.

Recorder and spokesperson

- Records team responses, discussions, and ideas for presentation to class and for team members.
- Organizes progress reports, team questions, and caucus discussions with instructor and other teams.
- Fills out this *Team Roles and Responsibilities* record sheet.

Monitor

- Takes responsibility for rock and mineral specimens.
- Picks up and returns team file folder.
- Ensures that team members have the necessary equipment and supplies during the workshops.
- Ensures that workshop activities for each week are complete and assignments are turned into the instructor by putting assignments into the team file folder.

Workshop Team Records

This RECORD SHEET will help your team manage time and the assignment of responsibilities more effectively. The Team Recorder fills this sheet out each week.

NAMES	ROLES	Date:	Date:	Date:
Attendance				
1.				
2.				
3.				
Homework				
1.				
2.				
3.				
Assignments for individual team members				
1.				
2.				
3.				
Assignments for caucus on April 3 & 4				
1.				
2.				
3.				
Assignments for final oral presentation on April 10–18				
1.				
2.				
3.				
NOTES: Meetings outside of the workshop session, etc.				

Annotated Bibliography

T his is a list of favorites. We believe a highly selected sample of books, articles, and internet materials on instructional design is more likely to be of use to college instructors than a ponderous coverage of the vast literature on college teaching. These are the books that we most regularly recommend to colleagues.

Active Learning

Bonwell, C.C. & J. Eison. (1991). Active Learning: Creating Excitement in the Classroom. *ASHE-ERIC Higher Education Report, 1*.

The former chair of our Molecular and Cellular Biology Department at the University of Arizona regularly gave copies of this fine little book to faculty in the hopes of encouraging good science teaching. It contains many useful ideas and exercises that will foster active learning in your classroom. If you have one book on college teaching on your shelf, this should be it.

Attitudes: Measures for Geology Course Assessments

Libarkin, J. (1999). Inquiry-Based Instruction in the General Education Laboratory. *National Association of Research in Science Teaching: Final Program and Abstracts, 72*(200).

Libarkin, J. (1999). The Science Education Assessment Project (SEAP): Evaluation of Science Teaching in Undergraduate Courses for Non-Majors. *GSA Abstracts with Programs, A410*.

Libarkin, J.C. (2001). Development of an Assessment of Student Conception of the Nature of Science. *Journal of Geosciences Education, 49*(5), 435–442.

As part of her NSF post-doc, Libarkin developed a series of scales that tap several attitude dimensions that are relevant to learning geology:

1) Conception that science is static
2) Conception that science is evolving
3) Attitude toward geology
4) Attitude toward learning geology

For further information about her measures, contact:

Julie C. Libarkin (Ph.D., Geosciences)
Science Education Department
Harvard-Smithsonian Center for Astrophysics
60 Garden St. MS-71
Cambridge, MA 02138
(617)496-4795
fax: (617)496-5405

Julie C. Libarkin (Ph.D., Geosciences)
NSF Post-Doctoral Fellow in SMET Education
University Learning Center
University of Arizona
Tucson, AZ 85721
(520)626-7734
fax: (520)621-5015

Cooperative Learning

Johnson, D.W., R.T. Johnson, & K.A. Smith. (1991). Cooperative Learning: Increasing College Faculty Instructional Productivity. *ASHE-ERIC Higher Education Report, 4.* Washington, D.C.: George Washington University, School of Education and Human Development.

The ERIC Digest version of this article can be accessed on the web.
http://www.ed.gov/databases/ERIC_Digests/ed347871.html

The web version describes some of the basic variations of collaborative learning (e.g. **informal vs. formal** learning groups) and cites relevant literature reviews (several of these reviews were cited in Chapter 4 of this manual).

The full article (available from ERIC for $17) provides training on collaborative learning in a format appropriate for college professors. Johnson takes a conceptual approach: he teaches principles one can apply to build one's own activities, lessons, and strategies. He encourages faculty to "branch out and try things on their own," using good principles of cooperative learning as a foundation.

Teaching Teams Program (University of Arizona)
http://hal.lpl.arizona.edu/teachingteams/

This site contains helpful ideas about how to make use of undergraduate preceptors as full partners in your classroom instruction. Some of these ideas concern cooperative learning experiences during large lectures. See the instructor section of the site for materials that will help you get started.

Michaelsen, L., L. Black, & L. Fink. (1996). What Every Faculty Developer Needs to Know About Learning Groups. In L. Richlin (Ed.), *To Improve the Academy: Resources for Faculty, Instructional and Organizational Development.* Stillwater, Oklahoma: New Forums Press.

Formal learning groups are collaborative groups that work together for an entire semester or project. Increasing numbers of instructors are finding this approach advantageous to learning. If such an approach interests you, you will find Michaelsen a very helpful reference. Many useful suggestions about setting up groups, structuring activities, and grading group projects are included.

Prescott, S. (1996) Trouble Shooting Cooperative Learning. *Cooperative Learning and College Teaching 6(3):10–11.*

Another useful reference for instructors who are considering formal learning groups. Susan Prescott is a nationally known expert on cooperative/collaborative learning. This article provides suggestions for dealing with students who say they do not want to be in a collaborative group, fail to contribute, make complaints about someone on their team, or visit with others during the team's work time. Susan Prescott has written many other helpful articles on cooperative/collaborative learning for this same journal.

Critical Thinking

Critical Thinking Consortium
www.criticalthinking.org
Helpful materials and professional development activities for college faculty interested in critical thinking.

> Lynch, C. & S. Wolcott. (2001). Helping Your Students Develop Critical Thinking Skills. *Idea Paper # 37.* Manhattan, KS: The Idea Center, 211 South Seth Child Road, 66502.
>
> Email: IDEA@KSU.edu

This very useful little paper lays out a model of how student thinking develops during the college years, relating student development to the design of educational experiences. A must read for anyone who is serious about teaching students to think clearly.

> Paul, R. & L. Elder. (2001). The Miniature Guide to Critical Thinking. *Foundations for Critical Thinking.*

A brief and helpful introduction to Richard Paul's critical thinking model. Contains useful materials you can adapt and hand out to your students. Available through the web site of the Critical Thinking Consortium (see above).

> Van Sickle, M. & W. Kubinec. (2000). Transformation Teaching: A Physics Professor's Thoughts. *Journal of College Science Teaching, 32*(4):258–263.

Moving from the traditional lecture style to teaching that fosters student learning and the development of habits of clear thinking is, to say the least, a challenging transition. This inspiring article describes the evolution of one teacher of physics. A good article to read when you become discouraged.

Evaluation

> Angelo, T. & K.P. Cross. (1993). *Classroom Assessment Techniques.* (2nd ed.). San Francisco, CA: Jossey-Bass.

Angelo and Cross are considered the primary source for practical approaches to classroom evaluation.

> *9 Principles of Good Practice for Assessing Student Learning*
> American Association for Higher Education (AAHE) Assessment Forum
> http://www.aahe.org/assessment/principl.htm

This site provides very useful ideas to guide your course assessment projects.

Internet Information for Students

> Wilkes, Glenda. *Information on the Internet.* University Teaching Center, University of Arizona, www.utc.arizona.edu.

Assignments requiring research on the Internet represent an exciting means of access to information for students. But students need guidance about how to think critically and how to judge the quality of information they find. Wilkes provides that guidance. She also includes valuable links to information about the capabilities of various search engines and how to cite information one finds on the web.

Learning Styles/Multiple Intelligences

Gardner, H. 1983. *Frames of Mind: The Theory of Multiple Intelligences.* New York: Basic Books.

While controversial, Gardner's theory of multiple Intelligences should be read by all who educate. Intriguing as theory, yet loaded with practical implications for what we do in the classroom.

Mathematical Class Activities for Geology Classes

Vacher, H.L. Computional Geology 13—Geological-Mathematical Activities for College Students. *Journal of Geological Education,* 1990–1999, *Journal of Geological Education,* 48(3). National Association of Geosciences Teachers.

This article presents a bibliography of 212 articles, published in the *Journal of Geological Education,* that describe and discuss exercises or projects that use mathematical computations and/or mathematical reasoning. These activities are for a variety of instructional settings, including the classroom, laboratory, field trips, and homework.

Study Skills Online Resources

Lecture Note Taking. Saint Johns College Academic Unit.
http://www.csbsju.edu/academicadvising/help/lec-note.html
Helpful one-page handout on note taking.

Editing Lecture Notes. Virginia Polytechnic Institute, Division of Student Affairs.
http://www.ucc.vt.edu/stdysk/editing.html
Helpful one-page handout explaining how to review and improve notes after lecture.

How to Study Math and Science. University of Texas at Austin Learning Center.
http://www.utexas.edu/student/utlc/handouts/862.html
Helpful one-page handout concerning how to study math and science.

Online Study Skill Workshops and Self-Assessments. University Learning Center, University of Arizona.
http://www.ulc.arizona.edu

Study workshops. You can send your students to online workshops that deal with study skills: Time Management, Note Taking, Exam Preparation, Memory Techniques, Goal Setting, and other study skills. Tell them to go to the home page, and click on Workshops.

Self-Assessment. Students can take a variety of assessments to help them evaluate their learning style, academic motivation, and other useful things. From the home page, click on Assessments.

Undergraduate Preceptors

Teaching Teams Program (University of Arizona)
http://hal.lpl.arizona.edu/teachingteams/
This web site is the best place to go if you are intrigued with the idea of utilizing undergraduates preceptors as full partners in your classroom instruction. In particular see the instructor area. There you will find descriptions of preceptor led activities that have worked in various

classes. Some of these ideas concern cooperative learning experiences during large lectures. There are even start-up materials that provide useful guidelines about how to recruit preceptors, supervise and train them, etc.

J. Groccia & D. Dibasio (Eds.). (2000). *Student Assisted Teaching and Learning: Strategies, Models, and Outcomes*. New York: Anker Publishers.

Oversight council members for the University of Arizona campus-wide program contributed three chapters to this book. One chapter was written by the undergraduate preceptors themselves. This is the best-written source of information about the program.

Larson, H., R. Mencke, S. Tollefson, E. Harrison, & E. Berman. (2000). The University of Arizona Teaching Teams Program: A Just-in-Time Model for Peer Assistance. In J. Groccia & D. Dibasio (Eds.), *Student Assisted Teaching and Learning: Strategies, Models, and Outcomes*. New York: Anker Publishers.

Stover, L., K. Story, A. Skousen, C. Jacks, H. Logan, & B. Bush. (2000). The Teaching Teams Program: Empowering Undergraduates in Student-Centered Research Universities. In J. Groccia & D. Dibasio (Eds.), *Student Assisted Teaching and Learning: Strategies, Models, and Outcomes*. New York: Anker Publishers.

Wood, D., J. Hart, D. DeToro, S. Tollefson, & J. Libarkin. (2000). The Role of Graduate Teaching Assistants in Undergraduate Education: Embracing a New Model of Teaching and Learning. In J. Groccia & D. Dibasio (Eds.), *Student Assisted Teaching and Learning: Strategies, Models, and Outcomes*. New York: Anker Publishers.